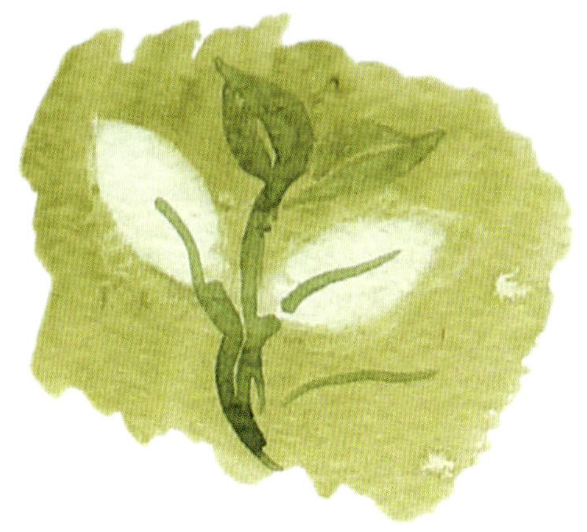

Painting with Watercolour

A Foundation Course

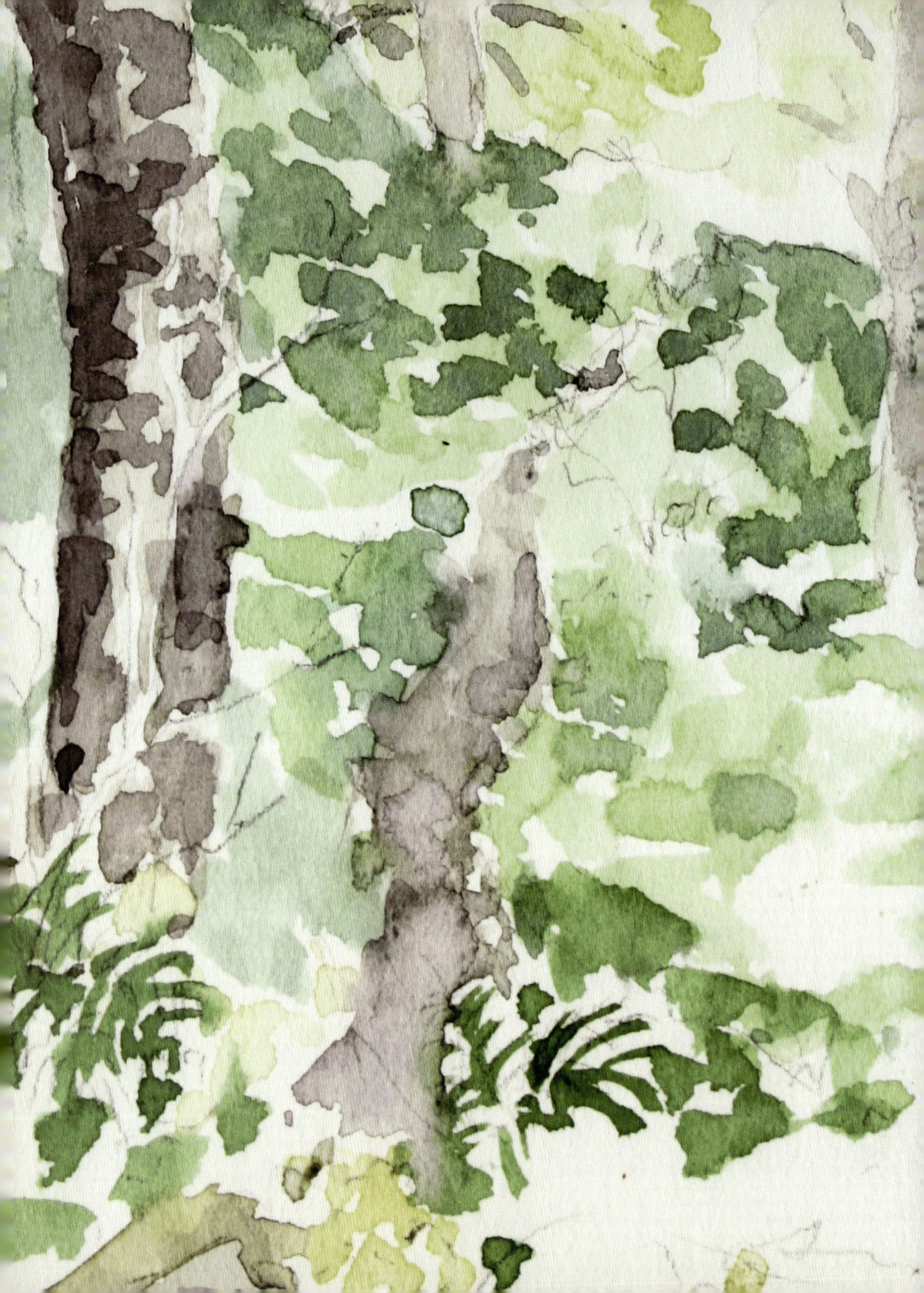

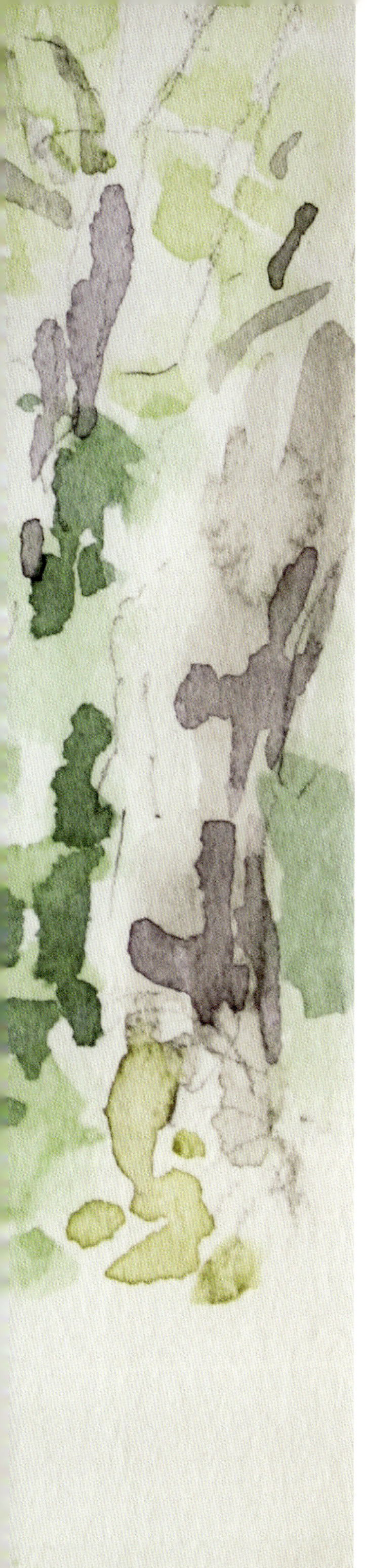

Painting with Watercolour

A Foundation Course

Debbie Flenley

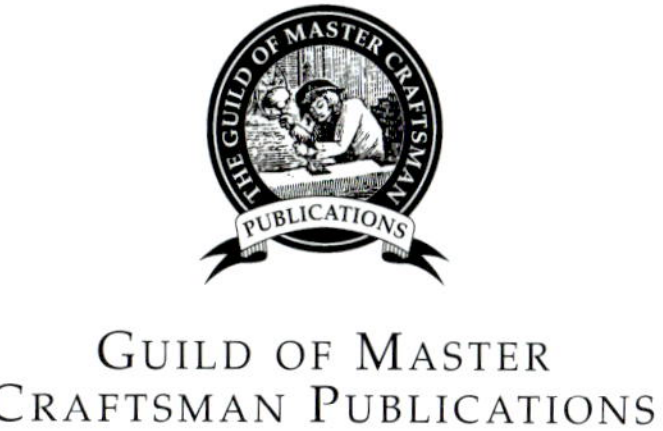

GUILD OF MASTER
CRAFTSMAN PUBLICATIONS

First published 2005 by
Guild of Master Craftsman Publications Ltd
166 High Street, Lewes
East Sussex BN7 1XU

Artwork: Debbie Flenley (debbie_flenley@yahoo.co.uk)
Apart from: Rebecca Mothersole: pp. 2, 55, 57
(x 3 bottom).
Jane Riley and Elaine Beeson: p. 71 (bottom).

Photographer: John Lynch (John-is@blueyonder.co.uk)
Apart from:
Anthony Bailey: pp. 13 (1, 3–7), 14 (6 and 8), 15
(13–15), 16 (x2), 17 (top), 25 (top), 36 (top), 38
(bottom), 43 (a, c & d), 44 (top), 45, 47 (top), 48
(top: 1 & 2), 53, 56 (x2), 68 (x 3), 84, 85 (5, 7–9),
91, 128, 146 (bottom).
Rebecca Mothersole: pp. 13 (2 and 8), 14 (1–5, 7),
15 (9–12, 17), 17 (bottom), 24 (top), 25 (bottom),
26 (bottom), 39 (middle), 43 (b), 48 (bottom), 85
1–4 & 6), 115 (top), 116 (bottom), 117 (bottom).

ISBN 1 86108 369 6

A catalogue record for this book is available from
the British Library.

Production Manager: Hilary MacCallum
Managing Editor: Gerrie Purcell
Project Editor: Gill Parris
Designer: Rebecca Mothersole

Colour origination by Altaimage Ltd
Printed and bound by Sun Fung, China

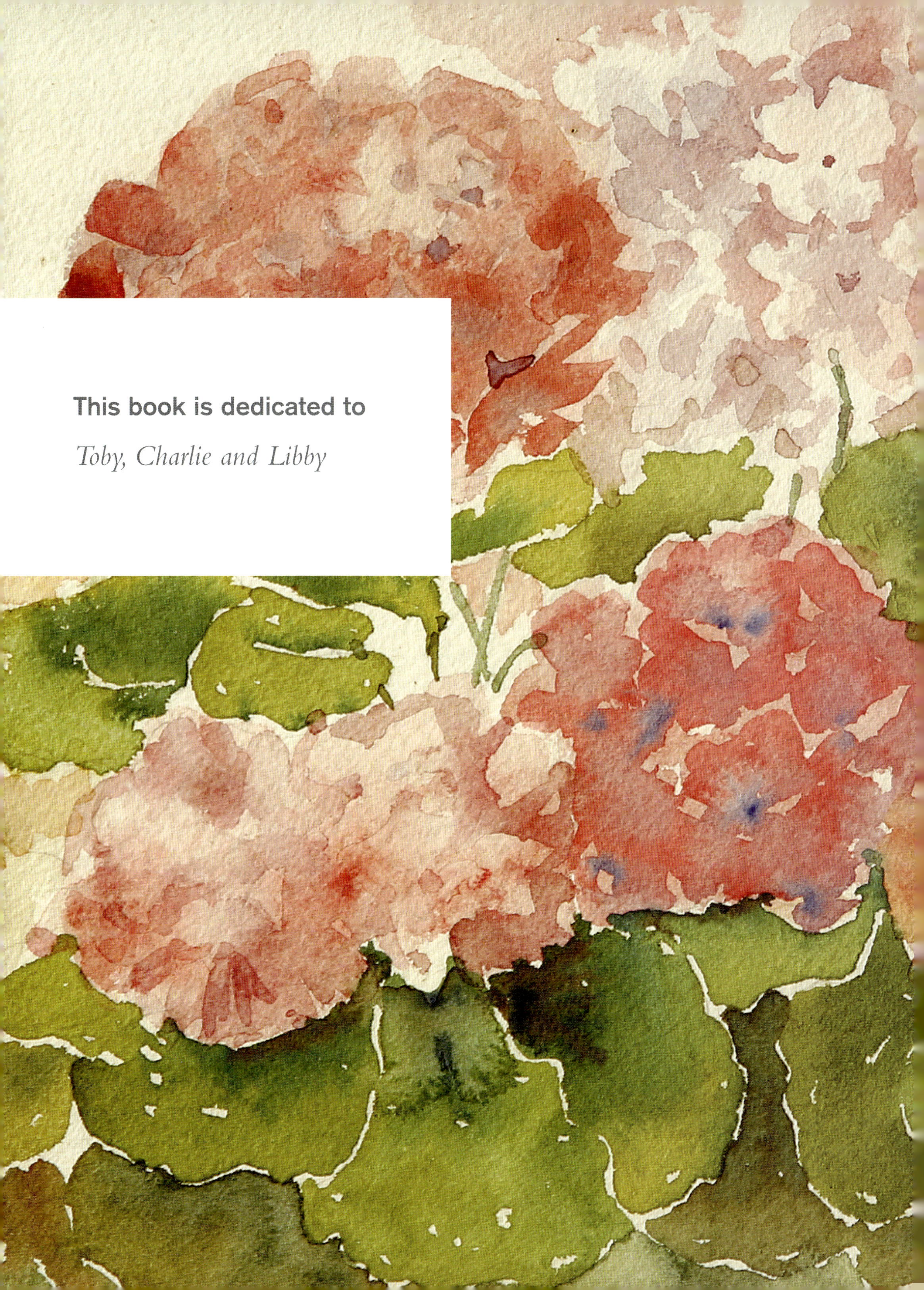
This book is dedicated to
Toby, Charlie and Libby

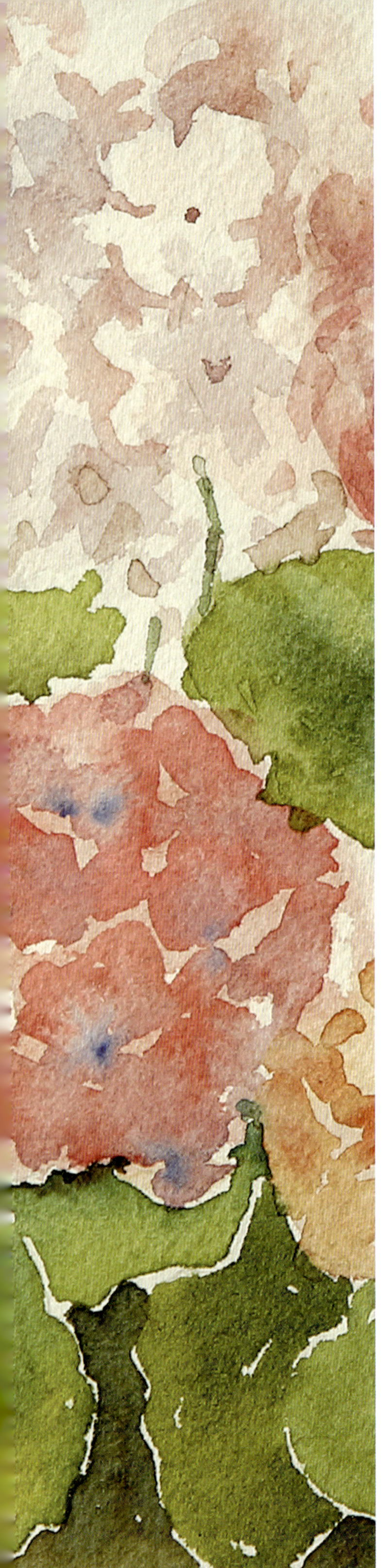

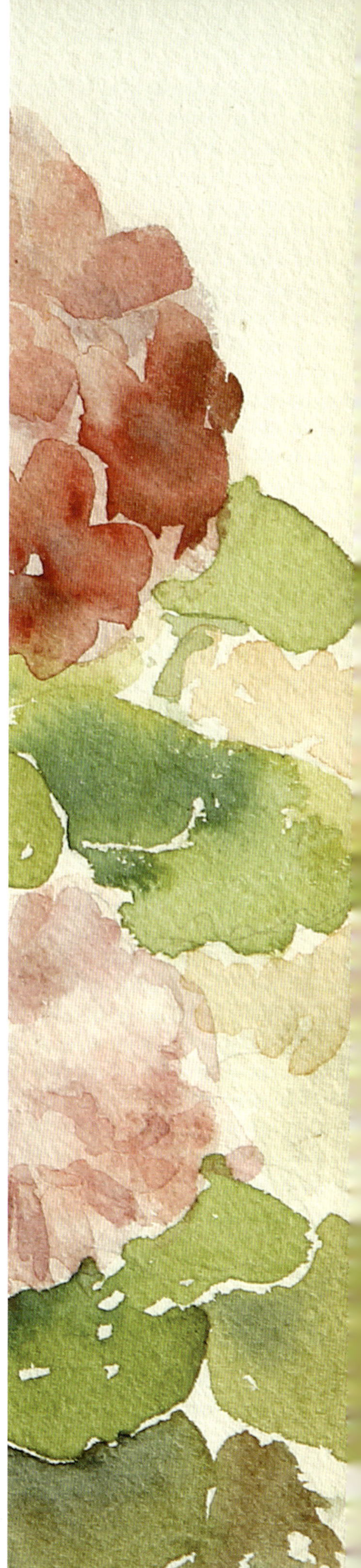

Colour

Theory of Painting

Becoming an Artist

Introduction

When I first started painting I was determined to learn everything about the subject, so for years I studied every book available, interrogated every artist I met, enrolled on every course possible, and – most importantly – painted every day. This book is a result of all that accumulated knowledge and, if you are a keen painter, it will be an essential book for you, as I pass on everything that I have learnt since becoming professional.

I went to art college, but found the emphasis was on 'expressing yourself', rather than learning the facts and basics, such as perspective and colour theory, and I longed to have someone simply tell me all that I needed to know. This book is my attempt to offer that to you, but I cannot offer you everything you need to become a painter. That requires drive and determination and the only place that will come from is your own hunger to learn to paint well. If you have that desire, I want to encourage you: paint every day, try out all the projects, study the 'Focus' points and take on board the advice – especially about developing your own style and not giving up.

Then, when you are ready, tackle the chapters on 'Becoming an Artist' (p.154) and 'Selling your Paintings' (p. 166) and, before you know it, you'll be there.

There is one area – hopefully the only one in my life – where I am a snob. I hate to see work hanging that is a copy of someone else's painting, especially when it is proudly framed, signed and passed off as their own achievement. My reasoning is this: when copying a painting you are already a step removed from the reality of the original scene and you will be copying any mistakes that have been made. But, more importantly, the interpretation of the scene and the style (which is the real work) is someone else's, not yours. By all means be influenced by other painters, see how they have tackled subjects and try and copy pictures to learn methods and techniques. But any painting you do should be truly yours and, even if it is technically inferior, it is still worth ten times any copy, simply because it is an original, so believe in yourself and your own ability.

If you are interested enough to be reading this, it will probably be because you are talented. All it takes is 1% talent and 99% hard work so, if I can do it, there's no reason why you can't too. You just need the determination to succeed.

So, get reading, get to it and good luck!

Debbie

Debbie Flenley

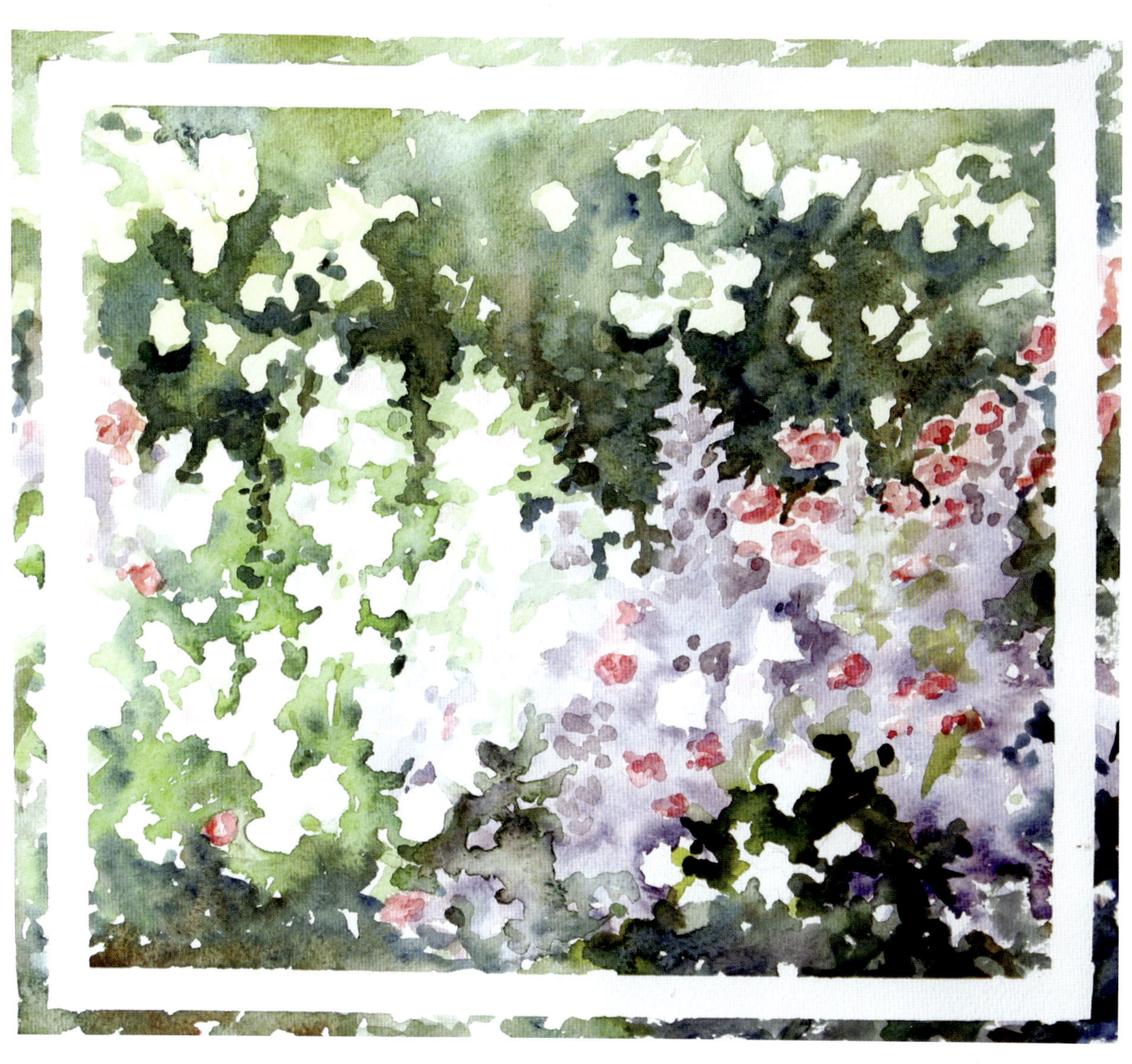

Getting Started

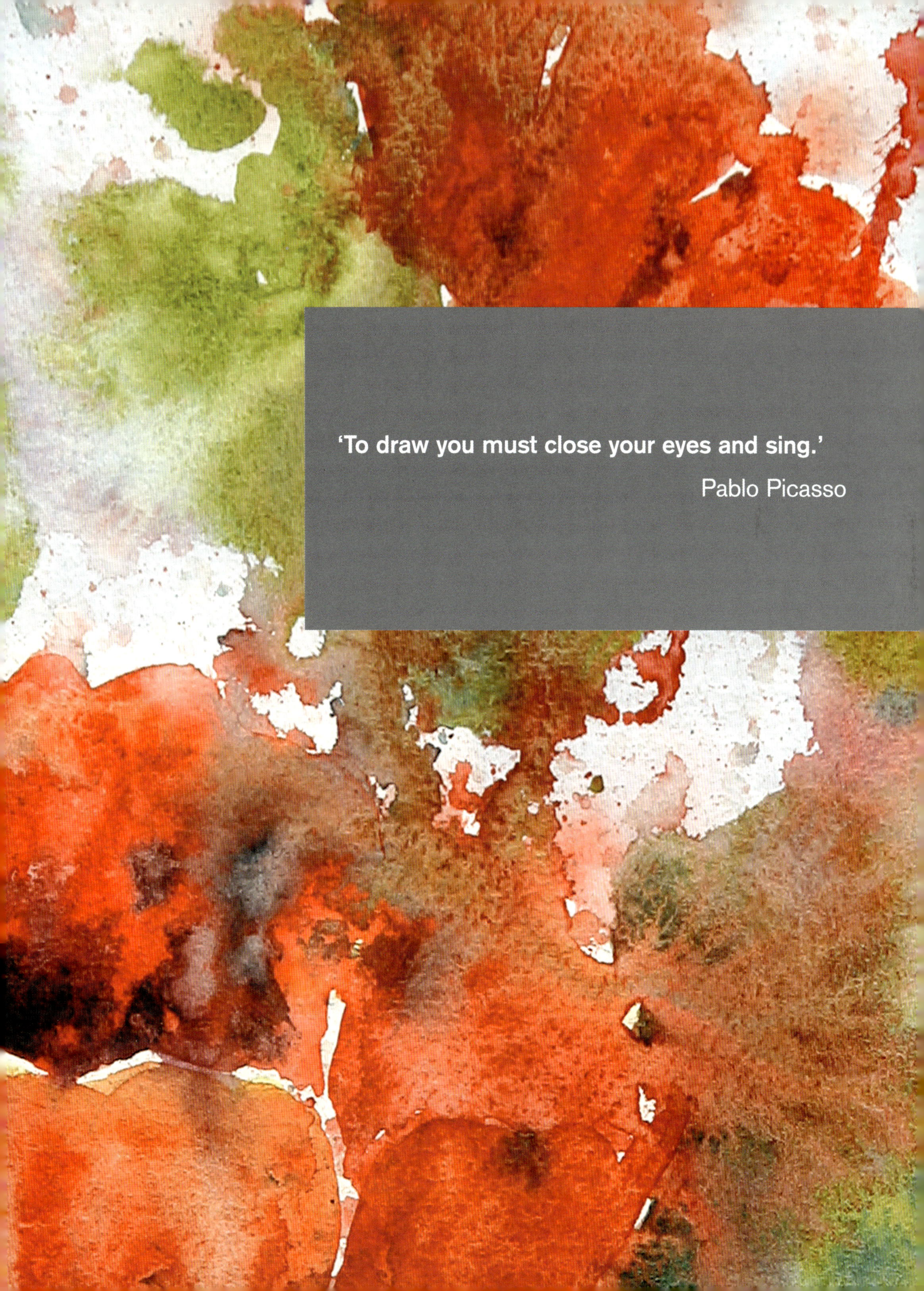
'To draw you must close your eyes and sing.'
Pablo Picasso

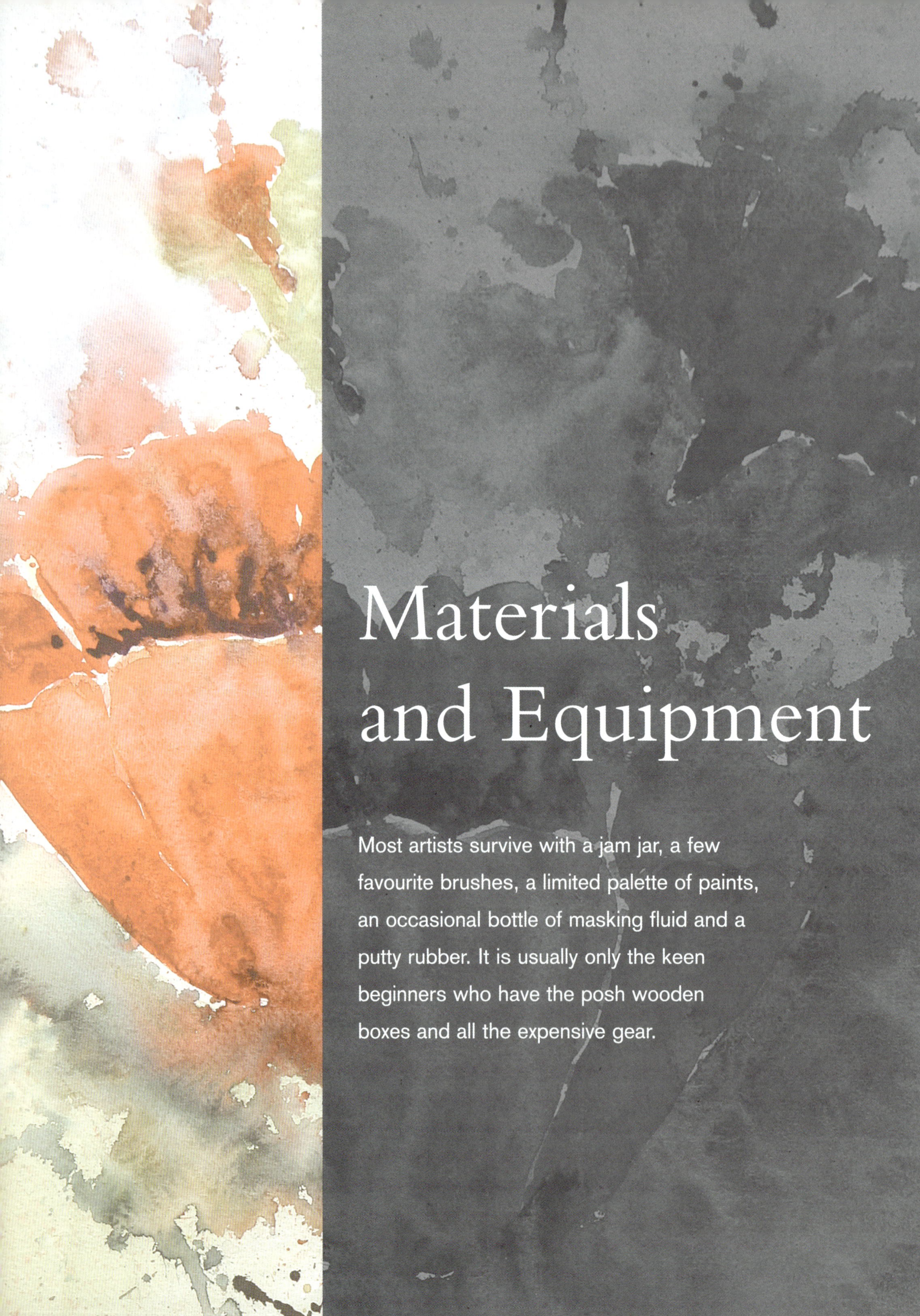

Materials and Equipment

Most artists survive with a jam jar, a few favourite brushes, a limited palette of paints, an occasional bottle of masking fluid and a putty rubber. It is usually only the keen beginners who have the posh wooden boxes and all the expensive gear.

Painting needn't be an expensive hobby. Once you have bought your equipment it will last for years, with just the occasional replenishment of materials – tubes of paint, paper and so on. The danger lurks when you purchase art materials for the first time and, as a beginner, you convince yourself that a new gadget, brush, or colour will be the one thing to turn you into a master painter.

My father – an artist from the old school – always said, 'If you can't get it into your pocket, you don't need it,' but as a beginner and as a daughter I didn't believe him. Instead, I was always in the art shop sampling new delights and, sure enough, years down the line I've found many of them remain unused. A lot of what I use is inexpensive or free so in this chapter I hope to save you a great deal of unnecessary expense.

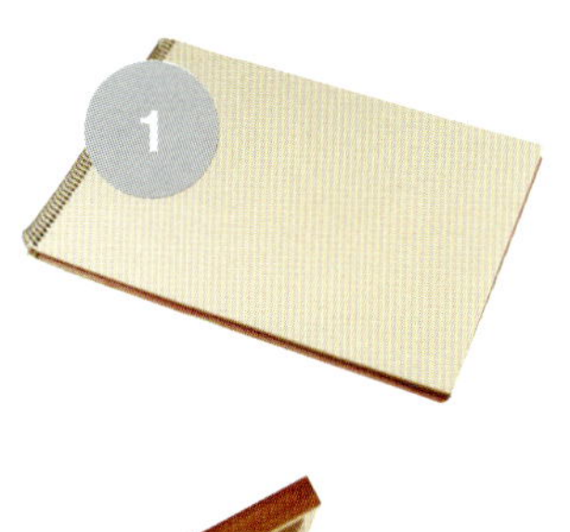

The absolute basics

These are the essentials that you will need to get started:

1   Pad of watercolour paper

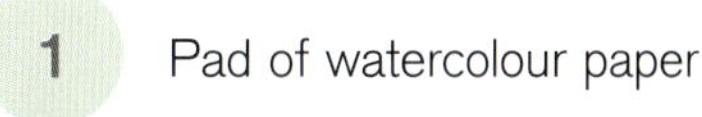

2   Box of paints with palette area to mix on

3   Eraser

4   Roll of kitchen paper, to mop up paint

5   HB pencil

6   Lidded jar for water

7   Piece of board to lean on

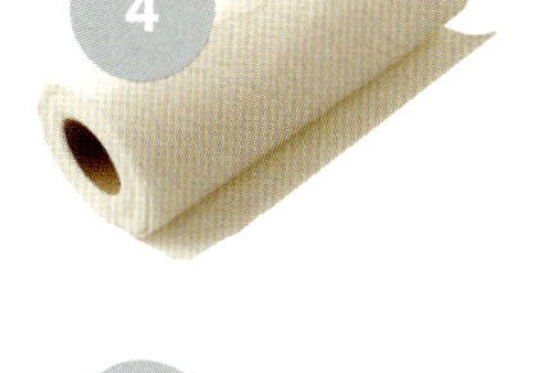

8   2 x watercolour brushes, sizes 8 and 12

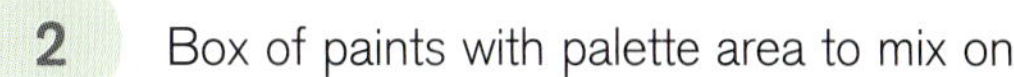

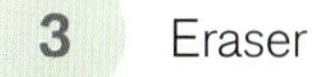

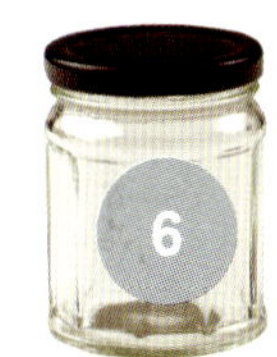

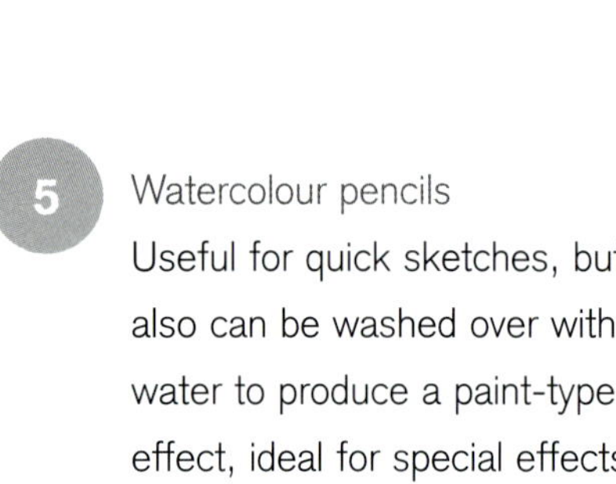

Additional materials

and equipment that I find useful

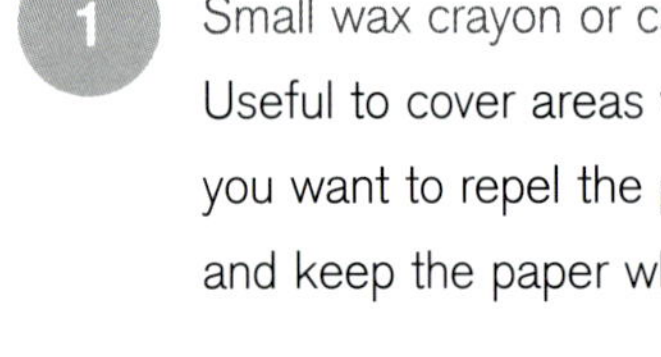

1 Small wax crayon or candle
Useful to cover areas where you want to repel the paint and keep the paper white.

2 See-through protractor
I look through this to measure angles, such as an open door. They can then be reproduced at the correct angle on the paper.

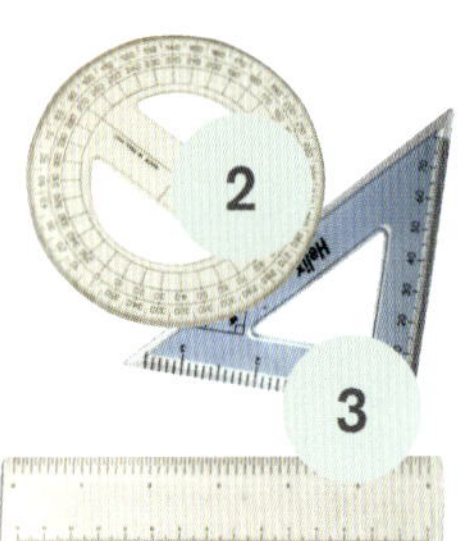

3 Ruler and small set square
I find a set square useful for still lifes. When drawing vases, for example, I draw one side of the vase, then flip the set square over and draw the other side. This ensures that the pot is upright and parallel.

4 Masking fluid
Bought in a bottle from art shops and used to 'mask out' the white of the paper.

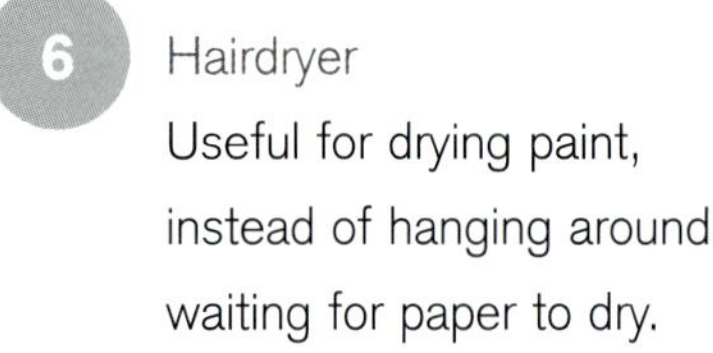

5 Watercolour pencils
Useful for quick sketches, but also can be washed over with water to produce a paint-type effect, ideal for special effects and planning paintings.

6 Hairdryer
Useful for drying paint, instead of hanging around waiting for paper to dry.

7 Mixing palette
A simple plate or white plastic tray is ideal – obviously it needs to be white so you can judge your colours accurately.

8 Easel, board-support or brick
When working at a desk or table, a brick is useful for propping up your board. By adjusting the position of the brick, you can achieve the angle required.

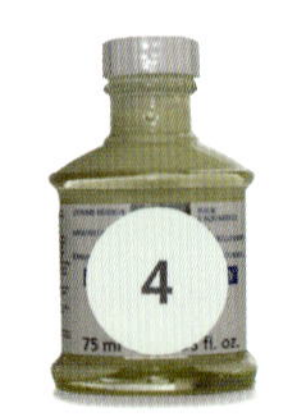

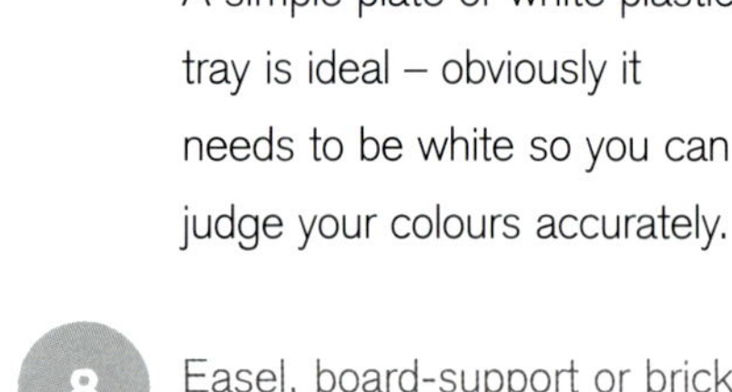

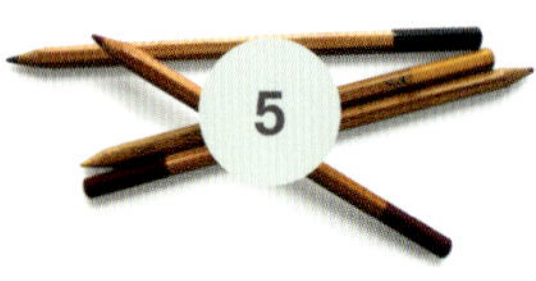

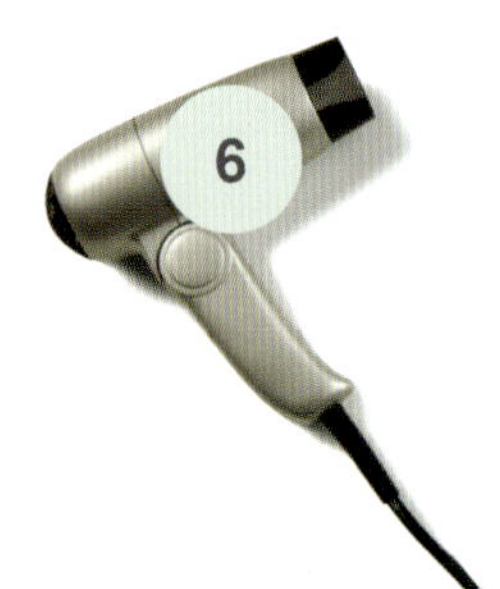

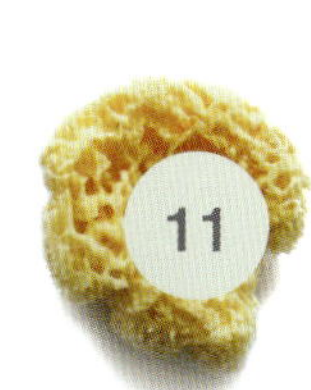

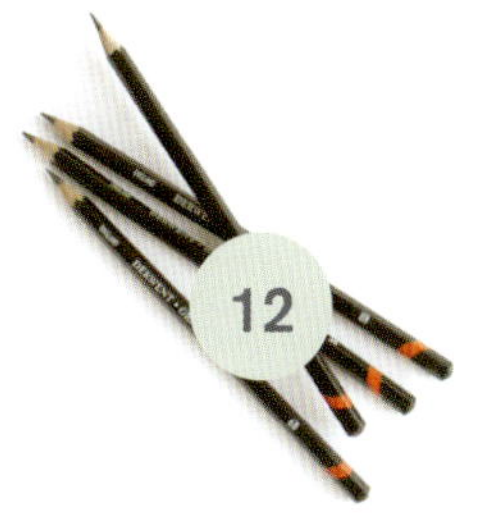

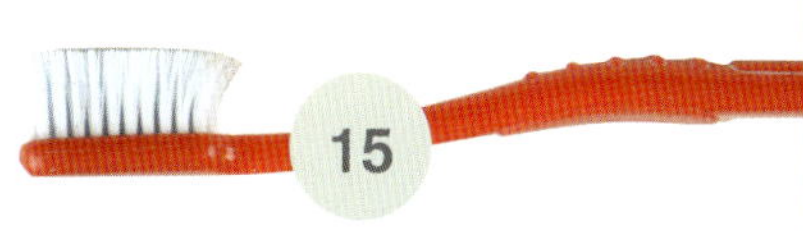

9 Pieces of card
A pile of these, ripped in different ways, is useful for 'masking out' areas of a painting before splattering paint.

10 Putty rubber
A traditional eraser can be harsh as you rub your paper, whereas a putty rubber is gentler for 'lifting off' the marks. It can also be moulded to fit the shape of the area you wish to erase.

11 Natural sponge
Useful for techniques when loaded with paint and dabbed on the paper to create a mottled effect.

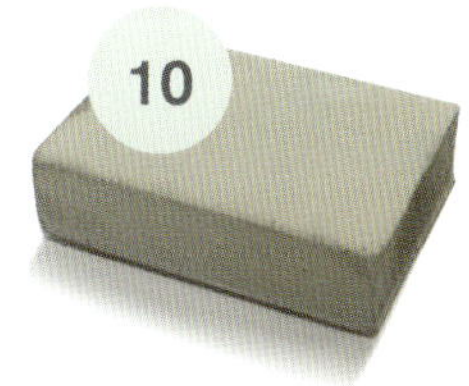

12 Assorted grades of pencils
Be aware of the different grades: HB is fine for drawing for watercolour but you may need softer grades, 2B–6B, for general sketching.

13 Mirror
If you look at your work in a mirror, it will show it in a fresh light and you will be able to see what's wrong with it.

14 Two x L-shaped Card mounts
Put these around your work: invaluable for ascertaining where to mount, cut work off, and see what it will look like when mounted.

Tip: new palettes, or anything plastic to be used to mix paint on, should first be washed with scouring cream, so that the surface is receptive to paint.

15 Toothbrush
For splattering effect – load the bristles with paint and flick the paint across the paper.

16 Viewfinder
This is essential for planning composition. You can simply cut a rectangular aperture out of a piece of card, or buy a see-through one with compositional lines on from an art shop.

17 A craft knife
For scratching out marks on paper and sharpening pencils. (A traditional pencil sharpener turns the lead in the wood and can break it, you also get a better point with a knife.)

Most importantly, you need a lot of enthusiasm

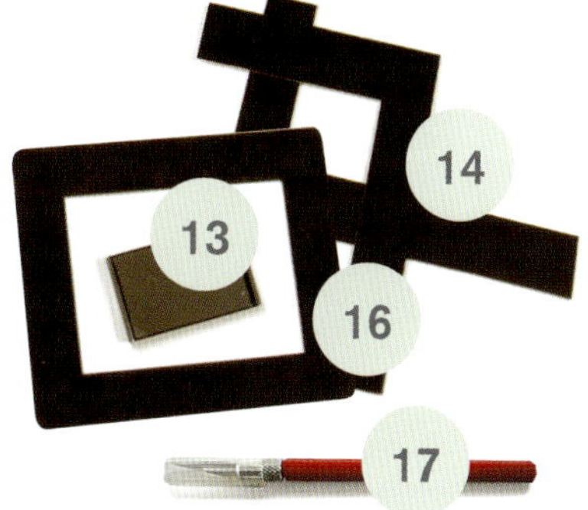

Paper

Which paper to use?

This might sound obvious but, whatever you choose, you do need to make sure it is watercolour paper – I've seen many beginners start to paint on cartridge paper and this is too thin: it will buckle when it gets wet, making it difficult to achieve a flat wash. Also, it will do nothing to enhance your painting as it has a flat uninteresting surface, which lacks the texture of watercolour paper.

In the early days your choice will depend both on what you can afford and on your level of ability – as some top papers can be very expensive and, with respect, would be wasted on a beginner. But gradually, as you begin to experiment, you will see the different textures and surfaces available and find that these do make a difference to the end result of your work.

It is a good idea to collect sample books of different papers from paper manufacturers and art shops and to paint a wash on each one using the same transparent colour paint, so you can compare the different effects.

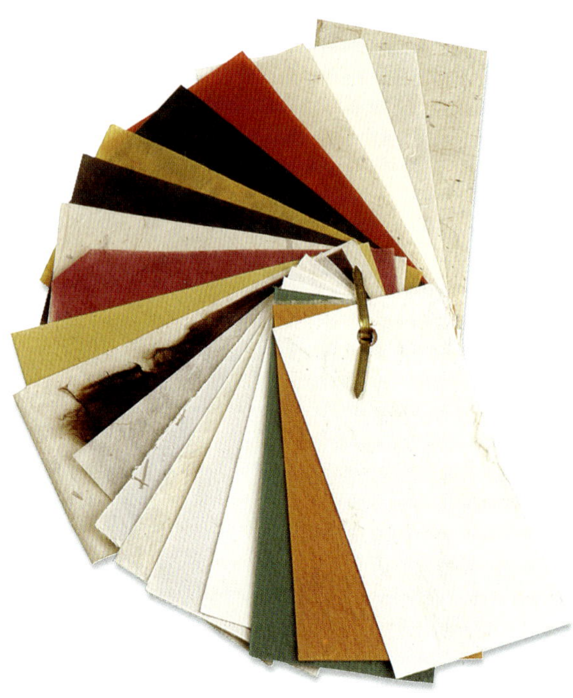

Tip: a group of you could buy one sheet of each paper and cut it up so that you each have samples at low cost. Keep the paper samples in your sketch book for reference.

Sheets of watercolour paper

Tinted papers

The choice of papers is wide and includes a variety of textures and weights: to start with I suggest a basic wood-pulp paper, which has a good texture, holds the paint well and is easy to buy.

At the other end of the market you will find rag papers made from cotton fibres. These are often in individual sheets, acid-free to prevent ageing, and forgiving in the surface, allowing mistakes to be rubbed out and changes to be made. There are many brands available.

When you find a brand that you like, I recommend buying it in bulk, as usually 10 or 20 full-size sheets will be much more economical per sheet than one. It is also advantageous to become used to the feel of a paper and to familiarize yourself with the way it behaves and interacts with your paint. This may sound strange but it can be significant, as you can get very varied results on different papers.

Once you have made your purchase, it is essential to store the paper somewhere free from damp and without mice – a lesson I learnt the hard way, when some mice used my best rag paper to make their nest!

It is worth noting that you can also buy coloured watercolour paper. This is tinted – usually a pale colour – which can be useful if you want to give your picture an overall hint of colour.

Paper Surfaces

There are three main types of texture or surface
for watercolour paper:

Hot-pressed or HP

This is where the paper has been 'ironed' through
a hot press and has a smooth surface like card. It is
similar to cartridge paper in its surface finish but it is
heavier in weight. It is not as 'thirsty' or 'textured' as
other watercolour papers, so it can seem odd at first
as the washes slide around on the slippery surface.
This smooth surface is suitable for detailed work, for
example botanical illustration, as it gives fresh, clean
and crisp edges.

'Not', or Cold-pressed

Here the paper is pressed but not so intensely, so
the surface has some texture. This is best for most
watercolour painters, as there is a slight interest to
the surface giving a 'watercolour feel' to the painting,
without it being too hard to handle. It is a good
compromise between the other two finishes.

Rough

As the name suggests, the surface of this paper is
heavily textured and has an unevenness about it as
the paper's fibres are left to dry without pressing.
This 'tooth' creates an interesting texture to paint on,
allowing the paint to be captured in broken/dry-brush
type marks from the brush. Interest also comes from
the granulating effect caused by paint settling in the
uneven surface, which is better for loose work where
the painter seeks texture rather than smooth detail.
This heavy texture can be advantageous when painting
large areas of sea, sky, or foliage, as it breaks up the
monotony of a brush strokes and gives shimmering
flickers of light showing through.

Whilst Rough gives exciting effects, I don't recommend
it for the beginner or the faint-hearted, as it can be
challenging to paint on.

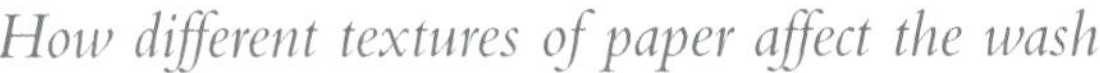

How different textures of paper affect the wash

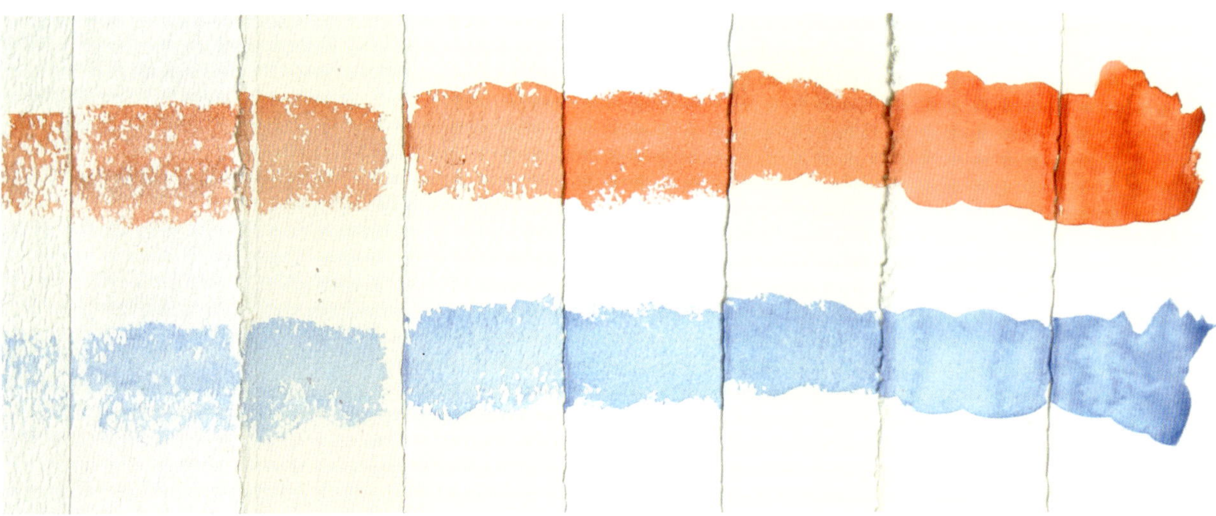

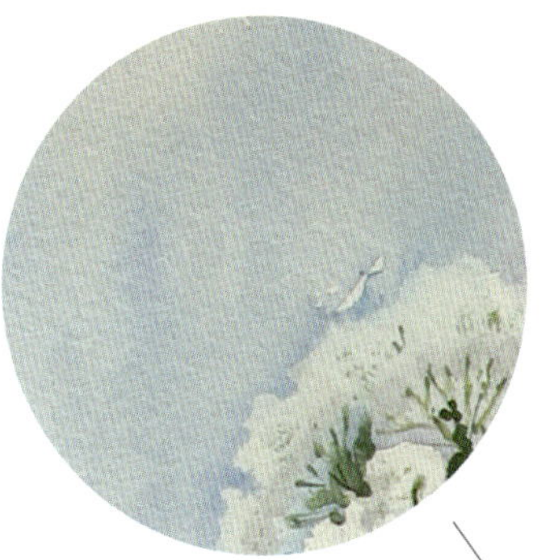

Rough paper that is not strongly sized can cause colours to appear dull and chalky and, because of the granulation occurring in the 'depths', paintings are liable to become muddy.

The advantage of blocks of watercolour paper is that they are bonded around the edges and don't have to be stretched – theoretically, the bonding holds the paper in place, as long as you don't remove it until it is dry. In practice, they do still buckle sometimes. It is convenient to have a pad ready to go, especially for painting on location, and set sizes can also be advantageous, as you can buy your frames and mounts to fit just one size.

However, I rarely buy my paper in pads, as I prefer the freedom of individual sheets: you can cut them to size to suit your mood and they are a more reliable surface to paint on. Also, if used whole, they have the lovely deckle edge around each sheet, which is lost with pads.

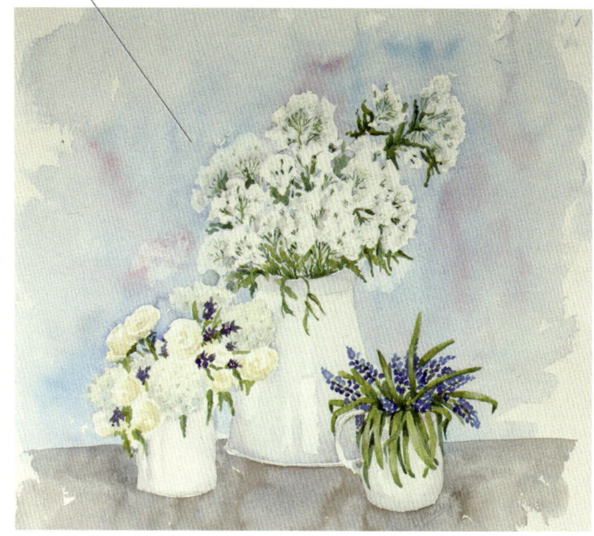

I used the same brushes and paint for these two paintings, but they are on different papers. Although the paintings were treated similarly, you can see that the overall effect is dissimilar, due to the difference in texture of the surface of the paper

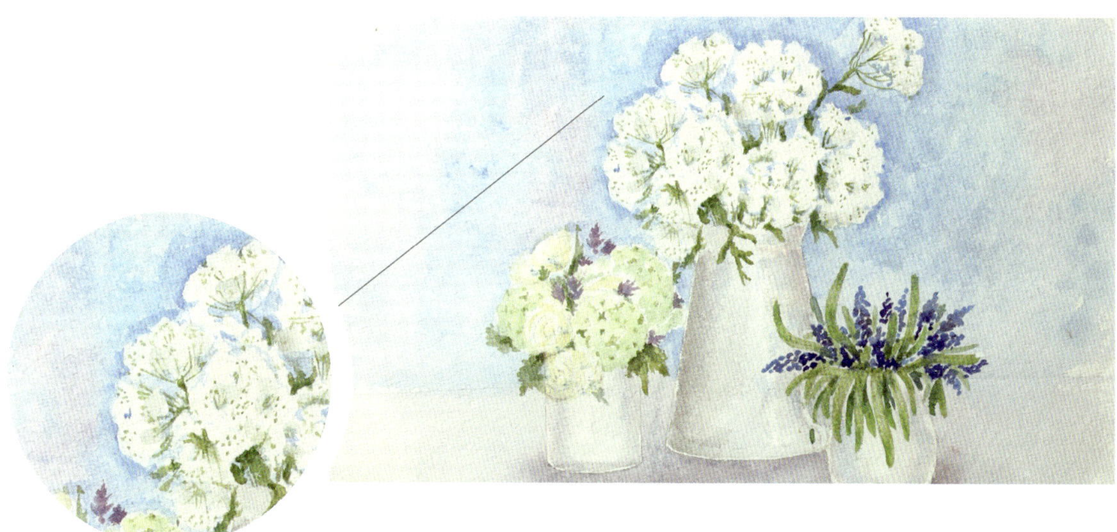

Paper weights

Watercolour papers are produced in varying weights –
these come in pounds/lbs which show the weight of
each ream which equals 500 sheets, or in grams/gsm
which show the number of grams per square metre of
paper. The most usual weights are shown below:

90lb / 190gsm	quite thin and tends to 'buckle' if not stretched.
140lb / 300gsm	the middle thickness, which I recommend to start with.
300lb / 640gsm	like card in its thickness and often won't need stretching before use, as its weight allows it to stand up to vigorous amounts of water without adverse effect.

Tip: For a beginner, I recommend the 'Not' finish. This will give you the slightly textured feel of watercolour paper whilst still being relatively easy to work on. 'Rough' on the other hand, would be too textured and difficult to paint on and 'Hot-pressed' would be too smooth and lacking the texture that gives watercolour its distinctive surface. Go for a middle weight of 140lb (300gsm).

Paper sizing

Special glue-like solutions are added to the paper
during manufacture to prevent the paper being too
absorbent. Without it the paper would suck the paint
off your brush like kitchen roll, and it would be
impossible to move the paint around smoothly on the
surface, or even remove it later if you make a mistake.

Papers can be internally or externally sized – the best
papers have size added both ways.

The difference in the way papers react to the paint
can usually be accounted for by the amount of size
that is added, which does vary considerably.

Brushes

It is an understatement to say a good brush makes all the difference – I think it's vital to have a good relationship with your brushes. As with friends, it may seem impressive to have lots, but a few good ones that you can rely on are all you need, so that you can trust them and know how they will behave in all situations!

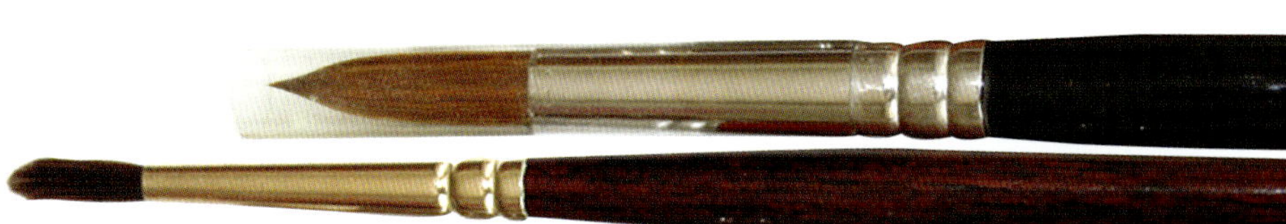

Focus on
Types of brushes

Having read all the pros and cons – and there is plenty of discussion about which brushes are best – you will have to decide what simply 'feels right' for you. With experience you will also find that different brushes suit different styles of picture and different occasions, and I suspect that you will gradually form an attachment to a couple of favourites.

This might sound obvious but, as with paper, make sure you buy *watercolour* brushes, which are softer than the stiffer hog-hair type brushes that are used for oils or acrylics. The two main shapes are:

'Round': for general work, landscape and flower painting and so on.

'Flat': for architectural work and for straight-edged objects such as stairs, or when the brush is turned on its side for lines for, say, telegraph poles.

You can also find:
'Fan': as its name suggests, this is a fan-shape brush suitable for painting tree shapes (I bought one of these in my enthusiastic early days but never use it).

'Hake': this is wide and flat and great used in large strokes for painting in a broad, free style, but you can't paint detail with one of these.

'Rigger': this has long thin hairs to paint lines, i.e. twigs on a tree or for 'rigging' on a ship. I have a large and a small one of these, which I find useful for painting the branches on winter trees (but I would use them for little else).

*This painting would not have
worked with a little brush –
I used sizes 16 and 24*

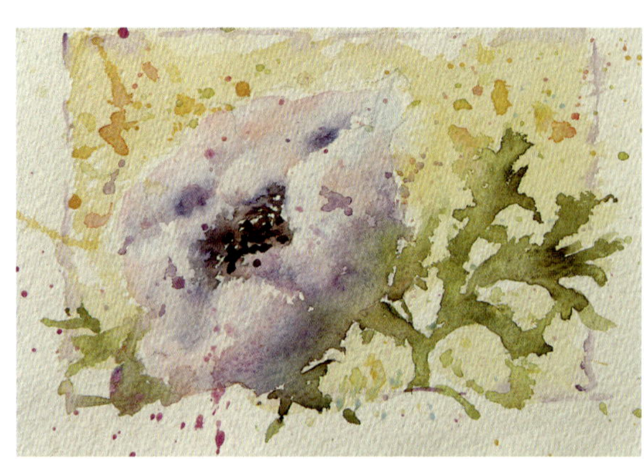

Whichever type of brush you choose, make sure it has a good fat 'belly' so that the body of the brush can hold plenty of paint and water; you then won't need to keep 'refuelling' and the paint will flow gently onto the paper. This is vital for laying a wash and keeping all your work 'fluid' – a telltale sign of an amateur is dry, bitty brush strokes.

A flat brush should have a sharp chisel-edge, so you can make accurate strokes.

Check that all the hairs lie comfortably in the same direction and that there aren't odd stray hairs sticking out at strange angles.

A round brush is for general painting where you need detail; make sure it has a fine point at the tip. Knowing this in advance might save you a fortune along the way – I spent my children's inheritance on useless brushes, including a couple of expensive sables, before I finally settled on my soulmate, a synthetic/sable mix.

Natural or synthetic?

Ideally, watercolour brushes should be made of animal hair as it is more absorbent than synthetic material. Sable is the best (Kolinsky red sable especially) with mongoose, ox and Japanese deer following behind. Unfortunately for us (but fortunately for the sable) these are very expensive.

Having bought sable brushes in the past, I agree that they are lovely, but the tip soon wears down and the brush loses its fine point, so it is then good only for laying a wash rather than for finer work. I also found they didn't have the strength and spring of synthetic brushes so I, personally, can't recommend them to you as a good investment, only as a luxury.

Squirrel-hair brushes are natural but less expensive than sable. These are very soft and hold lots of water, so are ideal for large washes. Their softness means they don't hold their shape, so they are little use for fine point-work (unless it is a small brush), but a mop-shaped one will be an ideal acquisition for large areas of paint.

Tip: if you are setting out, I advise buying larger

size brushes than you think you will need.

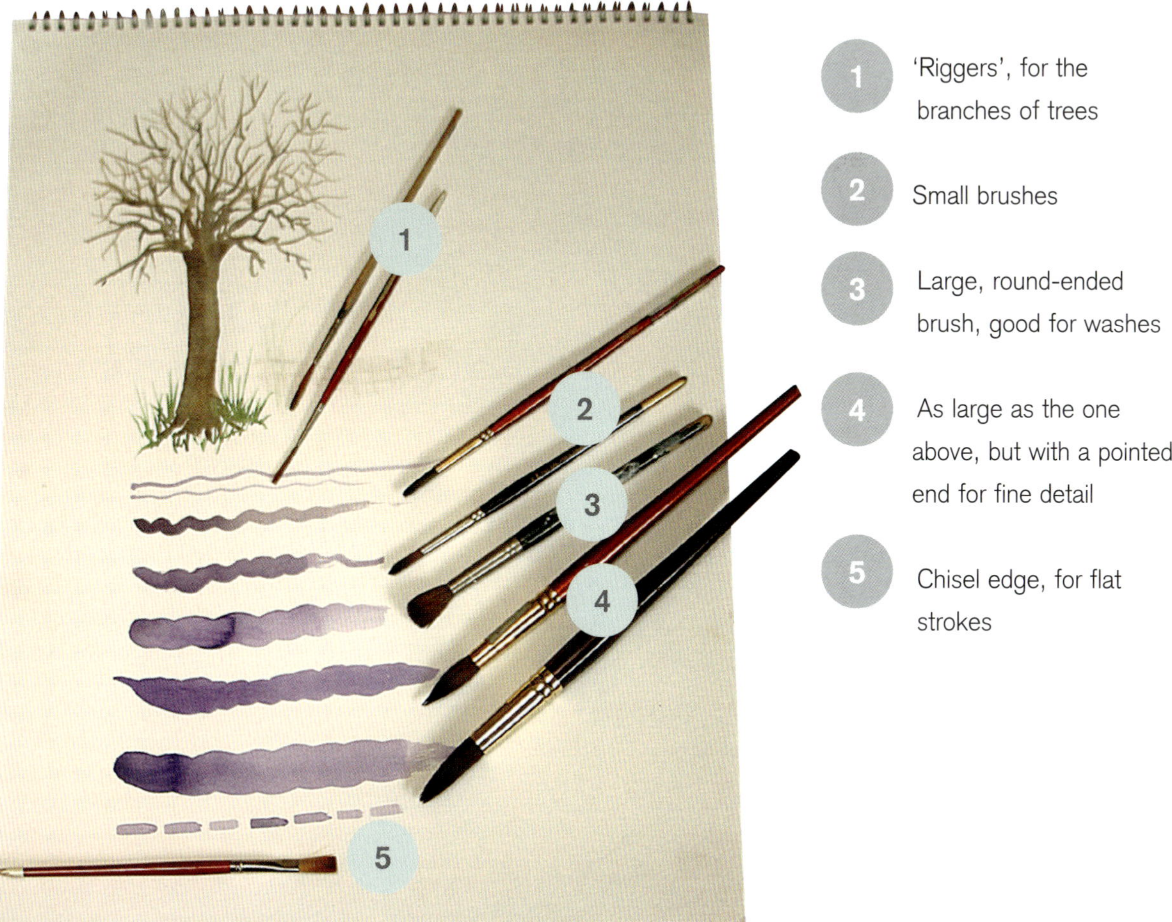

Synthetic brushes, on the other hand, are much cheaper, longer lasting and readily available. The downside is they don't hold so much water and are not as soft, but many are good and ideal for a beginner. If you have bought a 'beginner's set' you will probably already own one of these.

So, I have found it better to buy a brush which has a good mix of sable and synthetic. You then have the advantage of the absorbency and springiness of the natural hair, whilst the synthetic hair seems to give it more body and strength. I find synthetic hair easier to work with, as all-natural hair can be too soft, and with this combination you get a more balanced feel to the brush which is easier to control, cheaper and lasts longer.

Brush sizes

Often beginners have brushes that are much too small, probably because the brush that comes with a pre-packaged watercolour set is a size 2 or 3. This won't help your painting at all, as you will get little 'bitty' strokes instead of bold washes.

I recommend a few brushes, approximately sizes 8, 12 and 16. Most painters will tell you they tend to use the same few brushes all the time (I certainly do), so it is worth investing in good ones of a decent size.

Focus on
Care and storage of brushes

Having described brushes as valuable friends, it goes without saying that you will need to take care of them to increase their longevity and protect their tips from damage. Also, as it may take a while to 'wear in' a new brush and get it to the 'comfortable as a pair of old slippers' stage, it makes sense to value those that you have.

I've been taught that you should rinse brushes thoroughly at the end of every session in mild soapy water, then dab them dry and leave to finish drying upside down, so the water doesn't collect in – and rot – the hairs in the root. It sounds sensible, but I do not have the patience to follow that routine every day and so I cannot recommend that you do that either.

I keep the few brushes I use regularly with me, so I either have them in the middle of my roll of materials, or put them in a long pencil case. It is important to protect the tips whilst they are in there and I find a simple, quick and effective way to achieve that is to roll up a piece of plastic into a thin cone, secure it with adhesive tape, and use that to slide over the brush. This can be moved to the end of the brush whilst painting, then slid back over the tip after use, which is especially useful when travelling.

When I am in the studio I simply leave the brushes lying there on their side.

You can, of course, buy tubes to keep your brushes in, and yes, I admit that I bought one of them, too, but I've never used it.

- Never leave your brushes standing 'tip down' in water for any length of time, as the tip will become bent.

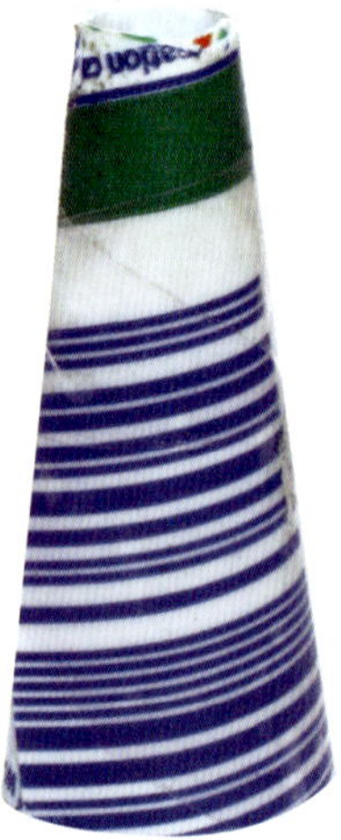

You can make a plastic cone to protect your brush tips using sections of spare packaging secured by clear tape

- Never throw brushes in your pocket or pencil case, as the tips will soon get ruined.

In addition, if you are meticulous:

After use, quickly rinse brushes in clean water, dry with kitchen roll, then pull the tips into a neat point whilst still damp before you leave them.

If taking the brushes with you when travelling, roll them in a breathable wrap (an old straw place mat or proper brush roll) to protect their tips.

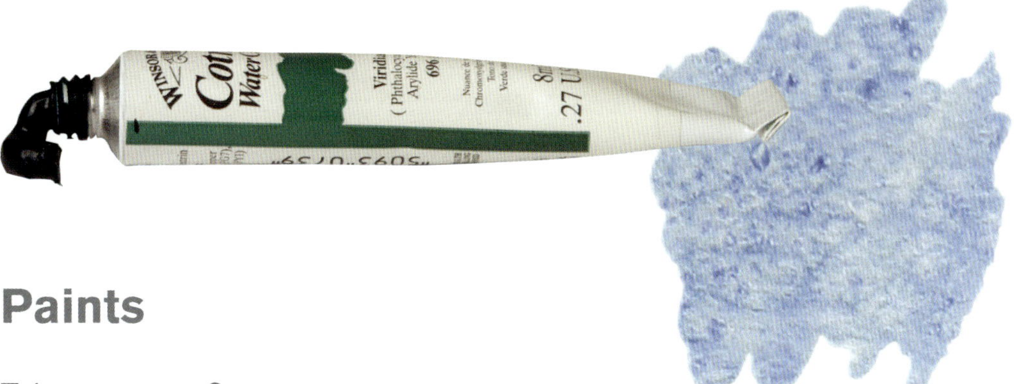

Paints

Tubes or pans?

Watercolours traditionally come in tubes or pans (the hard square ones). I am often being asked which is best. The answer depends on how you tend to paint and how you need your paints to serve you.

Tubes contain more glycerine, so are softer and more pliable than the hard pans. This makes them easier to manipulate than the solid paint, which sometimes requires a bit of rubbing with the brush to 'get it going', and to lift off enough paint if you are covering a large area. The advantage of pans, though, is that you can quickly get to the colour without having to anticipate in advance – and squeeze out – the colours you will need. For this reason I prefer pans and recommend them for the beginner.

I tend to use a combination of tubes and pans. For painting in the studio I have a large plastic palette and squeeze tubes into it around the edge. After painting I simply leave them – so there is no waste – and they dry like hard paint in the pans, so next time I use them just as I would use a pan of paint.

Paint in pans tends to be dryer than the glycerine-enhanced tube paint so, if you want them to be more pliable, simply pour on a drop of boiling water to soften them, or spray them with hot water using an atomizer/water sprayer.

For painting out of doors, when pans really are the most practical solution, I add paint from my tubes into the pans as they run out. I also buy empty pans and add my colour from tubes, or my own 'mixes' of colours from different tubes as I need to, which I find invaluable. For example, if I can't find a green that is dark enough, I mix paint from tubes of Prussian blue, sap green and a bit of red (green's complementary colour) in a pan and add it to my palette (see next page for example).

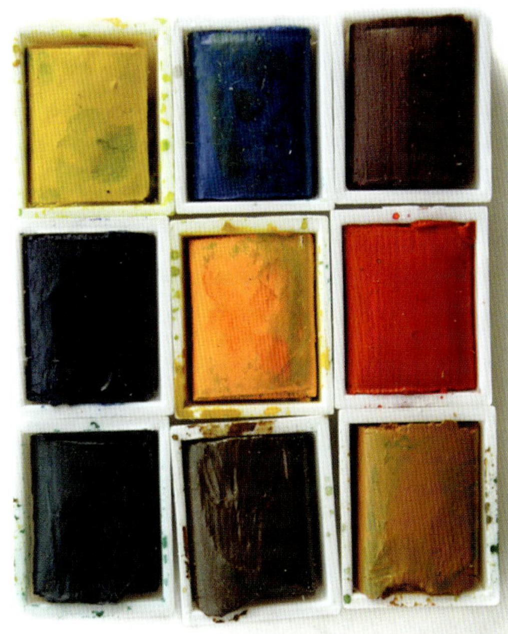

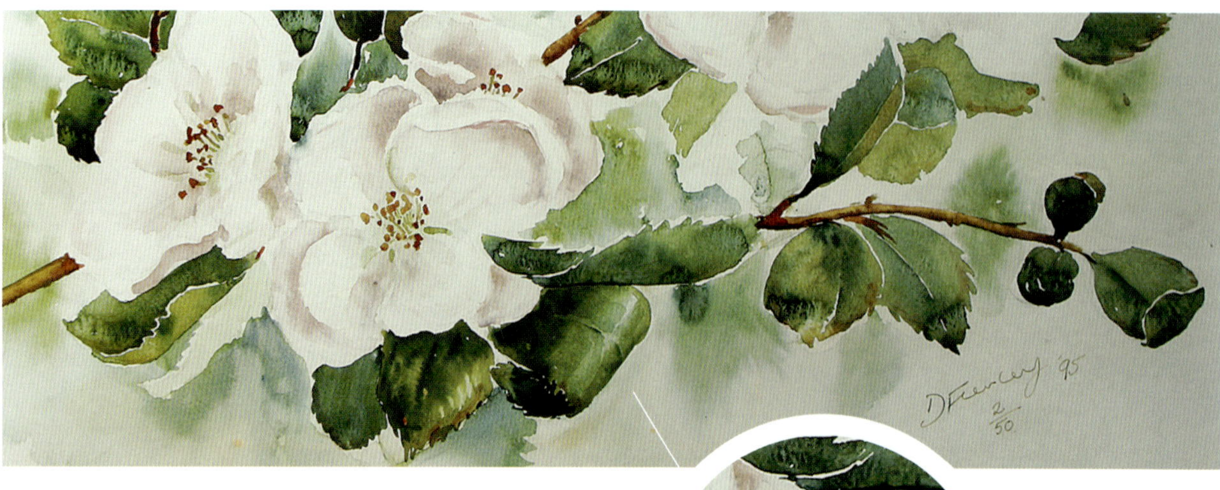

'Artist' or 'Student' Quality?

When you come to purchase materials you will notice that there is a vast difference in price between Artist and Student quality.

Dark green mixed from Prussian blue, sap green and a bit of red

Watercolour paints are coloured pigments that are expertly ground and then suspended in a medium. The discrepancy in price is because some are simple, individual pigments, whilst others are a blend of more than one. The Artist-quality paints have more colour pigment in them and so are clearer and more intense in colour. The Student quality have more filler in with the pigments, so they are chalkier.

Artist quality also have a high number of single pigments rather than the mix of pigments found in Student colours. The former claim to be more lightfast (although I've not seen any watercolour that stands up to being in the sun) and the latter may fade unreliably, as the mix of pigments may each fade at different rates.

Despite these differences, I would always recommend that beginners buy the Student range of paints, as the quality is fine and there is nothing to be gained

from paying up to four times the price when you are starting out. Make sure you use one of the major manufacturers though, and don't believe the words 'Artist quality' when it is on a box of 12 colours at a bargain price in a clearance bookshop!

The Student range of brushes tend to be synthetic rather than natural hair, and the paper not quite so robust as the Artist-quality paper, but these too are fine for the beginner.

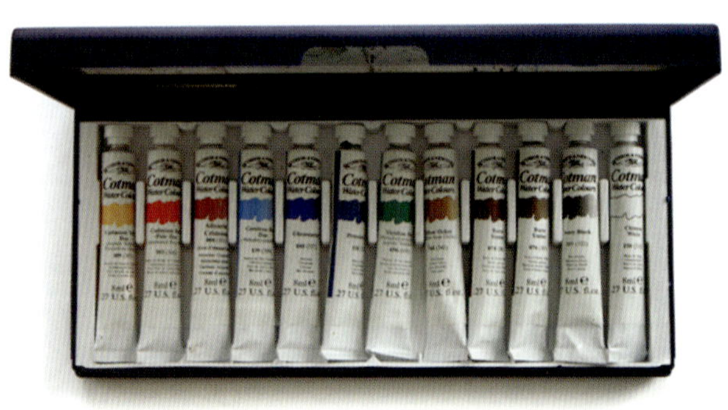

Basic palette of colours to buy

In 'Understanding Your Paints' (p. 54), I describe the properties of different coloured paints and explain how they 'behave'. For now I suggest this basic palette. It is similar to many of the boxes of paints you can buy with the collection of colours already chosen for you but, if you are buying one of these, do make sure you have a warm and cool of each of the primaries, as not all manufacturers include them. If you need to, simply ask your retailer if you can exchange one – and get rid of the black one – or buy another half pan the same size and squeeze it in at the end of the section where the brushes lie.

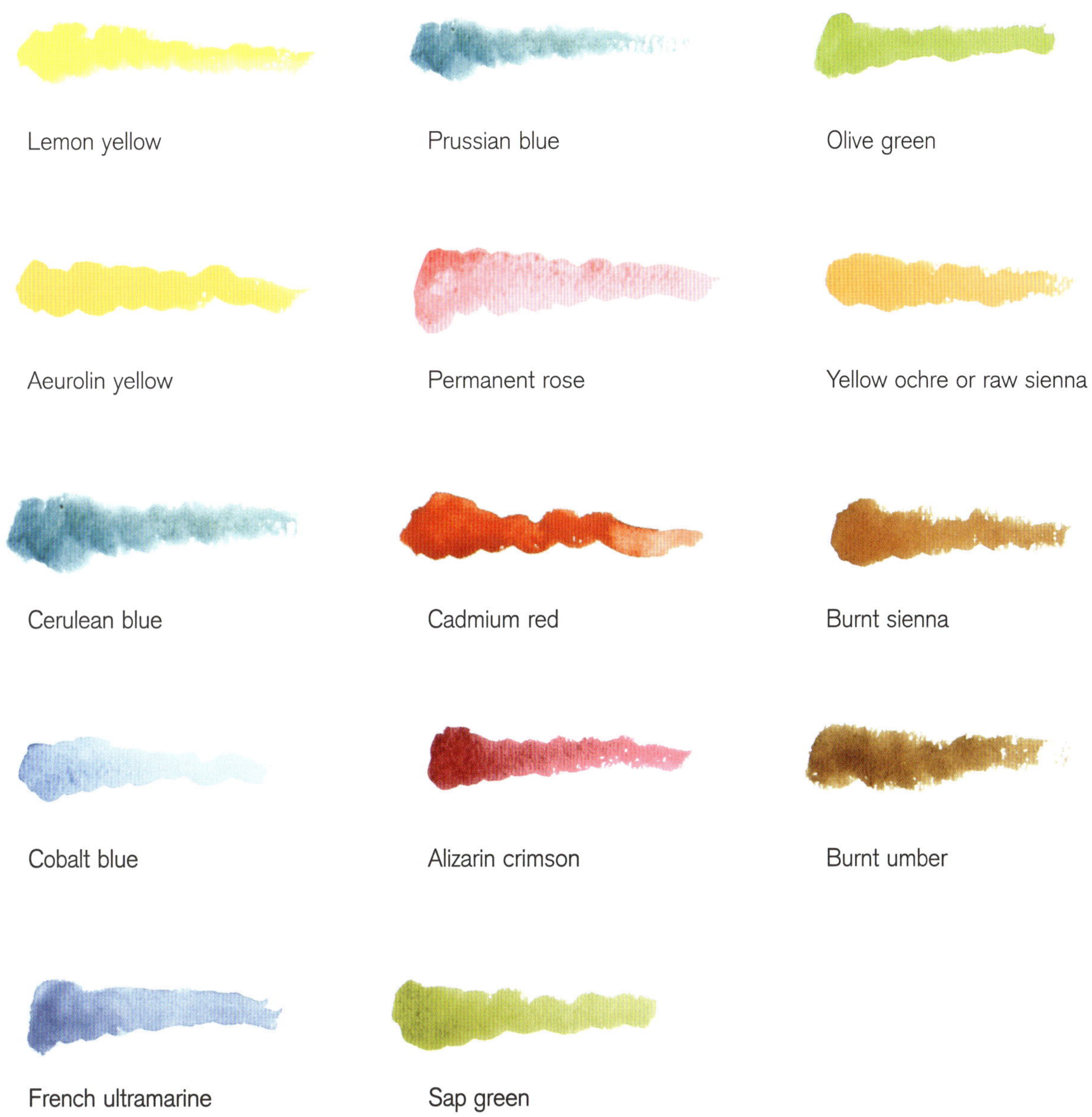

Lemon yellow

Prussian blue

Olive green

Aeurolin yellow

Permanent rose

Yellow ochre or raw sienna

Cerulean blue

Cadmium red

Burnt sienna

Cobalt blue

Alizarin crimson

Burnt umber

French ultramarine

Sap green

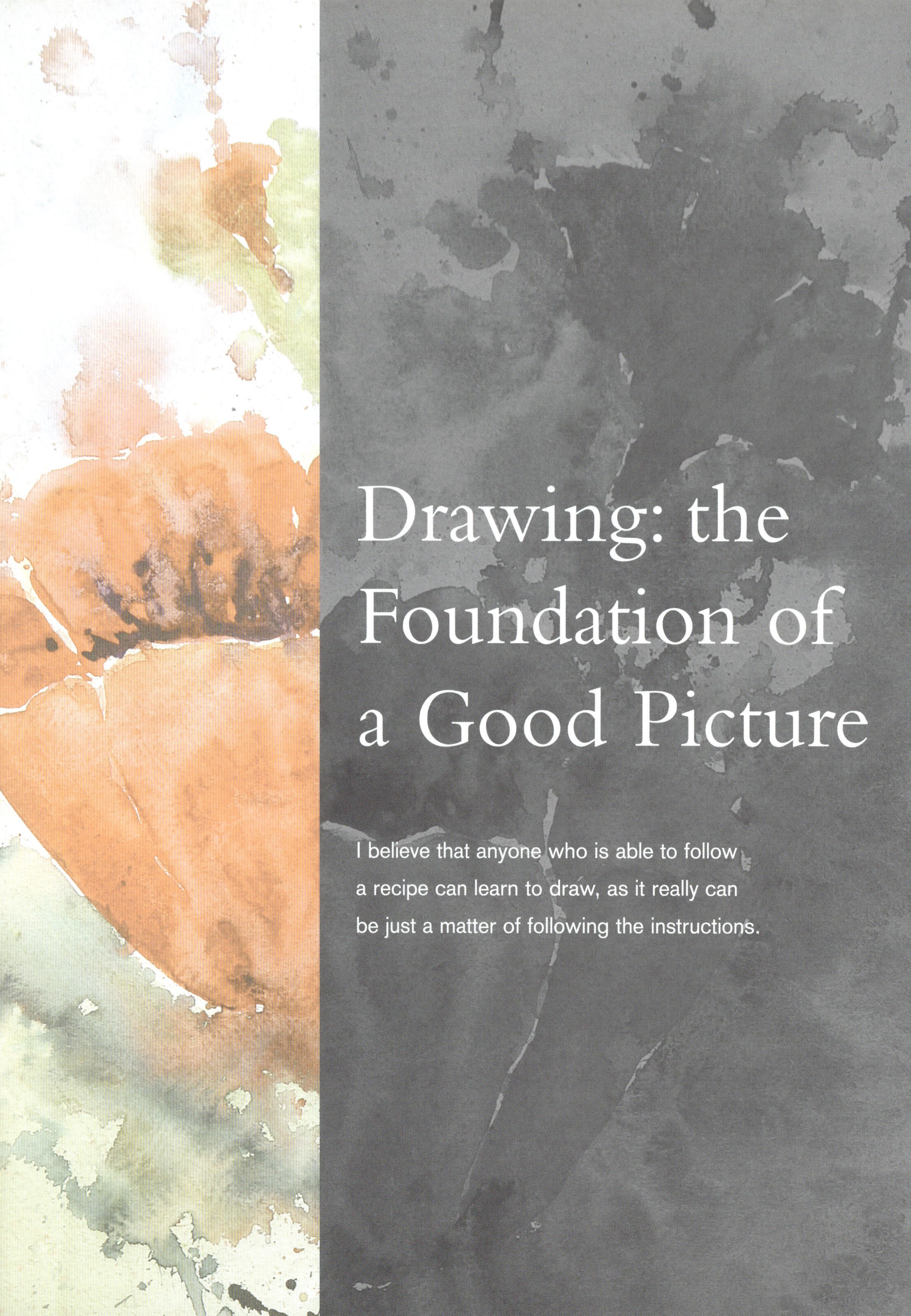

Drawing: the Foundation of a Good Picture

I believe that anyone who is able to follow
a recipe can learn to draw, as it really can
be just a matter of following the instructions.

Some people are intimidated by the whole drawing process. I've heard so many people say that they can't draw, yet I know these same people can follow recipes and complicated instruction manuals and I believe that anyone who is able to follow that kind of procedure can learn to draw.

It is easy to think that artists just throw a quick drawing together by magical instinct, but they too will have started by taking it a step at a time – looking, observing, measuring, comparing, simplifying the image by breaking it down into simple shapes and parts – the basic principles that all aspiring artists should follow.

Tip: don't be overwhelmed at what you see before you. Make it easier for yourself: simplify the image by breaking it down.

You may be eager to start painting – but wait a bit, as you will benefit from taking the time to study the basics of drawing. Remember that your drawing is the skeleton on which your picture hangs and if you get this – the foundation – right, it will pay dividends in the end result.

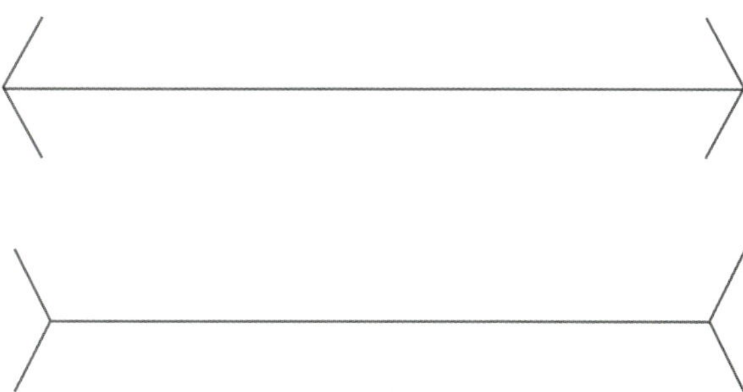

Take time to observe

Often we draw what we think we can see and what we expect to be the case, rather than what is actually there. The diagram above is an example of this.

Which of the arrows is the longest? You may think they are both the same, as you are so used to this popular visual trick. In fact I have just tested this out on my family and they all said, dismissively, that they're both the same size. But look again, and you will find that the top one is longer.

No matter how sure you think you are, always check things out visually, never rely on your preconceptions.

As would-be artists you can never look hard enough at what you are trying to reproduce. I made my students look and keep looking at a still life until they were passed the boredom threshold, and only then would they begin to see different aspects of the scene and view things in a new light. Try this yourself: look at your scene for five to ten uninterrupted minutes.

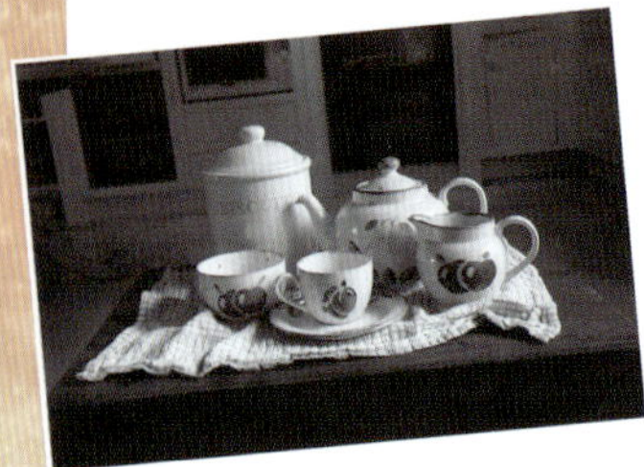

Let's use this tea set as an example
of how to apply the principles of drawing

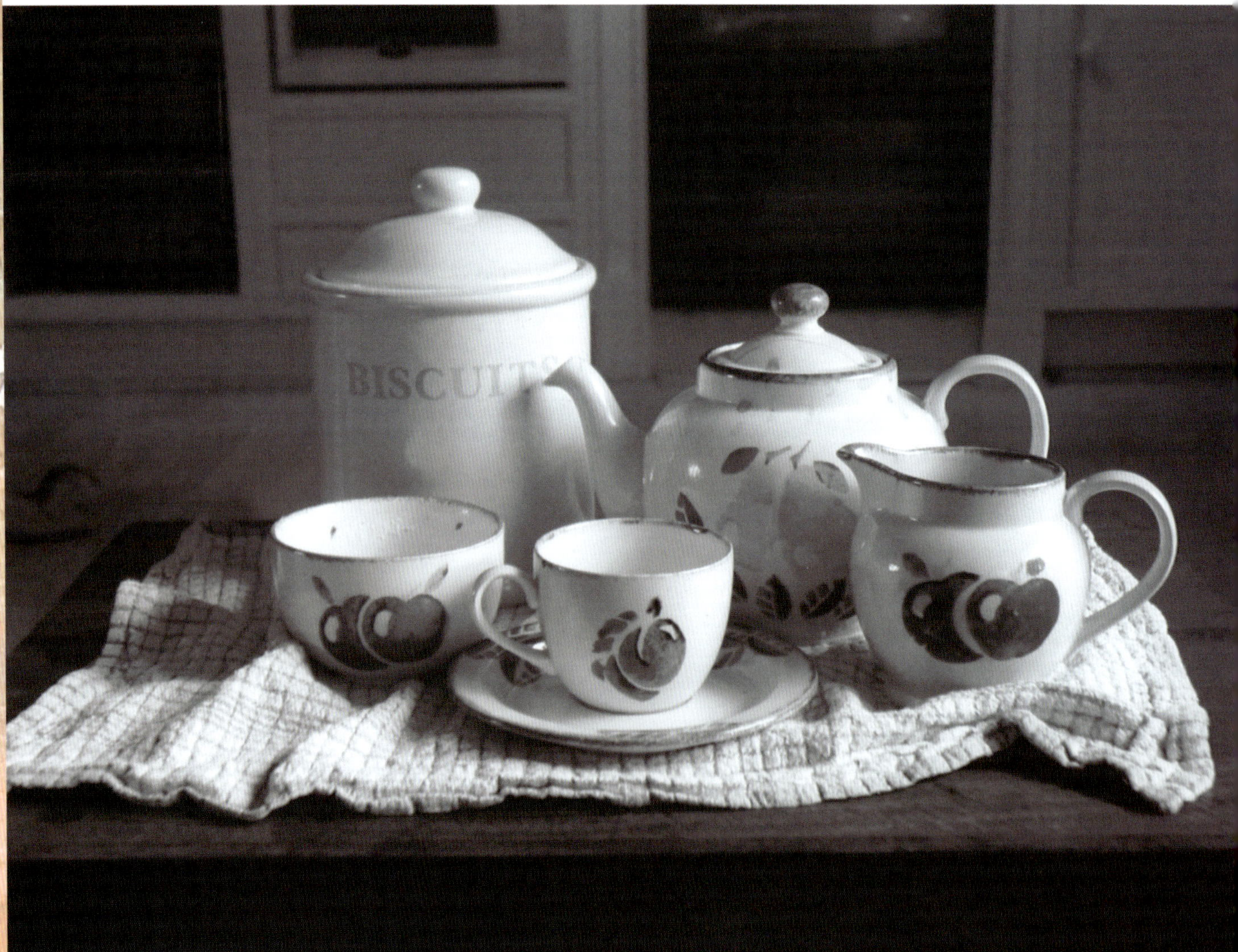

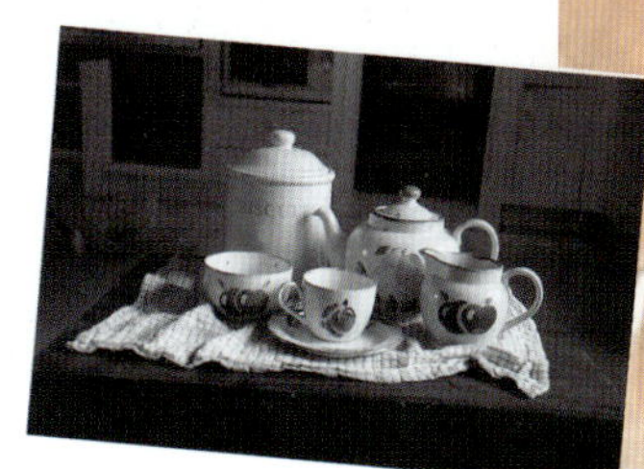

Reduce what you see to simple shapes

With a little imagination, most objects can be reduced to simple shapes. For instance, the teapot below is basically a sphere with lid, spout and handle added on, the bowl is half a sphere, the jug is a sphere, and so on. If you draw these basic shapes and get into the habit of thinking like this, analysing and breaking down the scene into more simple shapes, it is less daunting.

Once you have mastered this technique you will be able to cope with drawing most things. Admittedly, it may require creative thinking at times – for example, adding different shapes together and adapting them – but even the human figure, which is the most complicated thing you can draw, can be reduced to simple shapes of cylinders and a sphere.

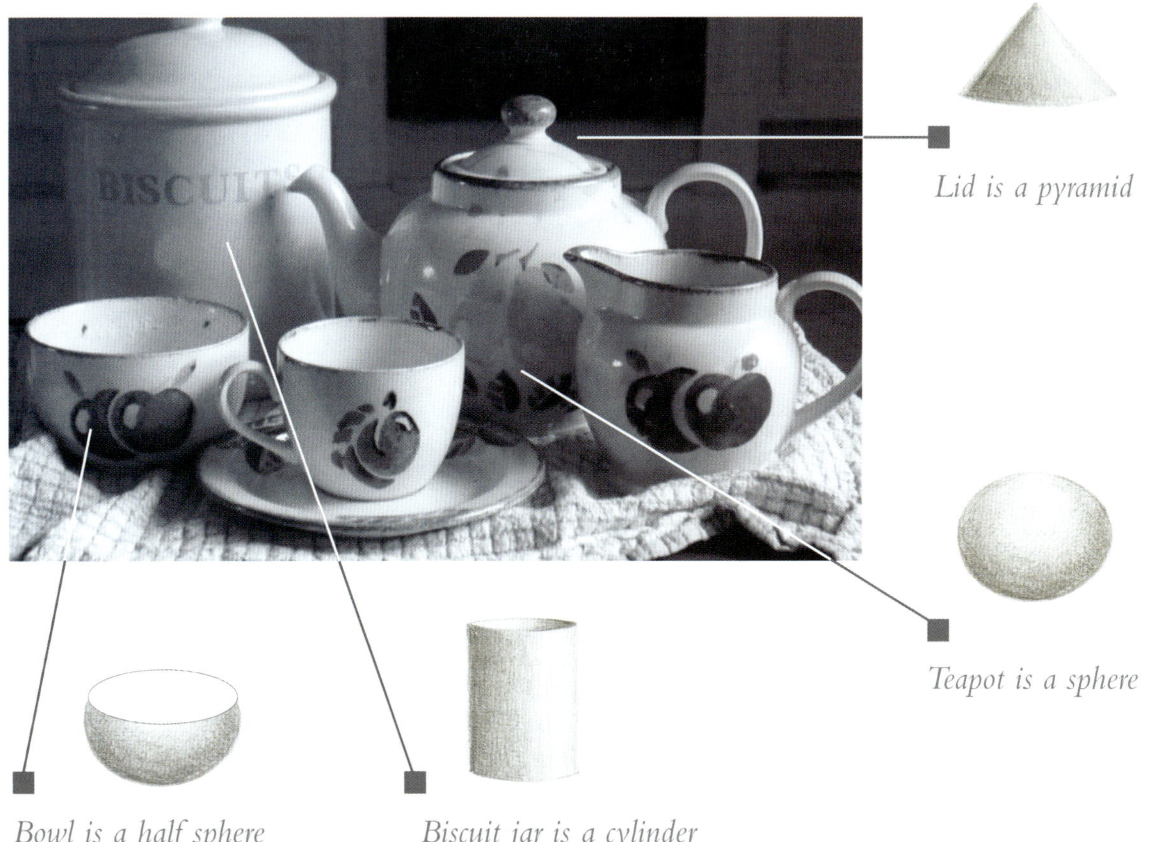

Lid is a pyramid

Teapot is a sphere

Bowl is a half sphere

Biscuit jar is a cylinder

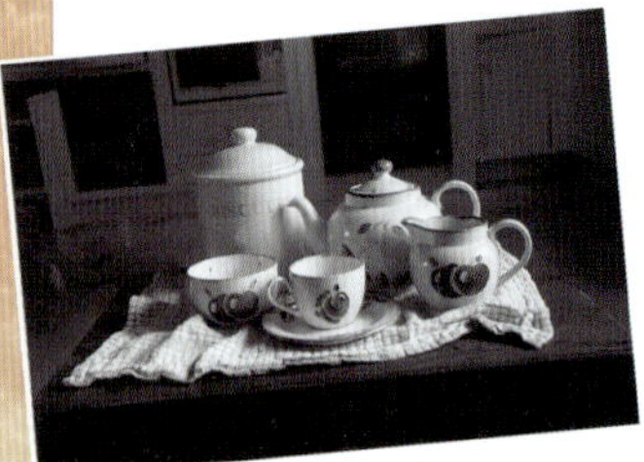

Measure and check areas against each other

To check whether areas are correctly proportioned in relation to each other, hold a pencil up at arm's length and use it as a measuring stick. Move your thumb along the pencil to mark the width or length of an object, keep your thumb in place so you have the measurement set, then move the pencil to another area and compare it to see if it is the same size. Keep looking, analysing and comparing like this as you draw. If you get the proportions of one part right, then you can use it as a unit of measurement for another part.

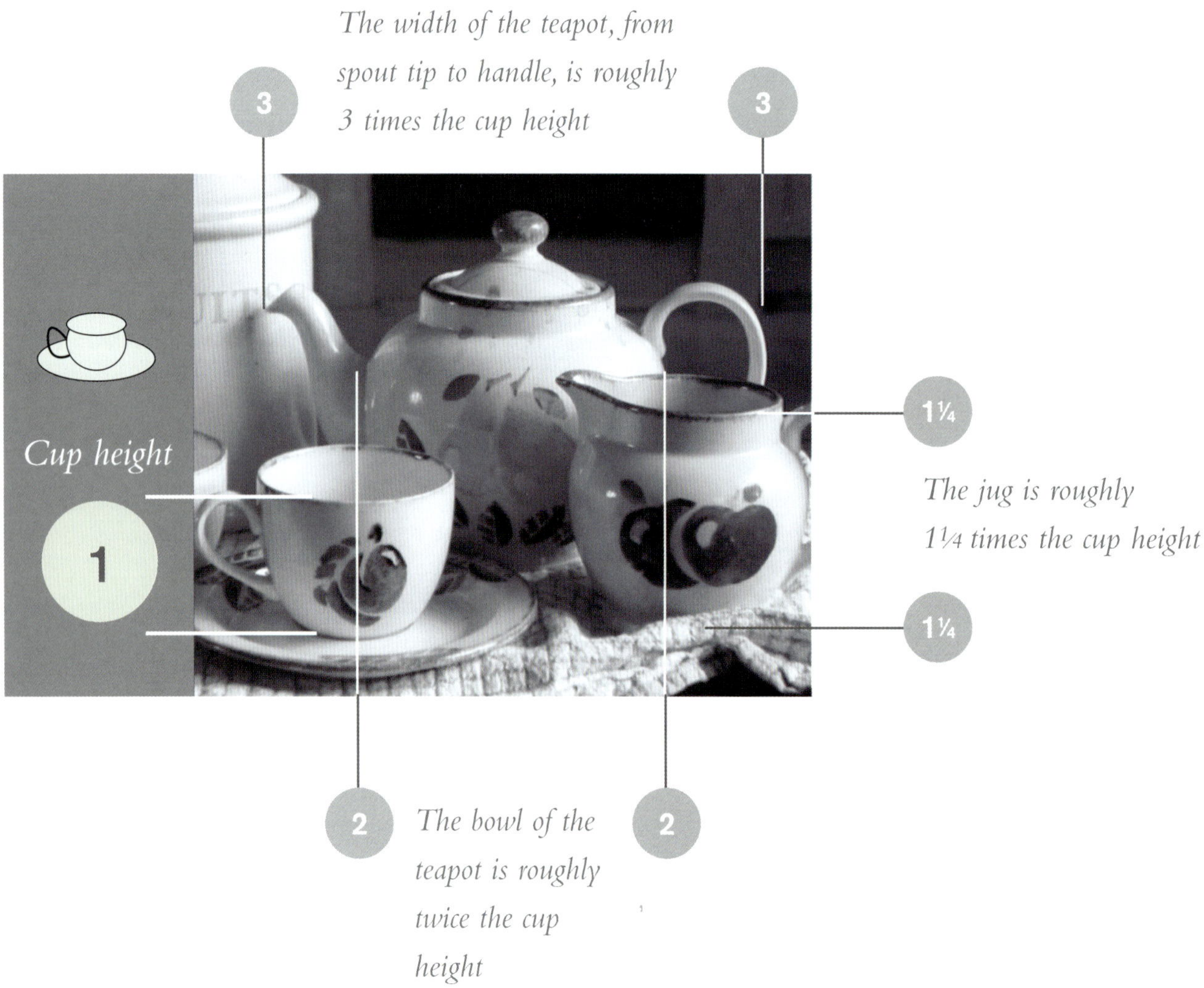

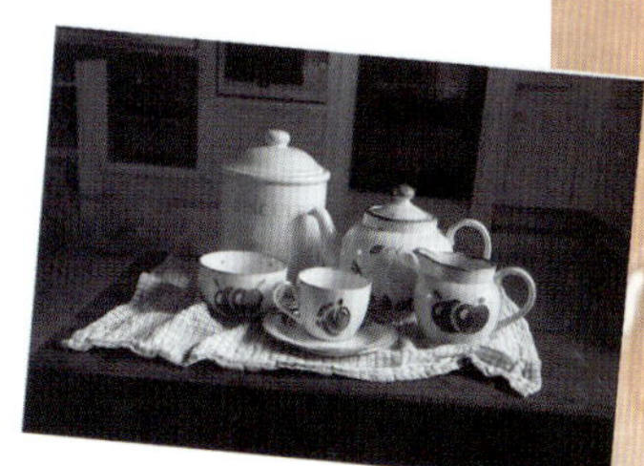

Relate the edges of objects to each other

Once your basic shapes are pencilled in, check that they are in the right place and double-check that they are the right proportions. To do this, compare and measure where objects are in relation to each other and how their sizes compare, as shown below.

Tip: keep your pencils sharp. A thick line could distort the area that you need to pinpoint and result in an inaccurate drawing.

The left edge of the saucer comes halfway across the biscuit tin

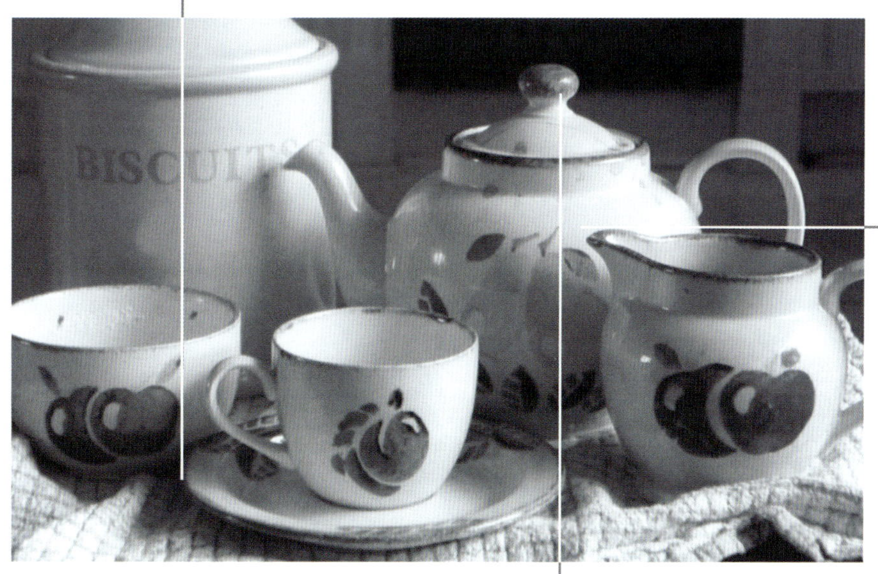

The jug intrudes a third of the way into the teapot

The lid of the teapot aligns with the edge of the saucer

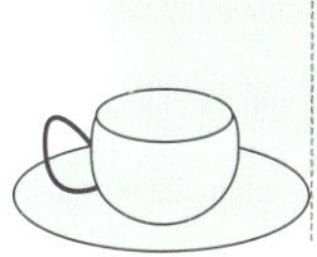

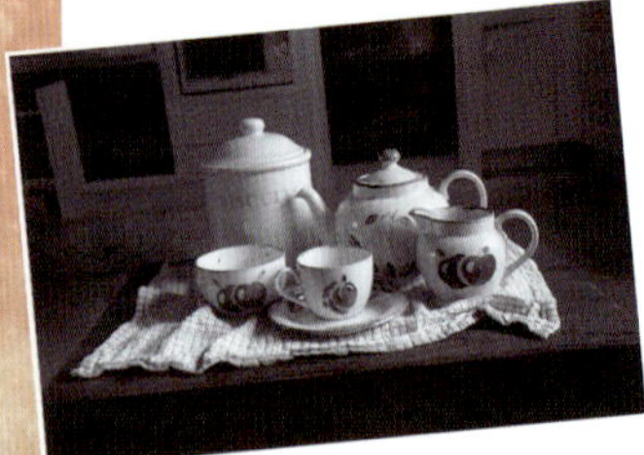

Ensure that your angles are correct

One badly drawn angle can let a whole painting down, but there are 'tricks of the trade' you can employ if you have difficult angles to include:

• Hold your pencil out at arm's length, either horizontally or vertically, and use it as a reference point from which you can note how many degrees the angle is away from the straight line.

• Make an 'angle deviser' by joining two strips of card with a paper fastener. Hold this up in front of the object you are drawing and move it around until it is at the correct angle. Then, keeping it set at that angle, transfer the card to your paper and draw the angle exactly as you have seen it.

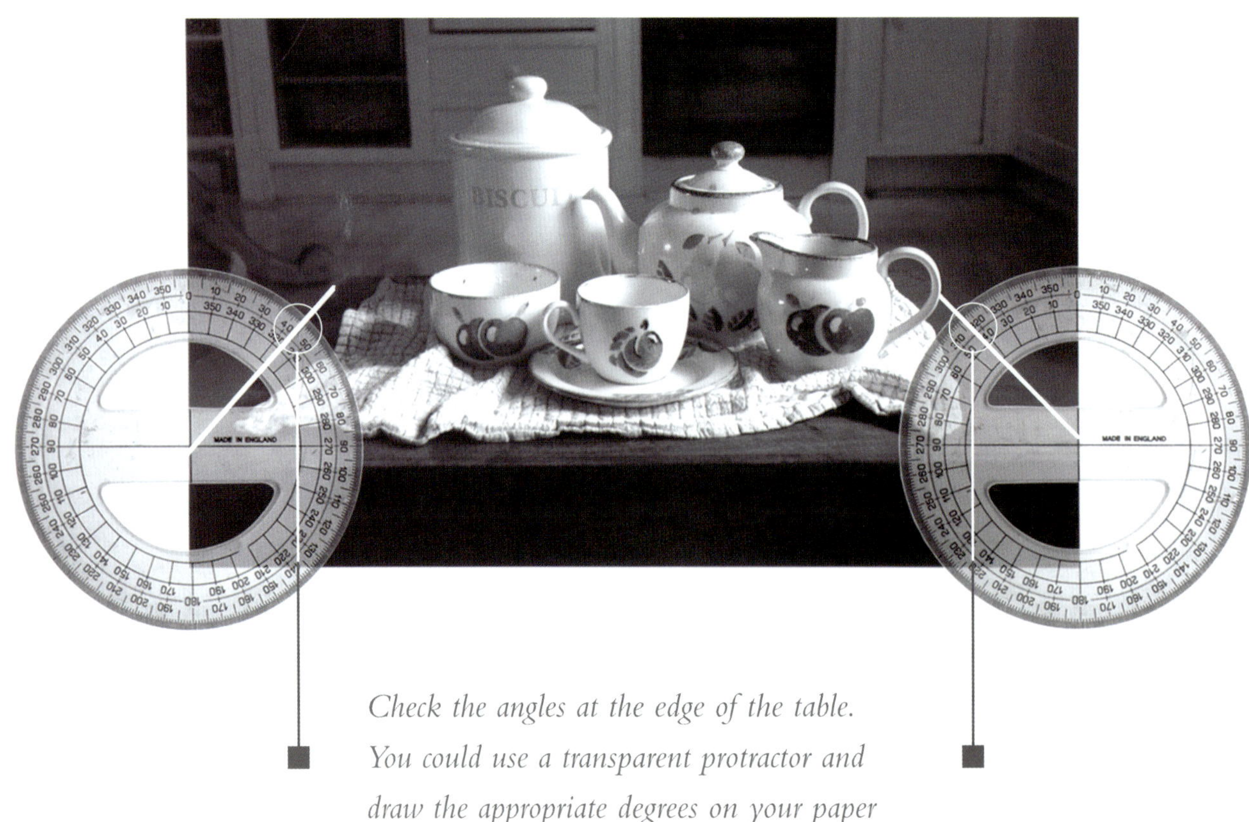

Check the angles at the edge of the table. You could use a transparent protractor and draw the appropriate degrees on your paper

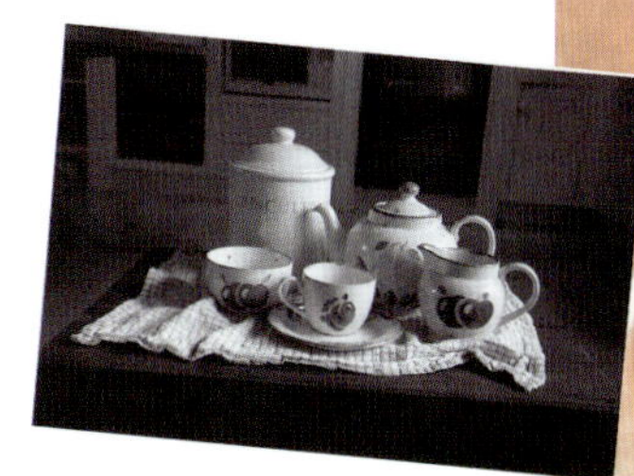

Using negative spaces

As well as looking at the shape of the objects you are drawing, notice the shape of the spaces in between them. If you draw those spaces (the negative shapes) correctly, the main objects will stand a better chance of being accurate.

Note the tiny triangle between the spout, biscuit jar and top of cup, and the shape created looking through the handle of the teacup – this places the edge of the sugar bowl in its correct position and establishes the base of the biscuit jar where it needs to be.

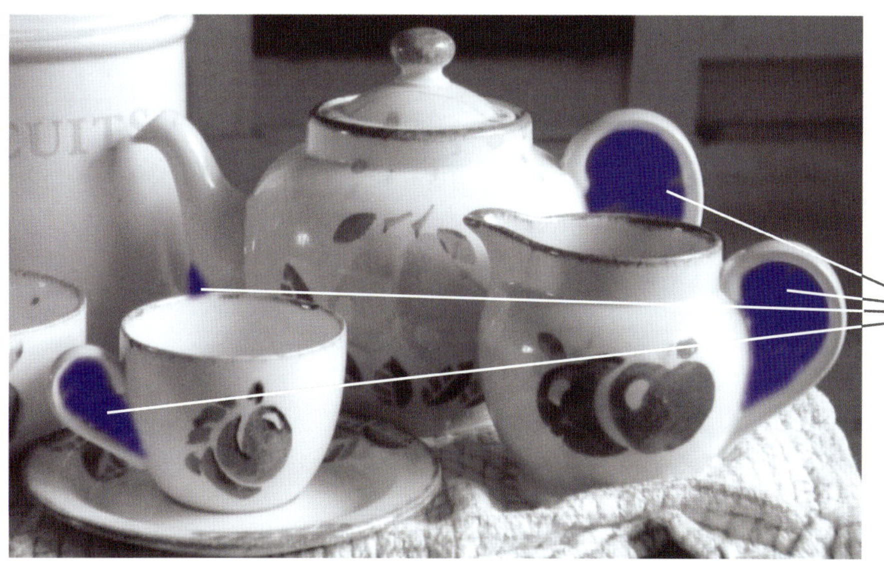

The negative spaces are highlighted

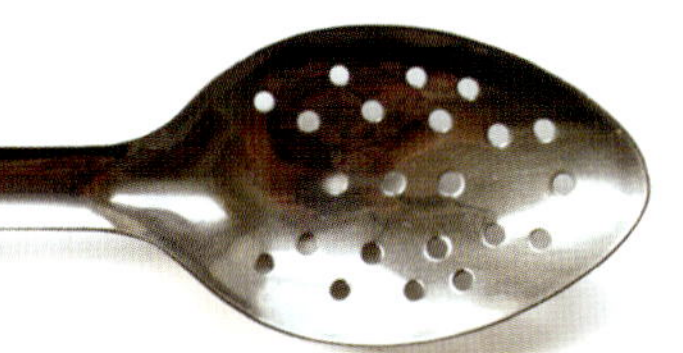

✱ Project: Negative spaces

Gather together some kitchen utensils which have holes in them. Arrange the objects together and just paint the colour of the surface they are lying on – i.e. all the negative shapes between and around the objects, rather than the objects themselves – and you will see that the utensils appear without actually being drawn.

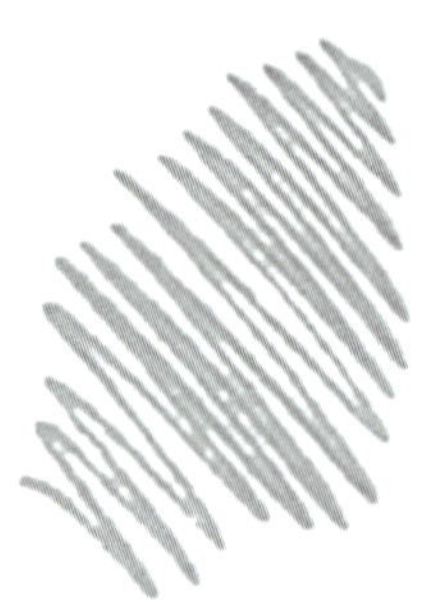

Making marks

When making observational drawings, start with gentle, light, planning marks, without any lines, so that the sketch can remain fluid and be altered as necessary. If you start drawing with firm lines it will be difficult to adjust the sketch as you go along.

Once you are happy with your sketch, you can finalize it with darker marks. If it bothers you that the sketch won't be neat, because of all the 'messy' lines, invest in a good plastic eraser.

It is useful to understand the various effects achieved with different grades of pencil, which in extremes range from very light, hard (9H) to very dark, soft (9B).

However, you certainly won't need all the pencils in the range, just an HB for drawing and 2B, 4B and 6B for shading, moving to these higher numbers as you need to get progressively darker.

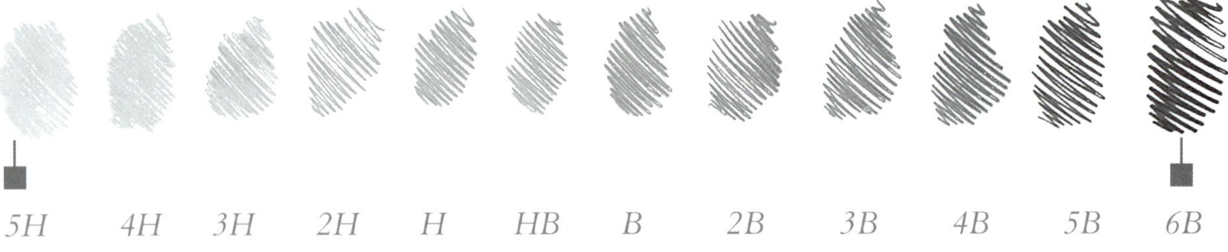

Keeping your eye level consistent

When you are drawing you need to keep both your eye level and the light source consistent. Notice if you are looking down on the objects, or whether they are level with your sight.

This factor makes a difference in the way you draw objects, for example the ellipse – the oval shape at the top of any cylindrical object that you draw – will vary in size depending on the angle from which you look at it:

the more level it is with your eye, the narrower it will be, and when it is at eye level, it will become a straight line as you can no longer see into it. Conversely, the more you look down on the ellipse, the wider it will be, until – if you are directly above it – it will be a full circle.

Be aware of this and keep your eye level consistent: make sure ellipses are uniform and all responding from the same viewpoint.

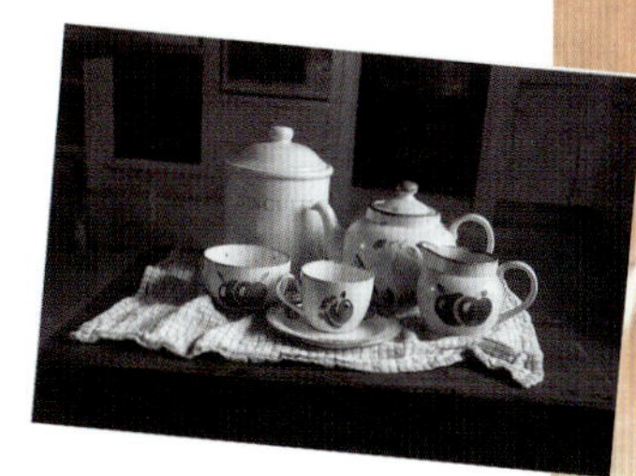

Shading (tone and value)

By adding shading to your drawing you will make it three-dimensional and turn an outline sketch into a picture.

First, note where the light is coming from and how it affects the objects. In the simplest scenario, they will be lighter where the light hits them and gradually become darker as they turn away from the light into shade.

Note that there will also be reflected light in the darkest areas, as on the left-hand side of the jug below.

Keep your shading consistent, make sure that the light is hitting objects from the same source and that your shadows all fall in the same direction (see also 'The Importance of Tone, p. 126).

Light source, hits the right-hand side of the objects

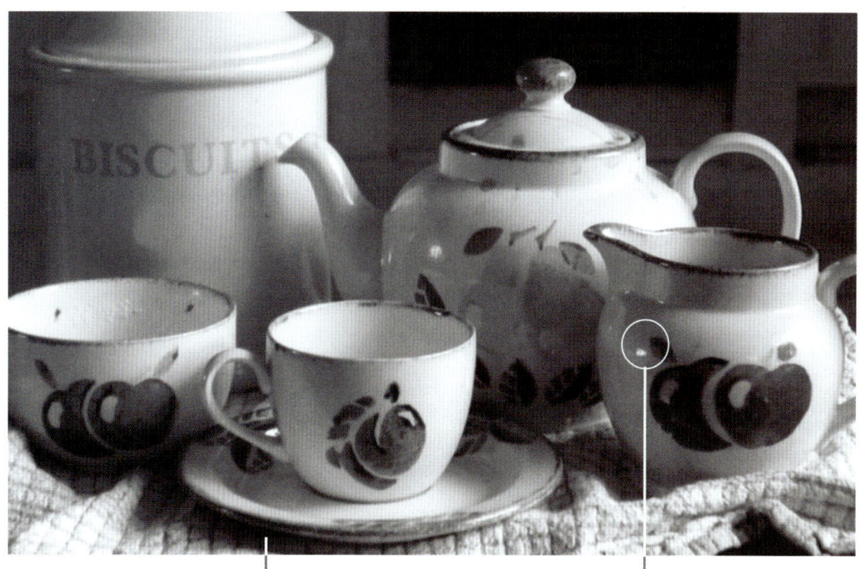

Look at the shadows on the cup

Reflected light

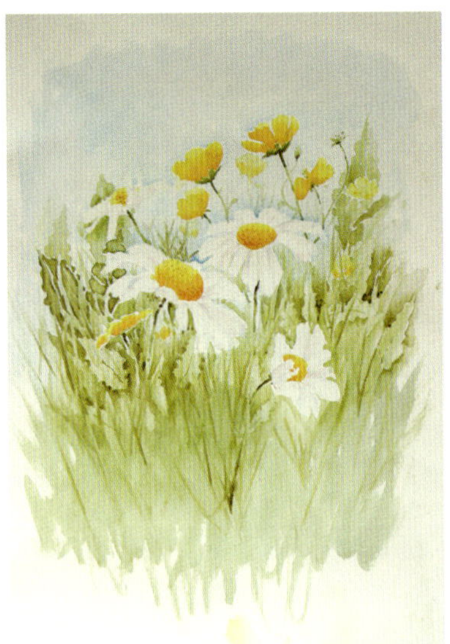

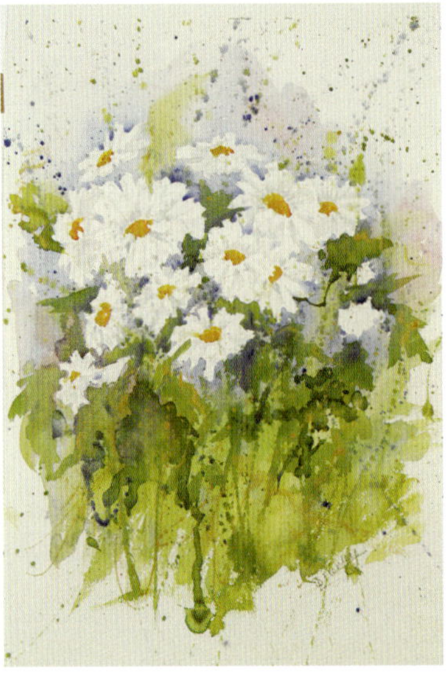

Here we have an early, traditional painting of a daisy on the left, compared to a looser, more exciting interpretation from later in my career on the right

Pushing the boundaries

When I first started drawing my main aim, as with most people, was simply to achieve a likeness. Consequently my drawings were tight and neat but had no excitement or spirit to them (see 'a' and 'b' on the facing page). Gradually I loosened up, and the process was more fun and the results more interesting (see 'c' and 'd' on the facing page, and page 161).

So learn to draw traditionally first – this is a vital foundation – but don't stay there, push yourself into new areas, aiming for excitement and expression. (See overleaf, and 'Becoming an Artist', page 154, for more advice about developing your style and loosening up.)

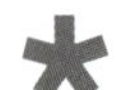 **Project:** Producing exciting drawings

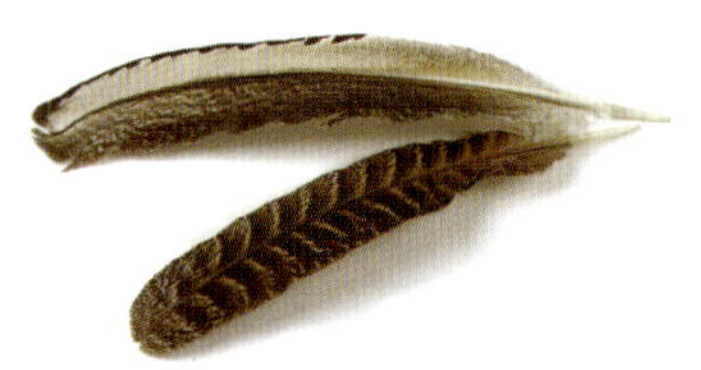

You can use your pencil in many different ways and it pays to exploit it as a tool to get as much variety, different texture and use out of it as you can: don't simply do shading with it, but also hatching, cross-hatching, scribbling, and so on. More importantly, don't confine yourself to just using a pencil. A friend used to leave the tops off felt-tip pens, until they were are half dried-out, as that gave a lovely feathery texture to her sketches. I love using unusual materials too, and suggest you try a variety of other materials, including:

- Old felt-tip pens

- 'Wrong' end of brush

- Feathers (both ends)

- Sticks – ragged and bendy, dipped in ink

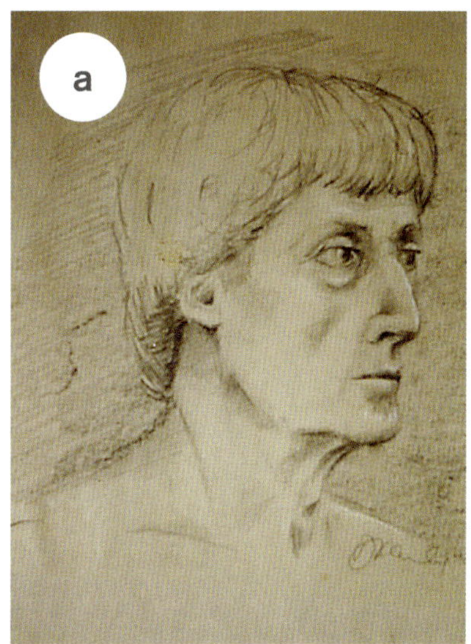

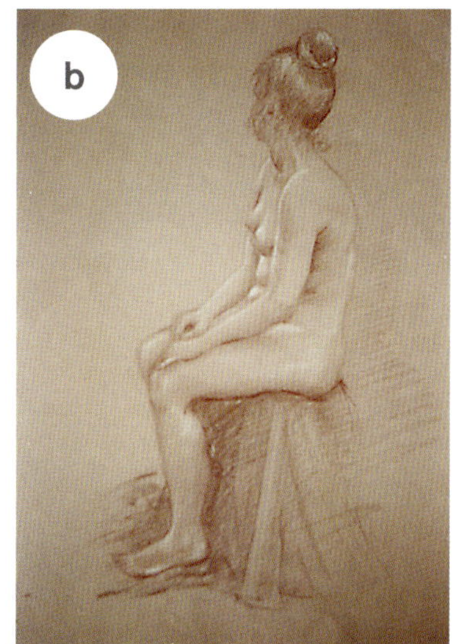

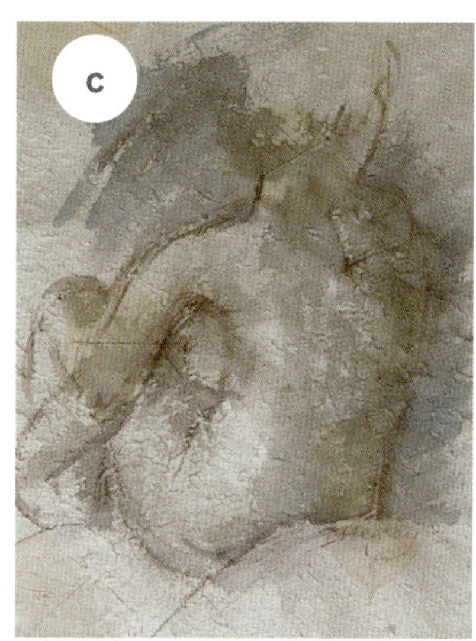

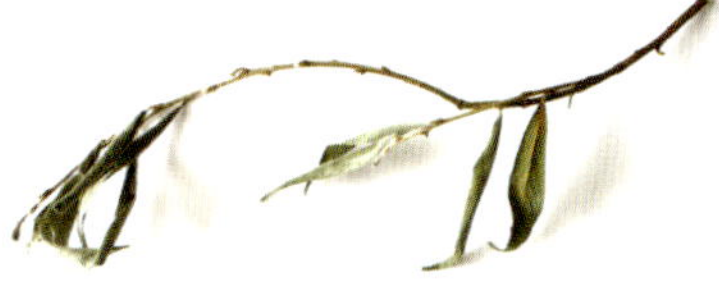

I was once seen picking up armfuls of sticks as my son and his friends came out of school, he said I looked like a bag lady and has never forgiven me. But it was worth it – the sticks were bendy willow and we had a great time drawing with them. We held them at arms length, dipped them in ink, then they bowed and bent with a mind of their own as we drew with them, giving lovely results, which you can see on pages 84 and 161

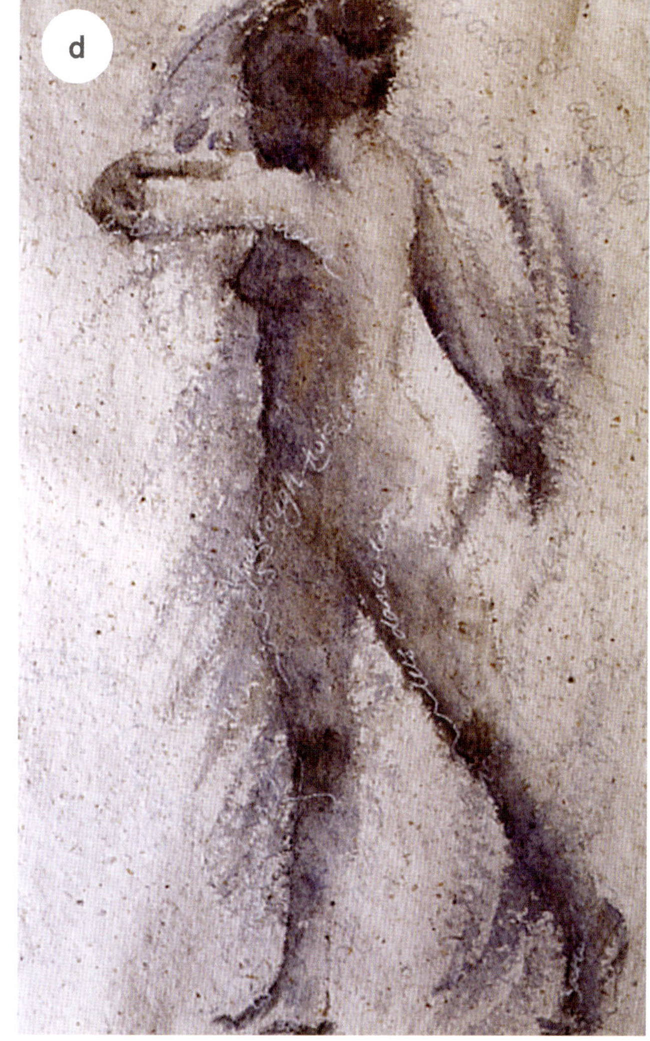

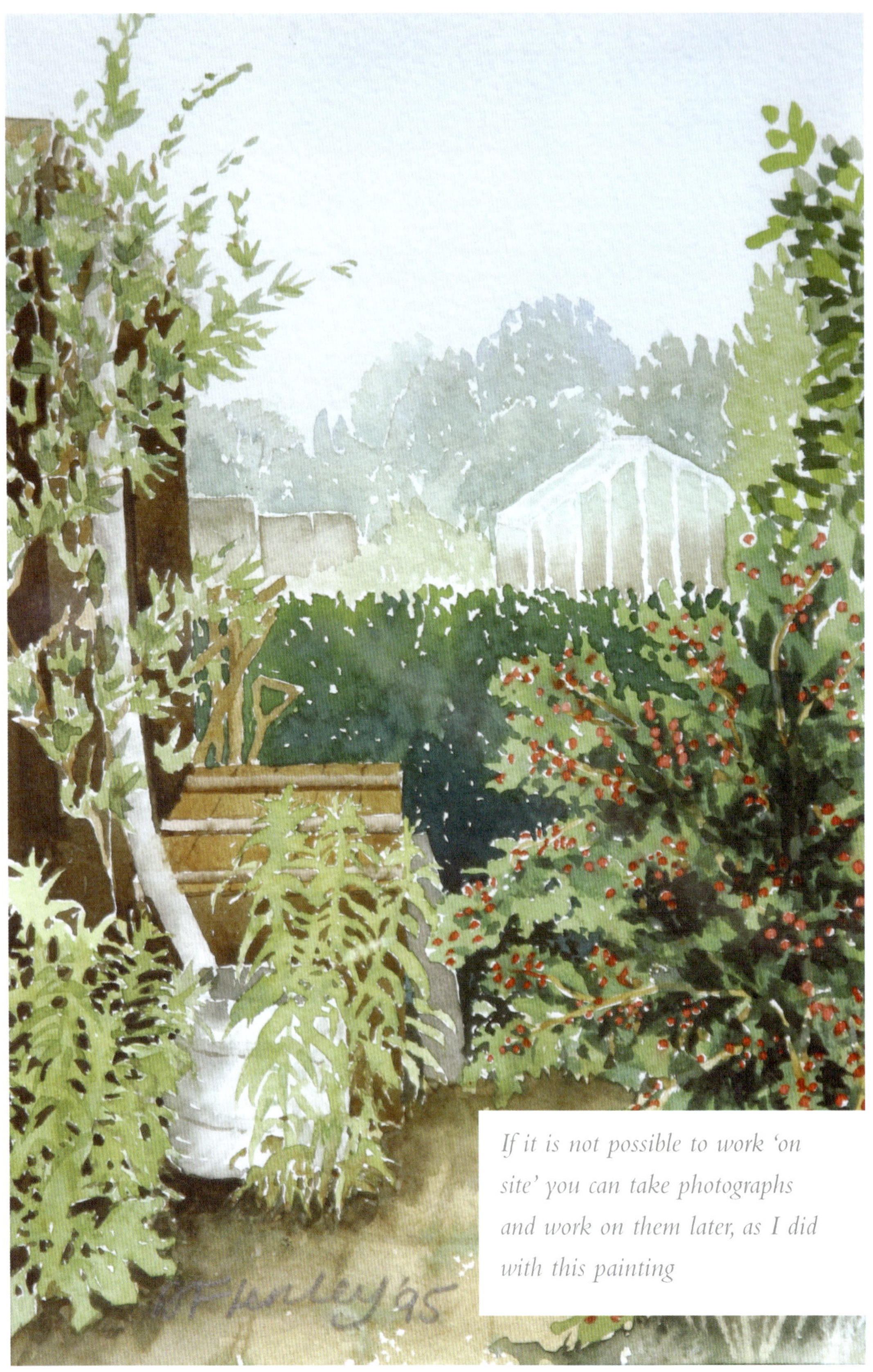

If it is not possible to work 'on site' you can take photographs and work on them later, as I did with this painting

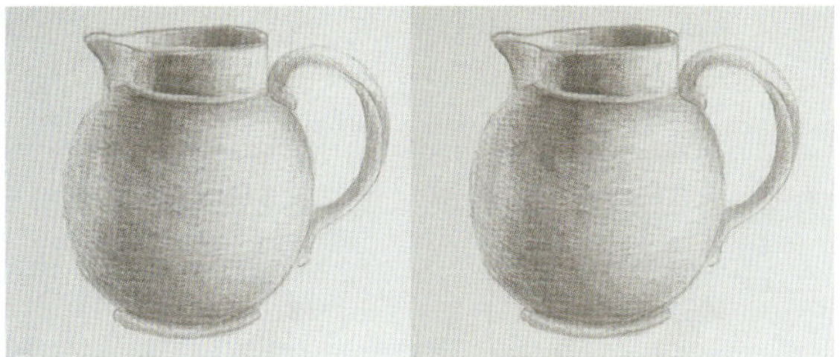

Transferring and copying work

Often you will need to transfer work or copy another drawing and there are a number of ways of doing this:

• You could use the simple, inexpensive children's toys available that reflect an image through plastic for copying. They only work up to A4, but could be a useful purchase if drawing really isn't for you.

• More traditionally, you could use a grid to help transfer, enlarge, or reduce an image.

Do you remember those children's puzzle books, where you were given a picture in a simple grid and had to copy it into an empty grid – usually on the next page – by drawing exactly what was in each square? Well, artists have employed this method for hundreds of years and so there's no good reason why you can't, too. If you have a picture you want to copy simply 'grid it up' by drawing lines over it and copy it out. You can reduce or enlarge your image by making your squares larger or smaller, as long as the proportions are kept

the same. If you don't want to damage your source material, simply draw your lines on see-through plastic and lay it on the picture.

• If you want similar help copying a scene in front of you, draw lines on a plastic sheet and hold it up at arm's length. If you frame this plastic sheet with a surround of cardboard you will have a viewfinder too, which will also help you with your composition.

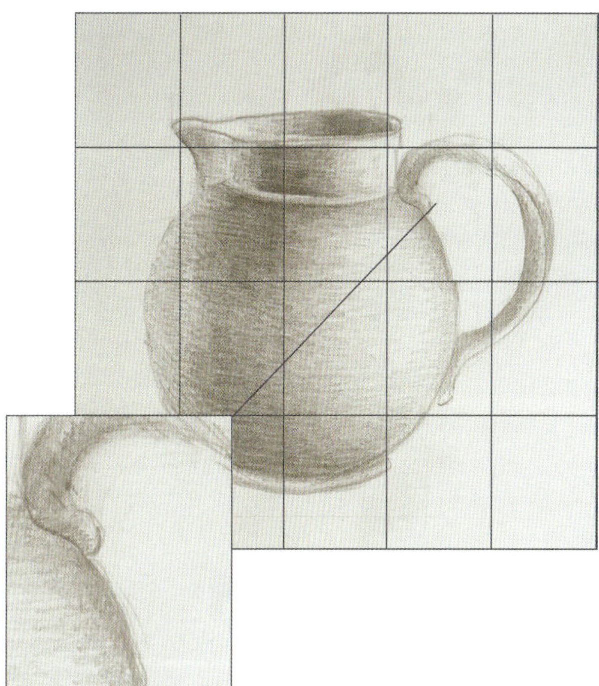

*While all these methods are great,
I encourage you to practise drawing freehand if
you can, rather than relying on 'props'*

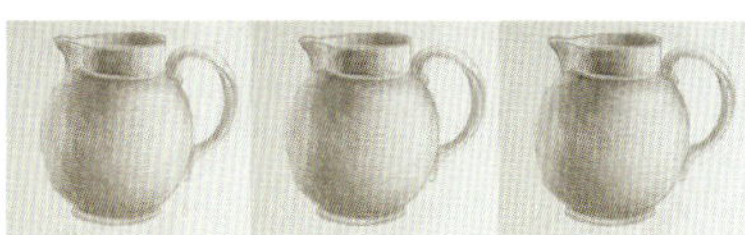

Preparing
to Paint

Before you start painting, I need to take
you through an initiation ritual: the process
of stretching paper.

Stretching paper

When paper is wet or paint is applied it expands and, if left to its own devices, will cockle. Cockling can cause difficulties, especially if you are trying to lay a wash in a large area, as paint will collect in pools in the valleys of the undulations. Stretching counteracts this, and creates a tight drum-like finish.

★ Project: Stretching Paper

To stretch paper, you will need:

a A sheet of watercolour paper

b Sponge, or a sink/ bowl of water

c A board slightly bigger than the paper.

d Gummed tape – it has to be the brown type that you wet, not adhesive tape

1 First, wet your paper: soak it in the sink, thoroughly sponge it with clean water, or spray it with a large atomiser. But don't get it too wet – there is no advantage in this, as it will take too long to dry.

If it does get too wet, roll the paper between two sheets of blotting paper, or lots of kitchen roll, to remove the excess.

2 When the paper is damp, carefully lay it on the board and tape the edges down with gummed tape.

I tear off a strip of tape the length of one side of the paper then lick just the half of the strip that will be sticking to the board: the 'paper half' will automatically be wet by the damp paper, and if it is too wet the tape won't stick.

3 Once the paper is stuck down, put drawing pins in the corners to stop the tape lifting from the tension caused by the paper drying. When the paper is perfectly dry and taut, it is ready for you to paint on it.

Leave your painting on the board until it is completely dry, then pull off or cut the tapes away carefully, to avoid taking any of the paper with it. Remove any remaining tape before using the board again.

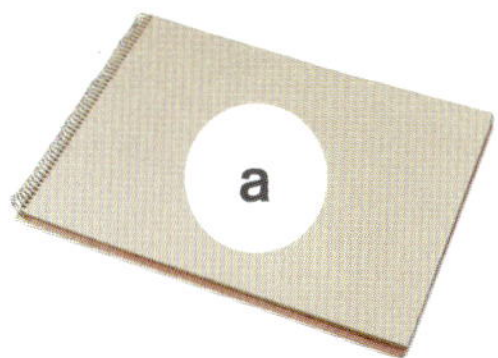

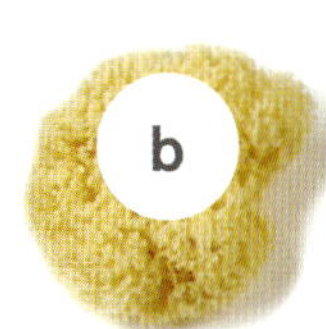

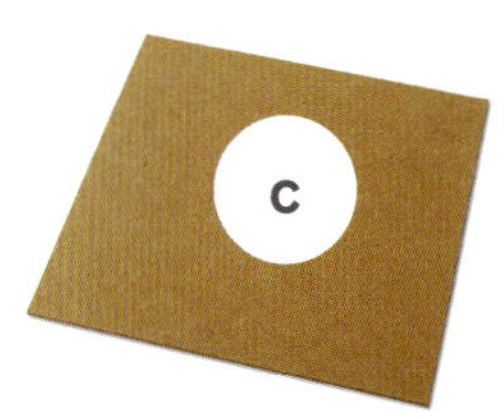

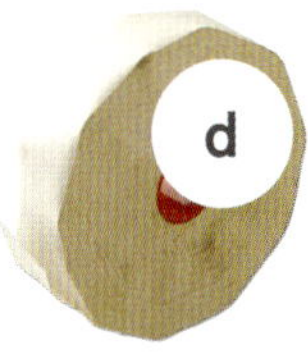

Tip: don't go buying expensive drawing boards – almost any flat piece of board will do. Go to a local sawmill with some painting friends and get a large piece of timber cut into lots of board-size pieces very cheaply. Take along your usual pad of watercolour paper to give you a rough guide to size, drill two holes in the top and thread rope through for handles.

While I admit it is a pleasure to paint on a lovely flat-stretched surface, personally – with apologies to all you purists – I rarely stretch paper, which is why I can describe it as a ritual rather than a necessity.

I find that if you use heavier papers –140lb or 300gsm and above – it is not essential and I don't have the time, organisation, or forethought to plan ahead.

Even if a picture has buckled, and is consequently difficult to frame, it can be stretched after painting, by turning it over, damping the back, sticking it down, and then allowing it to dry flat.

My best advice to you though is 'do as I say, not as I do' and have a go at stretching your paper. If you are just learning, a flat surface can only be a help and you can consider yourself initiated!

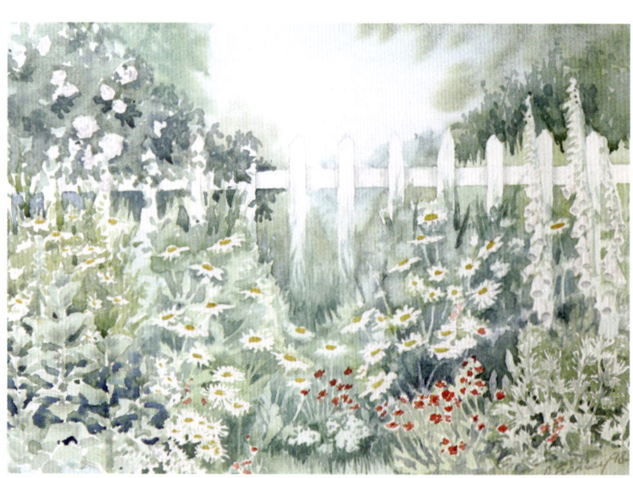

Drawing first

Unless you particularly want to go for a 'loose' painting I recommend that you sketch first. This will be the foundation for your piece and an accurate drawing, following the guidelines on pages 29–41, will go a long way to supporting a good painting. You don't need to do any 'shading in' with your pencil as the tones of your paints will define the form for you, you just need an outline to guide you.

I suggest you sketch lightly with an HB pencil. This is because the graphite from a heavier grade of pencil could pollute your wash as you paint over it, heavier lines would be too dominant, and the picture would become more like a children's colouring-in exercise.

Some painters are concerned about the lines showing through but I like to see the lines, especially if it is a loose, sketchy piece. Even if lines have had to be redrawn for correction, I like to see the original ones left: they show how the piece has been constructed and a 'warts and all see how the artist has struggled' approach makes it more interesting for the viewer – as long as the final outcome is pleasing, of course.

To avoid heavy lines under your painting, complete your drawing then use a plastic eraser to 'dance over' the pencil with random movements. This will eliminate the formality of hard, definite, lines but still leave you with a sketchy outline to follow. However, If you want your painting to look 'neat', get yourself a good plastic eraser.

This was a preparatory sketch and colour study for the picture on page 123

Tip: don't use a putty rubber

for your preliminary sketch, as it could

leave grease marks which will repel

the watercolour.

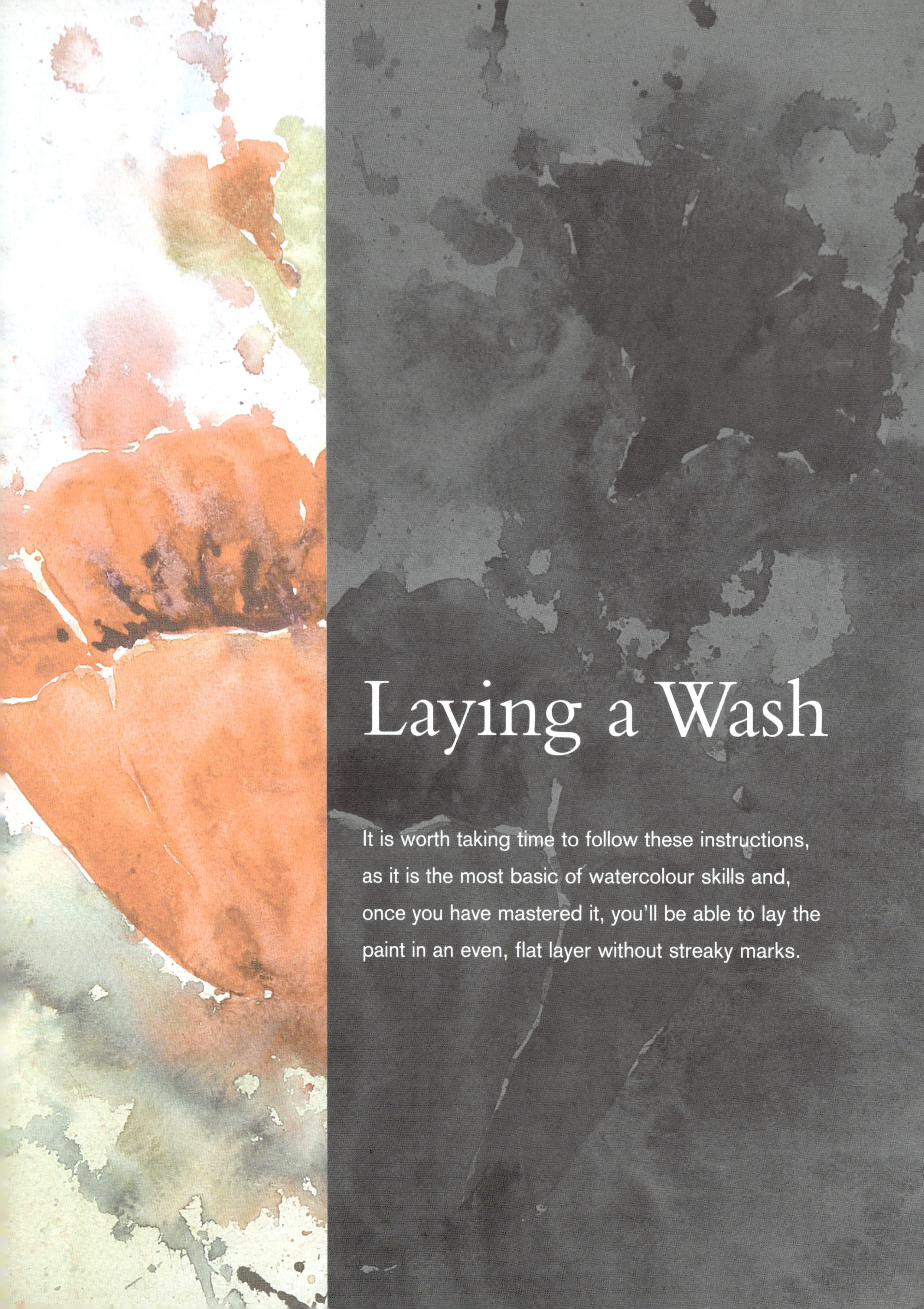

Laying a Wash

It is worth taking time to follow these instructions,
as it is the most basic of watercolour skills and,
once you have mastered it, you'll be able to lay the
paint in an even, flat layer without streaky marks.

This sounds like a very technical term but it's really just a pompous way of saying 'cover the paper with a coat (wash) of watercolour'.

Once you've sketched out your scene in pencil, 'reserve' any areas that will need to be kept white and free of paint (see 'The Use of White in Watercolour', page 66, for instructions on using masking fluid and white paint). You are then ready to lay a wash. This wash could become your sky, or the background basis of your picture, but it will often be the foundation that can be painted over.

A large 'wash brush' is useful, and most large brushes will do for this job, but using one with natural hair does help, because it holds more water. I prefer to lay the wash on dry paper, as it gives you more control over your paint, so with this method, make sure that the sheet of paper you have stretched is completely dry before you start. Some painters, however, like to wet the whole area first, as the water helps the paint disperse – you might like to try this to see how it works for you.

Be careful when handling the paper as the grease on your fingers will leave prints on the paper that will stop the wash adhering to the paper. See the example right, where the paper has been handled and the resulting grease mark left behind.

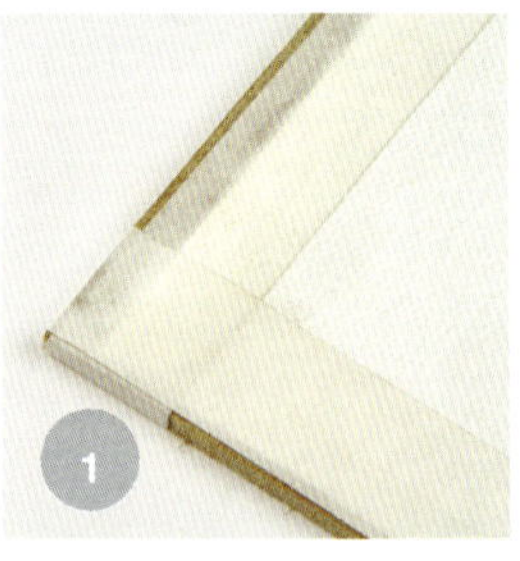

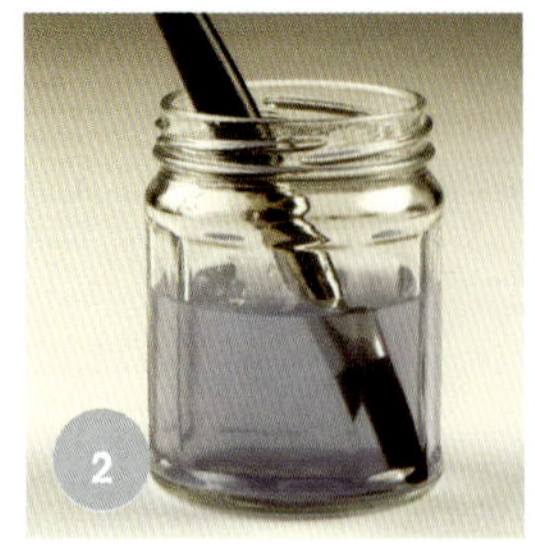

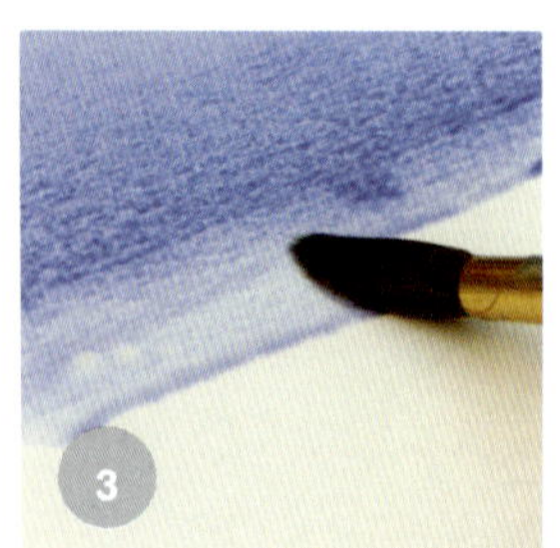

✳ Demonstration: Laying a wash

1 First stretch your sheet of paper, as described on p. 43, and leave it attached to the board. It can then be tilted to allow the paint to run down and 'collect' at the bottom of each brush stroke.

2 Mix up a generous amount of the paint mixture to be used, so that you don't have to stop and mix more paint halfway through. Include plenty of water in the paint-and-water mix, to dilute it and allow the paint to flow. This will ensure that the wash is light and suitable for a background and not too dominant to paint over later. If you want to change colour as you go, have that colour ready-mixed too.

3 Load your brush, then, starting at the top, take it horizontally across the paper from left to right. Once you have swept the brush across, repeat the process again underneath, joining with your previous stroke and picking up the paint collected at the bottom as you go. Your aim is to get a flat, even wash over the paper and this method should prevent any distinct lines between one stroke and the next.

Experiment: you can change colour at this point, add water, or more/less diluted paint to alter the effect, as shown (left).

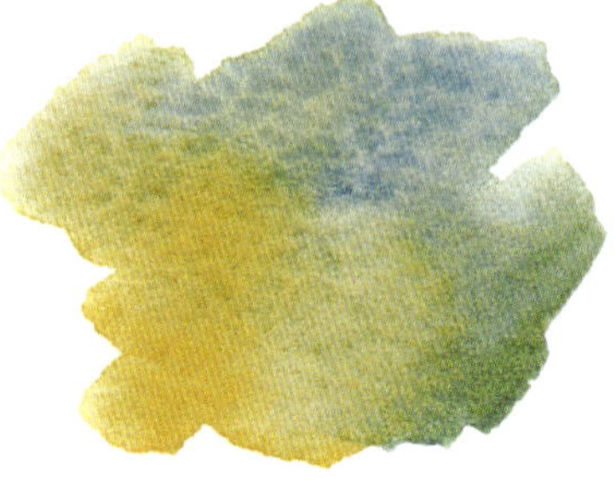

For a distant, out-of-focus style of background, use the 'wet-in-wet approach' and flood other colours in quickly, before it dries (see p. 82). Otherwise, once your wash is laid, leave it alone to dry. If you mess with it too soon you will get runbacks or 'cauliflowers' as the new paint you put on seeps into the damp paint and 'flowers out' into a pattern. In the right hands these can be used effectively, but for the beginner they can be a nightmare. If a run does happen, don't be tempted to try and stop it, as this would make it worse – deal with it later, when the paint is dry.

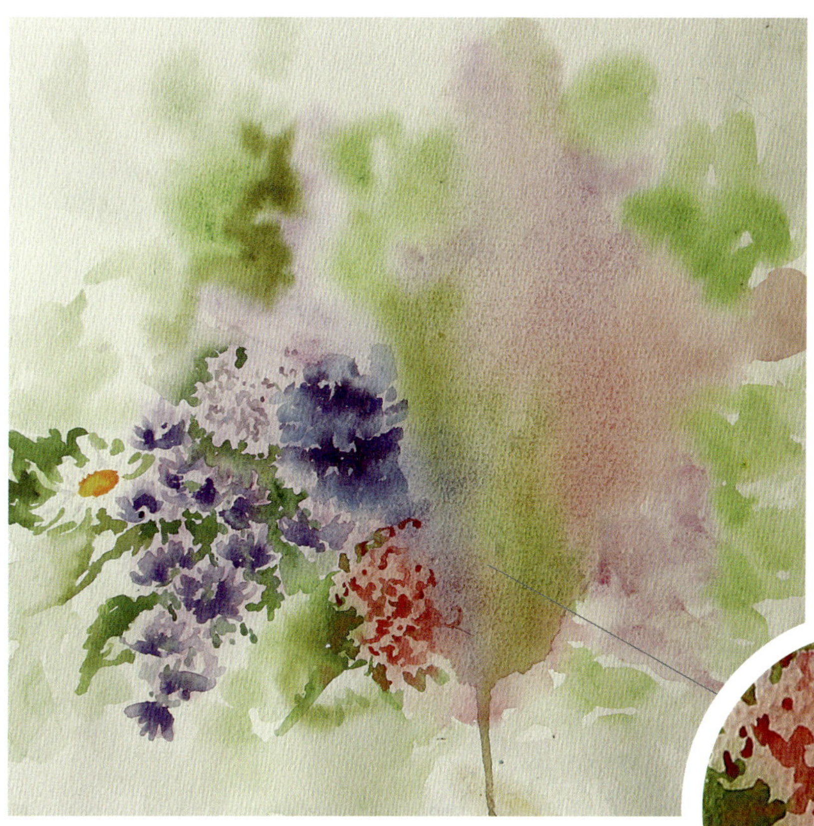

This half-finished painting shows how the underwash forms the basis of the picture. I planned the areas of colour with the wash, painted into it while wet and again when dry, led by the areas in which the paint had settled

Laying an 'underwash'

A general wash of colour laid down before you start painting can influence the feel of the colour for the piece. Obviously, you still have to consider if you want to save any white areas first, or use a colour that you know to be non-staining, so you can lift it out later if you need a white or lighter area.

You also have to consider if you want just one colour in a flat wash, or a graduated change of colour or tone. Bear in mind at this stage that the underwash influences the end product, so anything too fussy could be a distraction to your composition – not a problem if you happen to specifically want such an effect.

You need to be careful about which colours you choose, a staining colour is best – unlike granular colours, these will not 'dirty' other washes that you subsequently lay on top. (See 'How your paints behave', on p. 56, to identify which are granular and which staining.)

Alternatively, you could use a tinted watercolour paper (commonly available from art shops). These, like underpainting, will give an overall feel of colour to a work. The only disadvantage with tinted paper is, obviously, that you can't save white areas – as there aren't any – so any white would need to be added later with gouache.

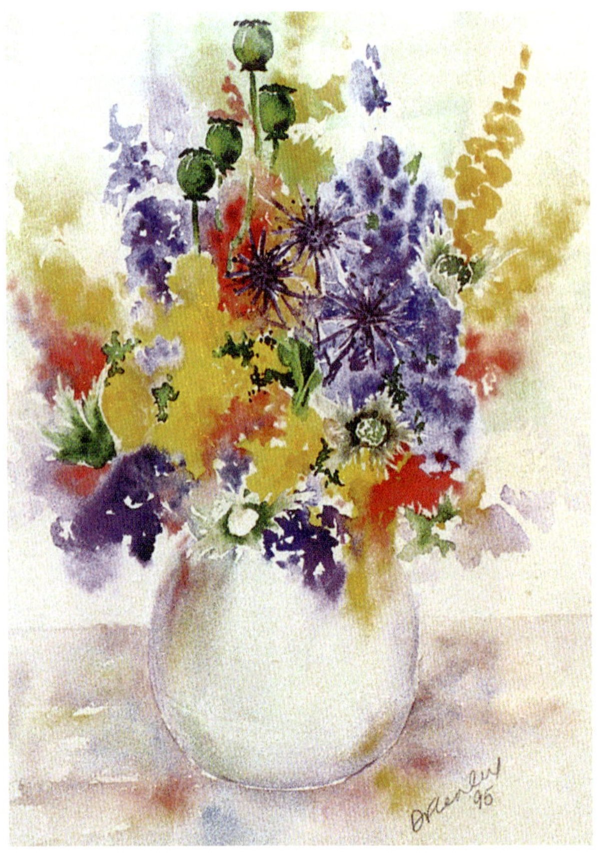

In this picture I flooded colour in the areas of the flowers wet-in-wet and let it dry. I then treated this colour as an underwash and painted the detail of the flowers into it

There is a story behind the painting on the right: when my children were little I sent some paintings to a competition and, as a result, was offered a week in London with members from the Royal Society at the Bankside Gallery. It meant leaving the family and taking lodgings for a week, and a long walk in every day to the gallery, lugging my portfolio and paints. But I did it and, by the end of a week of constant painting away from all distractions, I felt I'd broken through a barrier and my paintings had become more 'free'.

I treated myself to this bunch of flowers and painted this picture on the last day. I liked it because I felt I'd left out all the unnecessary detail and captured what really mattered. The composition is poor and I would tackle it differently today, but it meant a lot to me at the time. So do as I did: push yourself to step out of the box and go beyond your boundaries – it will pay off.

Another way of approaching this could be to flood a variety of colours and utilize a variety of textures then, when you have the finished result to play with, plan the painting around what you have created (see above).

With this method the detail of your painting enhances your original under painting, which becomes the most interesting feature of the work, rather than your under painting being like underwear supporting your picture.

For the painting on the right, I conditioned the paper with an 'underwash' of the cream colour of the lilies – it meant the lilies could be created simply, by painting the shapes of the leaves around them, and the background tied in with the flowers, giving a unified appearance

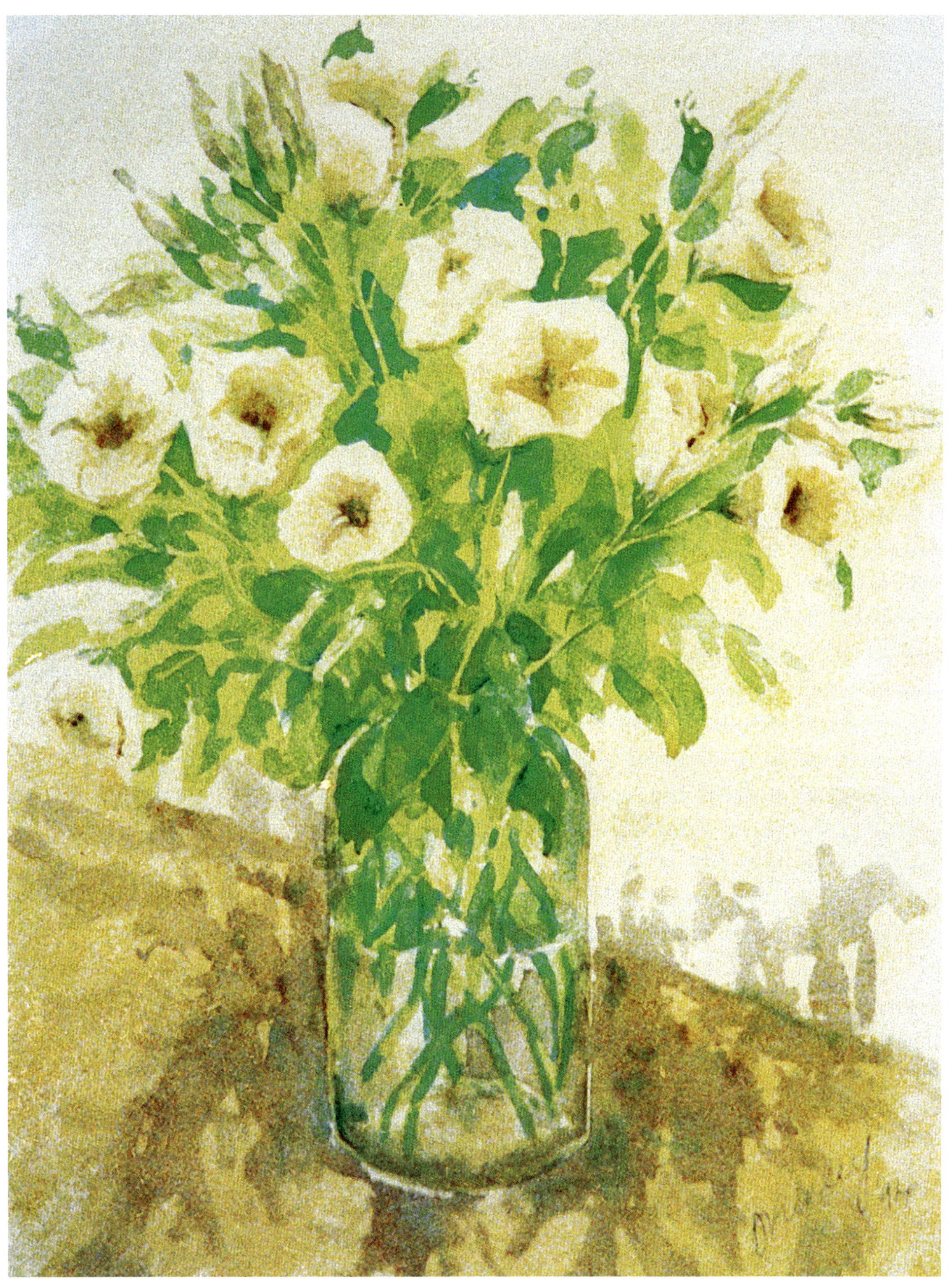

Handling Watercolours

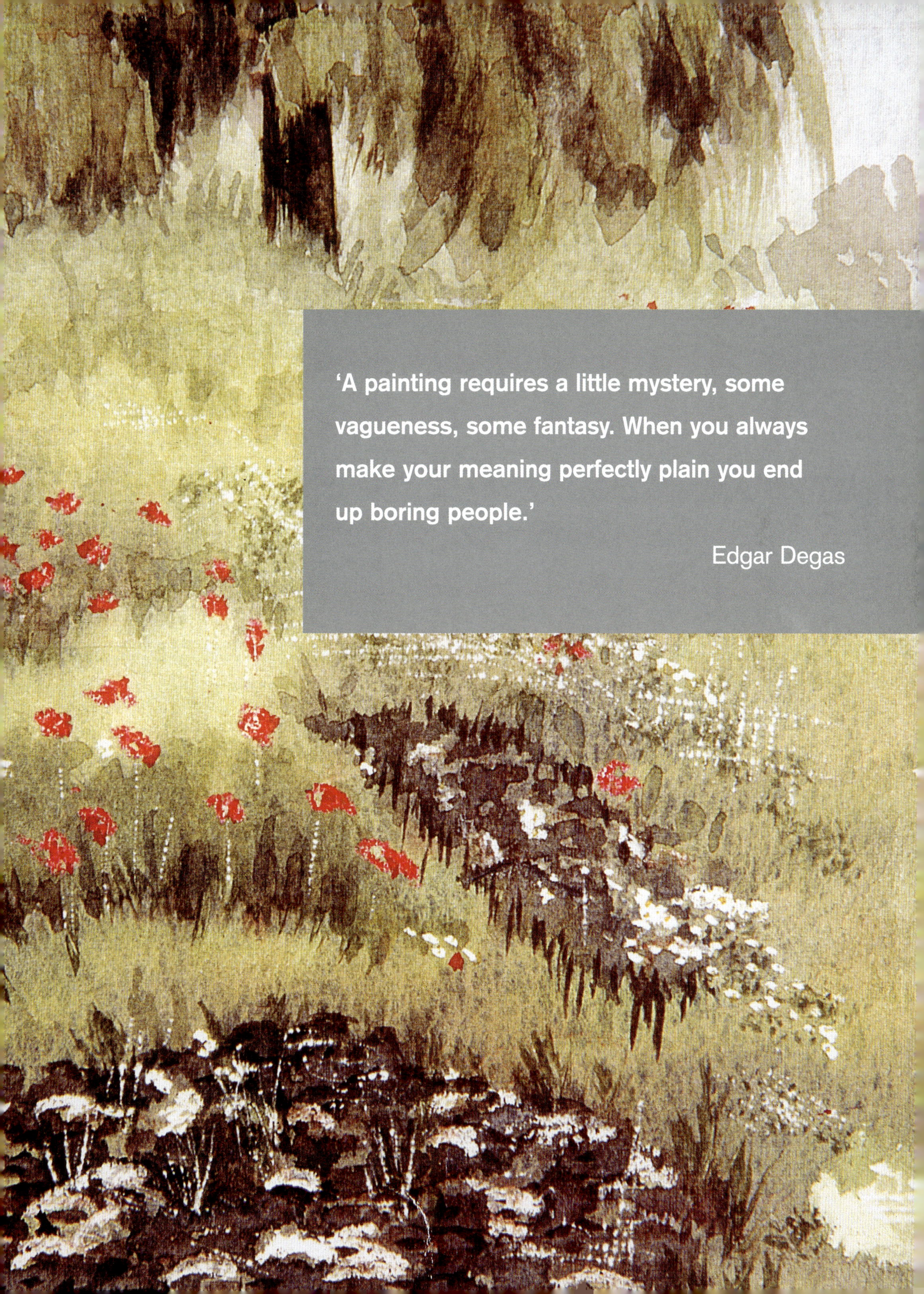

'A painting requires a little mystery, some vagueness, some fantasy. When you always make your meaning perfectly plain you end up boring people.'

Edgar Degas

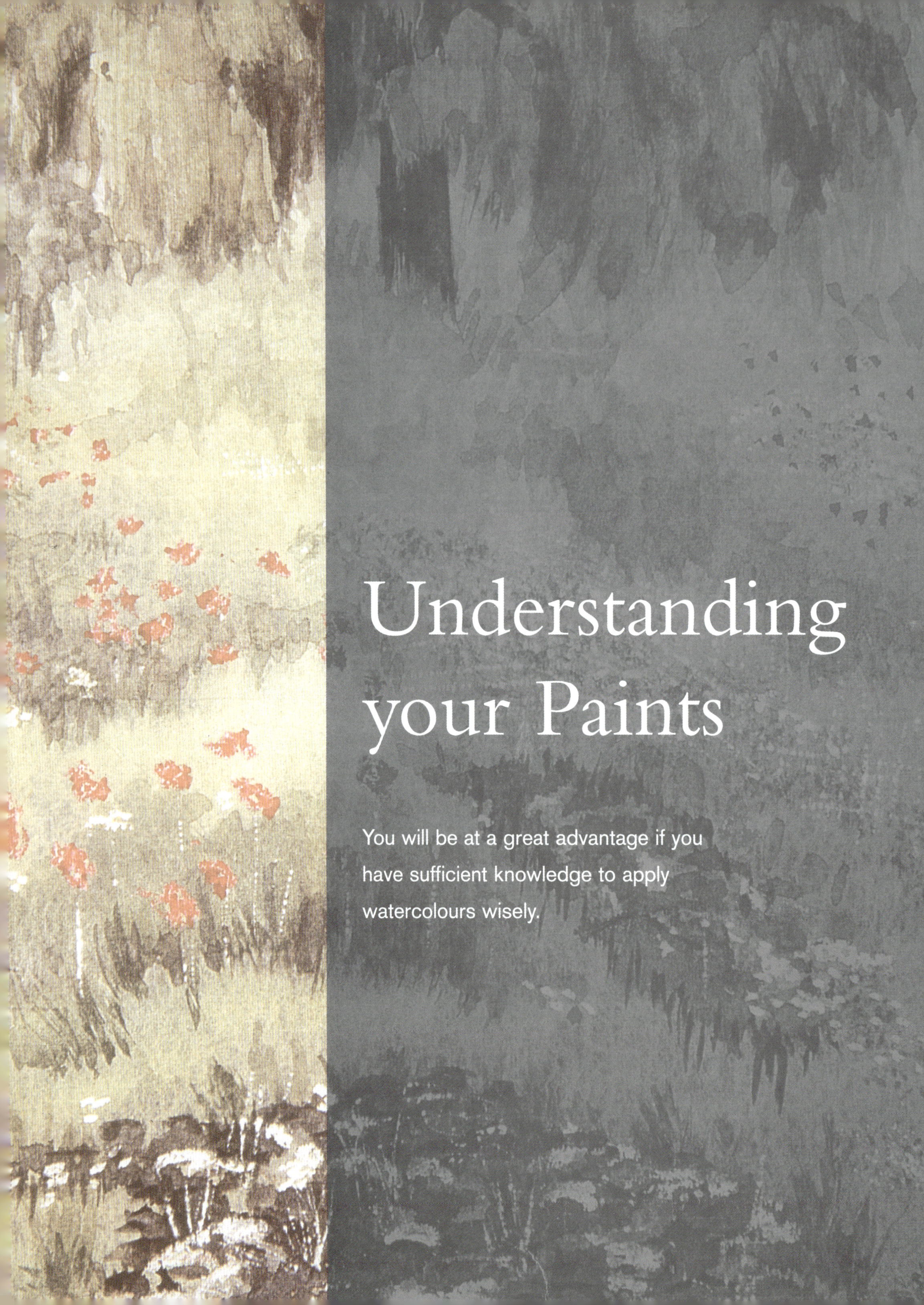

Understanding your Paints

You will be at a great advantage if you have sufficient knowledge to apply watercolours wisely.

The key to avoiding 'muddy' and 'heavy' paintings comes with an understanding of the nature of the paints, as not all watercolours 'behave' in the same way.

Some watercolours are transparent and/or staining colours and these colour the paper 'cleanly'. They are highly valued by watercolourists and I advise beginners to acquaint themselves with these very quickly.

Staining colours have terrific carrying power and can be very influential in mixes, so must be treated with caution. These are hard to wash off once they have stained the paper, so firstly acquaint yourself with them, then use sparingly. Test by laying strips of wash and letting them dry, then try and lift off the colour by scrubbing with clean water and a hog-hair brush. If it lifts it's not a stainer, if it stays, it is.

Others are semi-opaque, or sedimentary colours, sometimes called granulating colours. These leave a residue or sediment on the top of the paper.

Whilst it looks fine in one undisturbed wash, when you start to add other colours this not only stirs up the residue but, when mixed with a similarly semi-opaque colour, it renders the paper opaque and freshness is lost.

These do offer the chance to create some interesting textured washes though, where the sediment settles into the grain of the paper, or granulates into interesting patterns, especially when mixed with a staining colour. If you can find a couple of colours that 'argue', e.g. yellow ochre (granulating) and cerulean blue (staining), you can have a lot of fun. Again, experimentation is the key, so as long as you record your findings you can repeat them.

It is worth learning how and why your paints behave the way they do so that you can avoid mishaps and utilize the qualities. For example, when you want to 'lift out' colours to correct mistakes or make highlights, or to 'stain' the paper for a gentle background, it is useful to know which paints will do the job.

It is always useful to look in other painters' art bags to see what you are missing and, if you see a colour that you are not familiar with, ask if you can have a dab of it for your sketchbook.

Tip: To test the transparency of colours, paint strips of each paint over a black stripe. If they cover it, they are opaque, while the more visible the stripe is through the paint, the more transparent you know it is.

I have a sketchbook full of dabs of paint which have been scrubbed at to see if they will 'lift out', and that have been painted over writing to see how opaque they are. I strongly recommend that you also keep a sketchbook with paint samples in – it helps to see how they behave and they are useful for when you are looking at particular colours and mixes, for example for limited palettes.

Make sure, though, that you record not only the name of the paint, but the make too, as different brands can vary enormously. I keep two brands of both olive green and alizarin crimson as they are both so dissimilar it is like having two different colours of each, both of which are invaluable. Once you have them in your book, do the project below to check to see if they are staining, or 'lift out', and keep that information for reference.

How your paints behave

This list is not definitive and the qualities of paints can vary for different manufacturers, but these paints can, sometimes, be found in the following categories:

Transparent colours	alizarin crimson, cobalt blue, Prussian blue, hookers green, sap green, rose dore, permanent rose, Winsor violet, cobalt violet, sepia
Staining colours	alizarin crimson, pthalo blue, Winsor red, Prussian blue, Winsor violet
Opaque/semi opaque colours	Naples yellow, cadmium red, cadmium yellow, cadmium orange, lemon yellow, yellow ochre, cerulean blue
Granular/sedimentary	burnt sienna, burnt umber, raw umber, French ultramarine, yellow ochre, olive green, Venetian red, light red

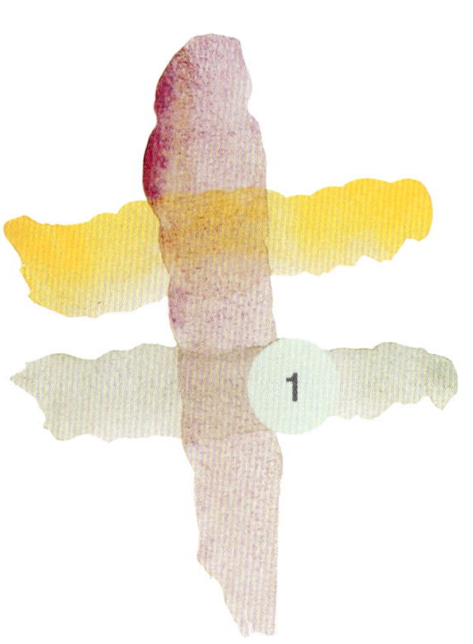

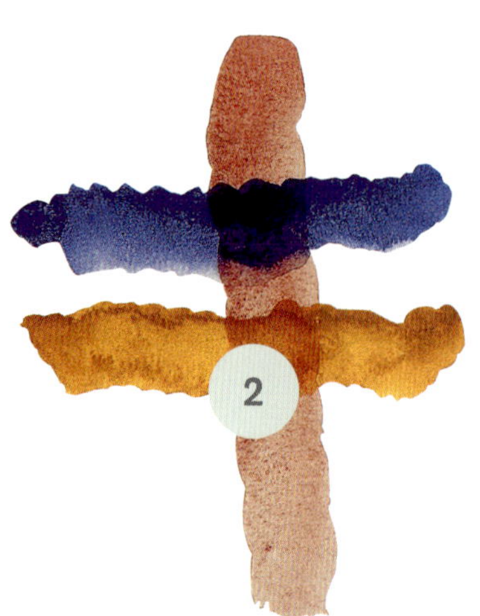

1 *Three staining, transparent colours laid over each other*

2 *Three granular, semi-opaque colours laid over each other*

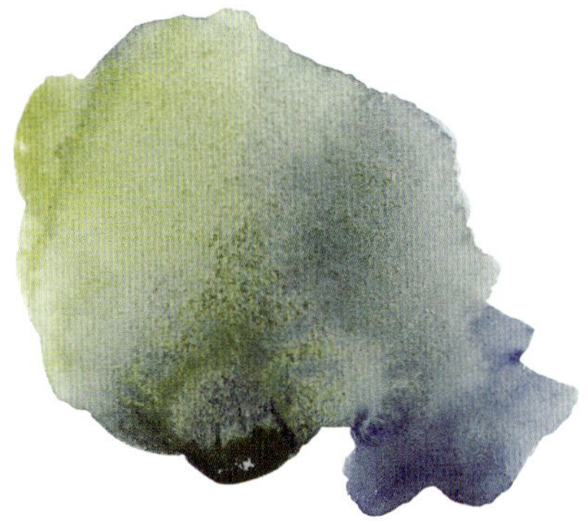

Tip: to avoid 'muddiness', don't:

• use more than three pigments together at any one time

• use a tertiary colour in a mix (see p.103)

• overlay sedimentary colours and semi-opaques

• mix more than two opaques.

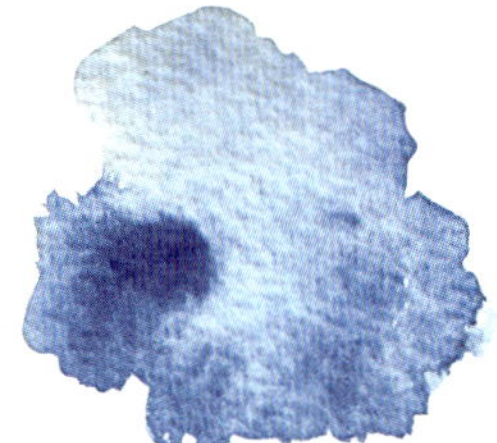

✱ Project: Transparency: getting to know your paints

• Make your own chart, laying out lines of each of your paint colours and allow them to dry. Record them in your sketchbook so that you have them for future reference.

• Make a note of the name of the colour and the manufacturer for each paint.

• Dip a hog-hair brush (stiffer than a watercolour one) in clean water then brush it across the surface of each dried colour, separately, using the same amount of pressure and the same number of strokes for each one, to give a fair comparison.

• Dab the paint with a clean piece of kitchen roll. This will show you which paints will lift out and which will stain.

• Once you have identified which colours are staining or granular, practise mixing them (recording all results) to see which go 'muddy' and which stay clear.

• Wait until mixes are dry before you judge the results.

Properties of paints

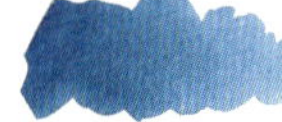

French ultramarine: warm, slightly opaque
Darkish, soft blue. Because of its warmth, suitable for mixing autumnal greens. Makes a good range of greys and browns when mixed with neutrals. Granular – so beware when mixing with other granular or opaque colours as it could go 'muddy' easily.

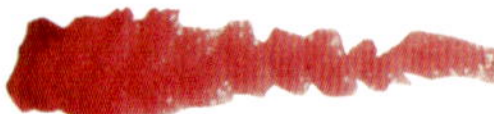

Alizarin crimson: cool, transparent, staining
Great for mixing as it is strong and stains, and its transparency means that mixes don't go muddy. Useful for mixing purples as it already has a blue bias: mix with cerulean blue, pthalo and ultramarine blue for good purples.

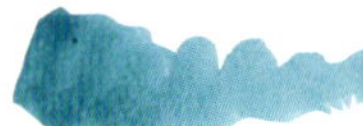

Cerulean blue: cool, permanent, sedimentary, opaque
A cool, light, bright blue, good for skies and atmospheric affects. Can be dominant in a mix. Argues with yellow ochre if you want interesting effects.

Prussian blue: cool, transparent, strong
A favourite of mine for getting dark mixes without mud due to its transparency.

Raw sienna: transparent, non-staining
Similar to yellow ochre in colour but 'cleaner' in mixes. For me this is an essential.

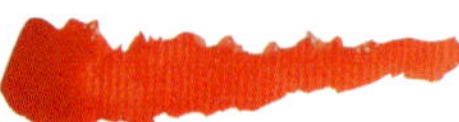

Cadmium red: warm opaque, strong
A bright red which can dominate and 'muddy' a mix if you are not careful with it. Some would say it is an essential, but I prefer less strong reds unless I want impact, for example in poppies.

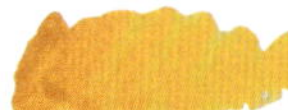

Cadmium yellow: warm, strong, semi-opaque, sedimentary
Some artists would say this is an essential. However, due to its opacity, I prefer to use gamboge, as it is less dominant and transparency is high on my agenda. If it is not such an issue for you, I would recommend it.

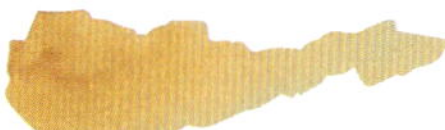

Yellow ochre: permanent, sedimentary, semi-opaque
I prefer to use raw sienna as an alternative, as it is more transparent, but I still recommend this as it has great qualities, especially as a mixer. Produces subtle autumn greens and 'dulls down' a variety of mixes if they are too bright.

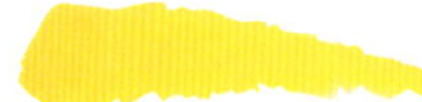

Cadmium lemon: cool, semi-opaque, strong
This is a good, strong, cool, yellow and many artists would argue it is an essential but, as with all the cadmium family, I prefer more transparent alternatives, so I would choose lemon yellow, Winsor yellow, or aureolin.

Aureolin: cool, transparent
A favourite of mine. Its transparency gives a light, clear yellow, less dominant than the more popular cadmium lemon, but similar in colour. It looks a dirty colour when it is in the tube but paints to be a clear yellow.

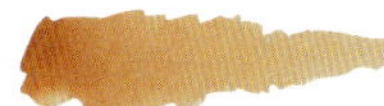

Burnt Sienna: transparent, warm, slight sediment
This is a lovely orangey brown and, as with so many
of my colours, I love it for its transparency. A good
mixer as it doesn't muddy. Great for brickwork, but
adapt it with other colours, as its distinctive colour
could be too 'obvious'.

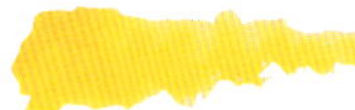

Gamboge: warm, transparent
An essential of mine, I prefer it to the more popular
cadmium yellow. Its transparency makes it a good
'clean' mixer. Good for fresh greens due to its cool bias.

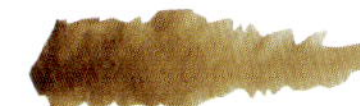

Sepia: transparent
A clear dark brown. Another favourite of mine that you
probably won't find on many lists of essential colours.
I prefer it to other browns for its transparency. Other
dark browns can cause mud when mixed due to their
sedimentary qualities, this doesn't.

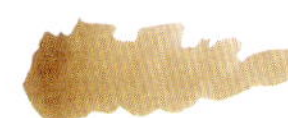

Burnt umber: sedimentary, permanent
This will appear on most lists of essential colours.
It is a dark subdued brown that mixes well into neutral
colours and gives autumnal colours in mixes. I prefer
sepia to this though.

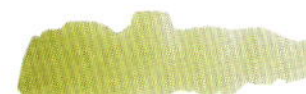

Olive green
This is a muted green as though it has been mixed
with yellow ochre – ideal for more natural greens that
are in shade. I use two different brands, as they are
so different, but both are essential to my palette.

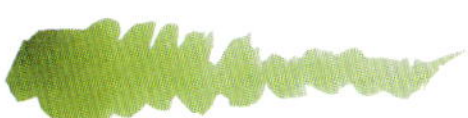

Sap green: a clear neutral green.
Ideal as a mixer, with warm, cool, yellows for spring
greens and with ultramarine for warm, deep, green.
An essential in my palette.

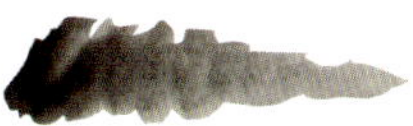

Paynes grey: thick, heavy, semi-opaque dark grey.
If you think that I don't like this colour you're not
far wrong! It is on many 'essentials' lists but I find its
heaviness can kill a painting. I've seen recommendations
that it be used in mixing but I find it too dominant.

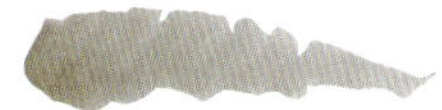

Davy's grey: if you must use a grey this is a gentle,
pale, one which is easy to mix with other colours. It is
more transparent and paler than Paynes grey and so
is more versatile.

Black and white
You don't need either, you really don't. You can always
mix a more interesting dark than black. And in
watercolour your paper will be your white and the paper
shining through colours will lighten them. Never try
and lighten a colour by adding white, as you will get
a chalky mess. White gouache can be used to add
highlight or lighter areas when needed, after the main
painting is complete and dry.

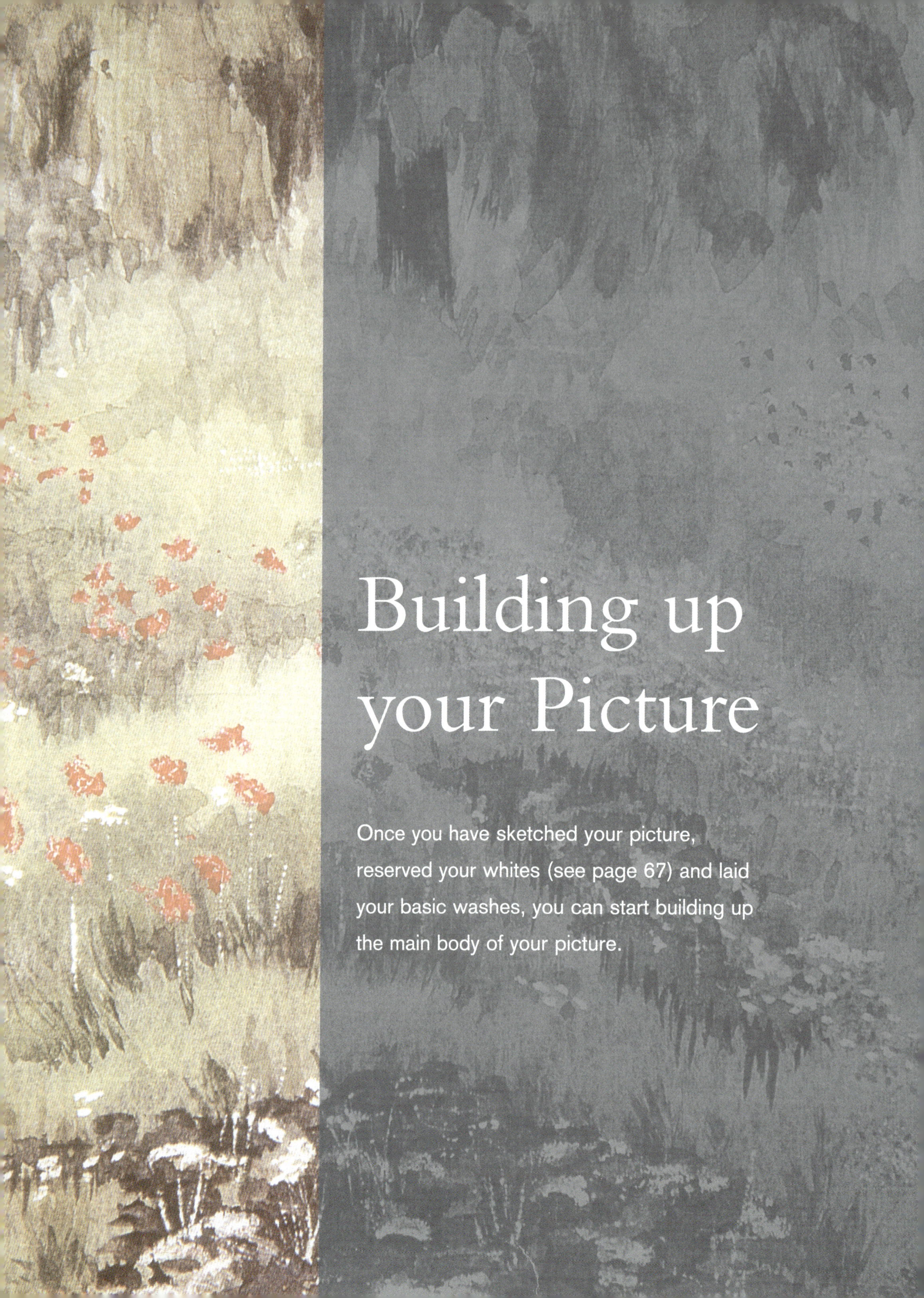

Building up your Picture

Once you have sketched your picture, reserved your whites (see page 67) and laid your basic washes, you can start building up the main body of your picture.

When you start painting the details, you can either get your darks in first, so that you can see the tonal balance of the picture from the beginning, or paint your lightest colours first, then work from light to dark, so that you can lay progressively darker layers over each other. I prefer the latter approach.

Working in layers gives a more harmonious feel, as then the areas are not 'separate' and isolated from each other. If, for example, you are painting a landscape, you can bring the wash for the sky down beyond the level of the hills in the far distance. This will help to unify the picture and prevent too hard an edge forming between the sky and land (see picture below and the Demonstration overleaf). Be careful to keep your layers thin and transparent – if they get too heavy you will lose the freshness of your watercolour and it will become 'muddy'.

Use plenty of water and just 'tint' it with paint pigment. It's very hard for beginners to believe just how much water can be used, but it is important to load up your brush and make confident washes.

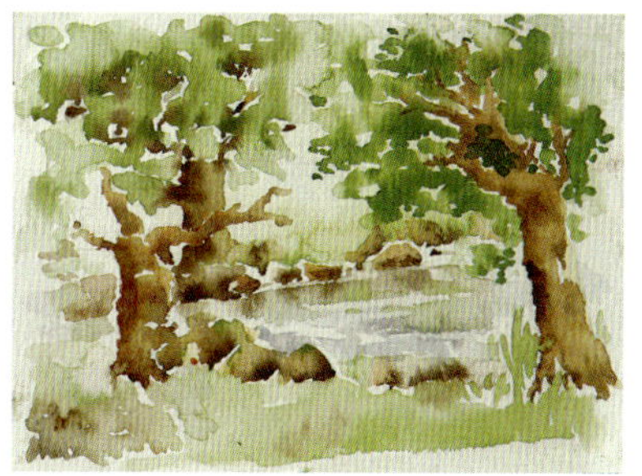

This sketch was painted quickly, using a large brush and plenty of water, creating a looser interpretation

So, my preference is for a large brush and lots of water, then fewer strokes are needed and you avoid the 'bittiness' that results from lots of dry brushstrokes. However, artists who like to include a lot of detail may prefer a dryer approach.

Remember: the rules are that there are no rules. There is no one way to do things, so all art manuals and art teachers need to be approached with the same caution. I can tell you what I do, but you should only use what suits you and ignore what doesn't.

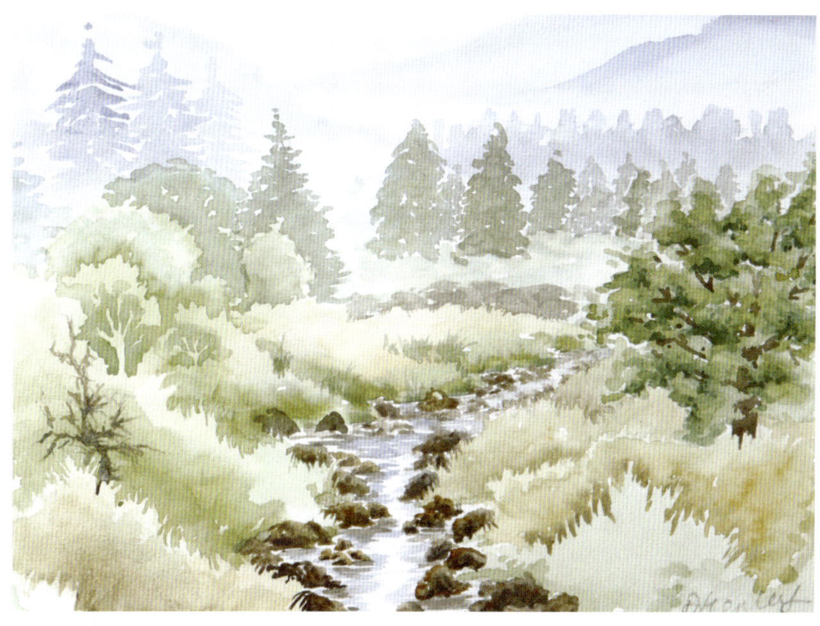

This scene was built up in layers, giving it a sense of distance. The foliage has been treated loosely, eliminating unnecessary detail

✳ **Demonstration:** A simple picture

To get yourself started, try this quick exercise:

1 Mix up plenty of blue paint and lay a wash. Start at the top of the page, and add more water as you progress down the page. This will make it lighter nearer the horizon and stop the sky looking flat and uninteresting. It also allows you to paint the ground over the bottom of the sky at the next stage and, in so doing, unite the two areas.

2 When the blue wash is dry, lay a green wash for the ground. Make the green stronger by adding more paint and less water as you move down the page, to add a sense of depth and make the landscape paler in the distance. Put in the road, again making sure it gets paler and thinner as it recedes in the distance.

3 Paint an area for the foliage and the trunk of the tree, and create an area for a bush.

4 Again, wait for the paint to dry, or it will run (unless you want to work 'wet-in-wet' for the foliage) then add some dark areas to give the tree and the bush form. Imagine areas of foliage and shade underneath each one. Finally, darken the edge of the trunk, to give it shape.

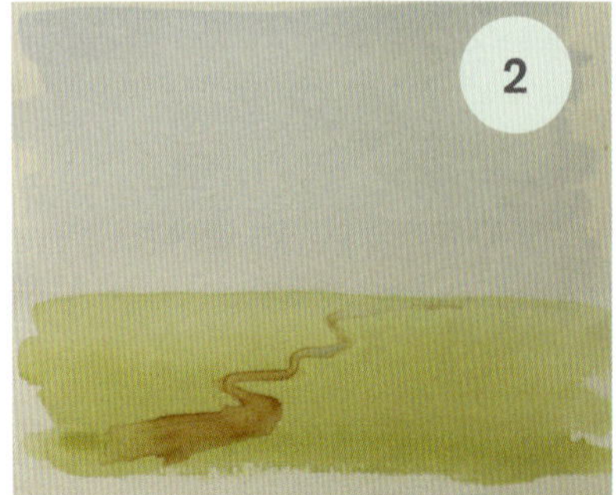

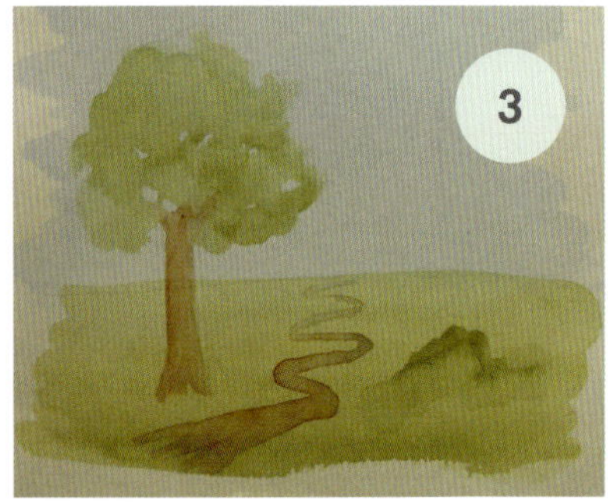

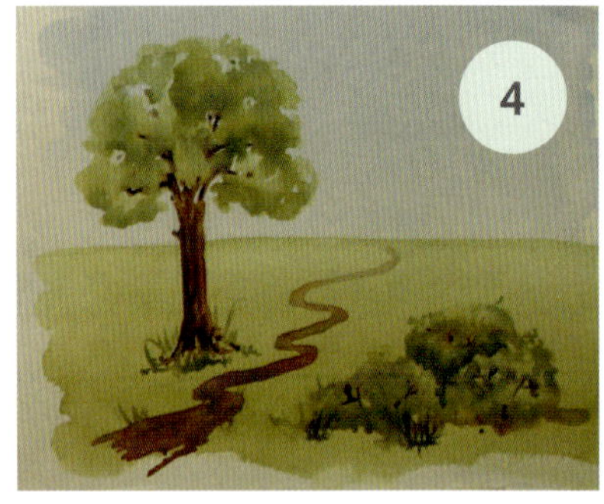

Tip: to get the right amount of water, think of it as adding a bit of paint to the water not a bit of water to the paint.

Focus on
Starting painting

• Have your board at an angle (about 20–30 degrees), as it is generally easier to paint like this and your paint will then run downwards for your wash.

• Put a brick or a box on your desk to rest your board on and to create the angle – cheaper and more efficient than buying a table easel.

• Organize yourself before you start – there is nothing worse than having to stop and rush off to get things – especially when the base of the board is on your lap.

• Have paints, water container and paper towels to the side of your work (right side if you are right-handed and left side if you are left-handed, so you won't drip paint across your paper).

• Keep plenty of water in the pot, to prevent it getting too dirty too soon, and keep replacing the water to keep it fresh (fresh water = fresh painting).

• Make sure that you have plenty of clean palette space available for mixing, but don't clean away all old mixes, as these are useful for re-using or adding to new colours. (Don't let the mixes get muddy – see 'Capturing Transparency', p. 74, for further advice on this.)

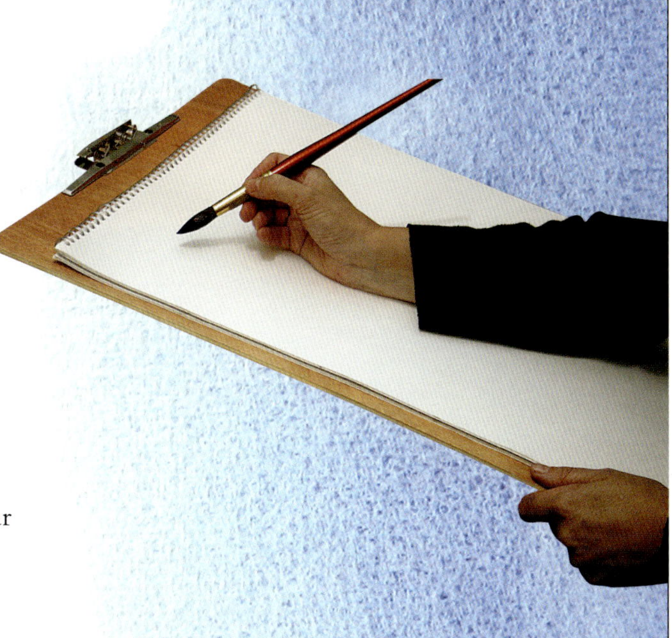

• Get up and walk away from your work to see it from a distance. Look at it again when you have been to do something else, such as make a cup of tea. This will clear your expectations by giving you other images to look at in the meantime and you will see it afresh. If you don't have time to do this, use a mirror – this will give you a reversed image and show up any mistakes.

• If you are unsure of the composition or tone, try looking at it on the floor between your legs – this different angle eliminates the detail and again presents the work in a fresh way.

• Think of the painting as a whole. Don't worry about detail in the beginning – only progress if it feels right first.

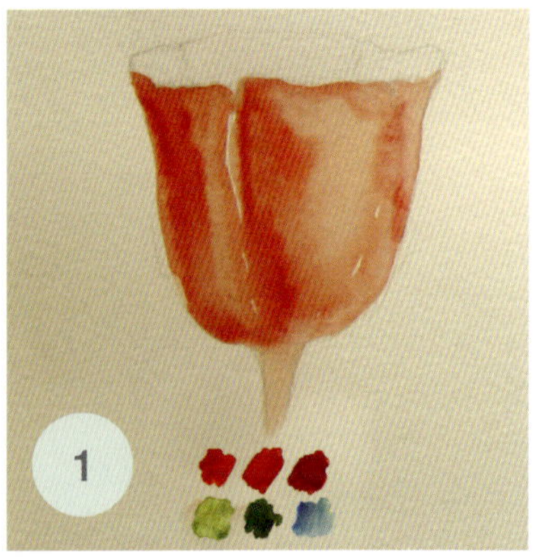

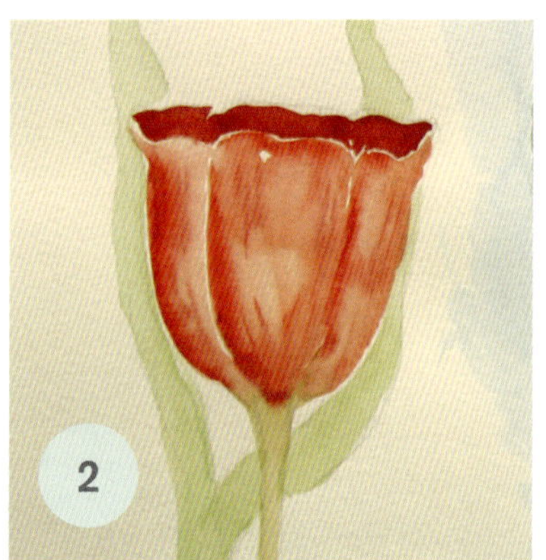

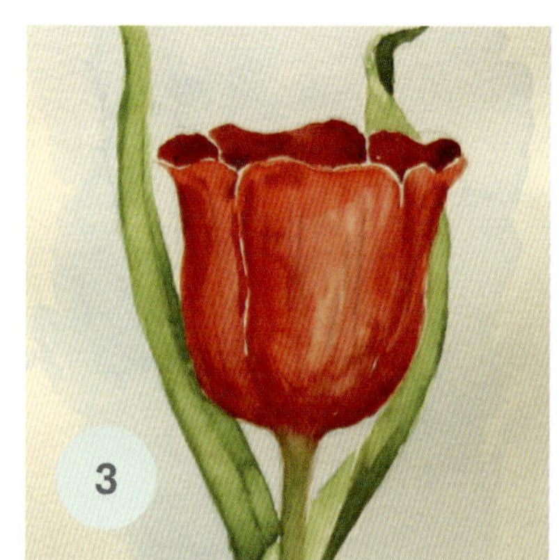

✹ Demonstration: A tulip in three stages

For this quick study of a tulip head I used three different reds: Winsor red,
scarlet lake and alizarin crimson. You could use any three interpretations of
a colour, as long as one is light, one medium and one dark. I also used olive
green and sap green and cobalt blue.

1 First, sketch your tulip shape in pencil. Wash in your lightest colour first (Winsor red, in this example), then darken around the edges away from the light. Where the petals overlap, make the underneath darker.

2 Whilst the paint is still wet, add your next darkest colour (scarlet lake), so that the 'wet-in-wet' process enables the colours to blend. Emphasize the shape of the flowerhead, using the tones of the colours to model the form. Put your first wash of olive green in for the leaves.

3 Again, whilst the paint is still wet, add your darkest colour (alizaren crimson) to the inside of the flower and underneath the tulip head. It should be beginning to dry, by now, so keep the paint mixture that you add quite dry.

Use the sap green to model the leaves, making sure the area behind the overlapping leaf is a darker shade than the one in front.

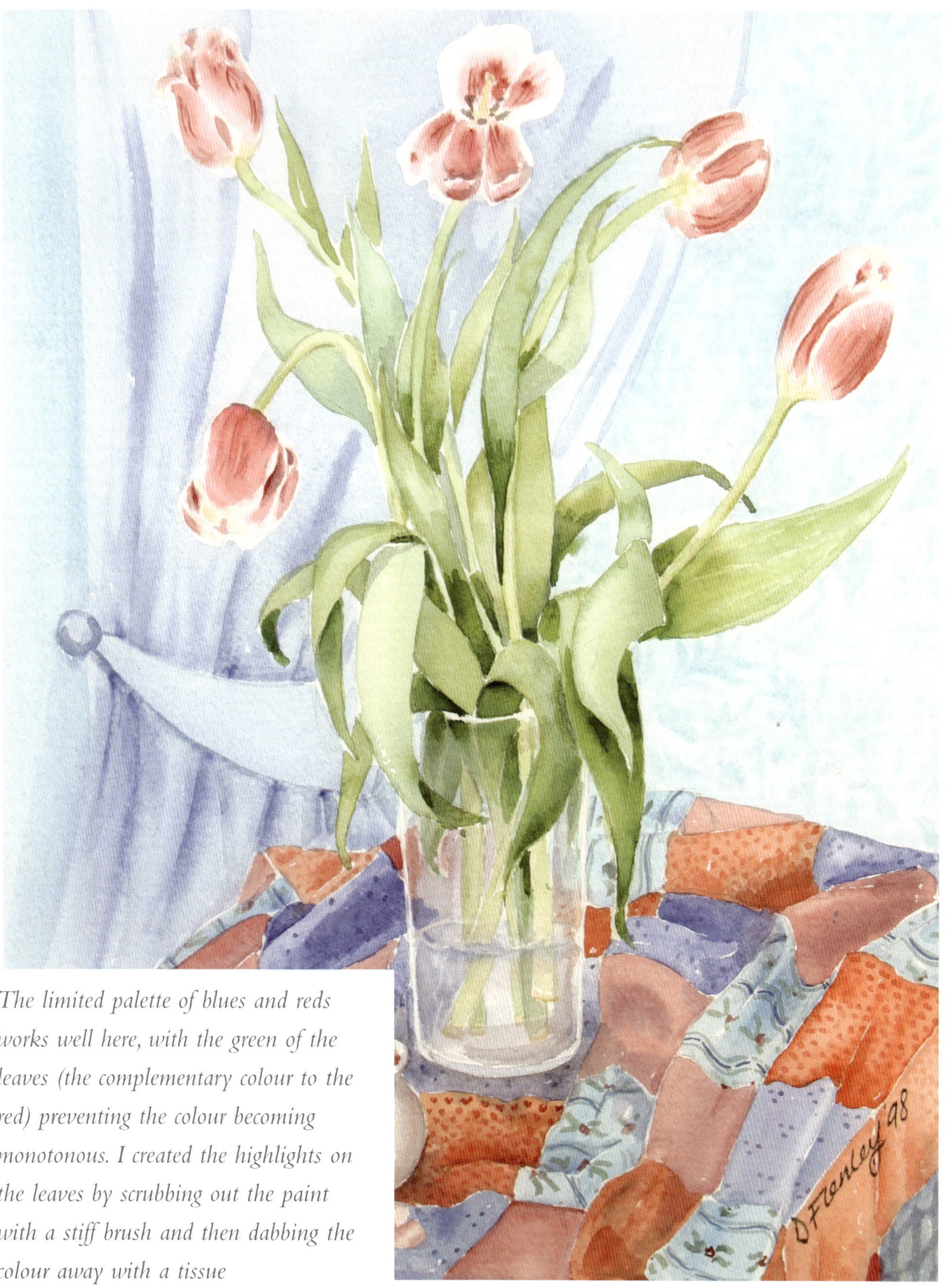

The limited palette of blues and reds works well here, with the green of the leaves (the complementary colour to the red) preventing the colour becoming monotonous. I created the highlights on the leaves by scrubbing out the paint with a stiff brush and then dabbing the colour away with a tissue

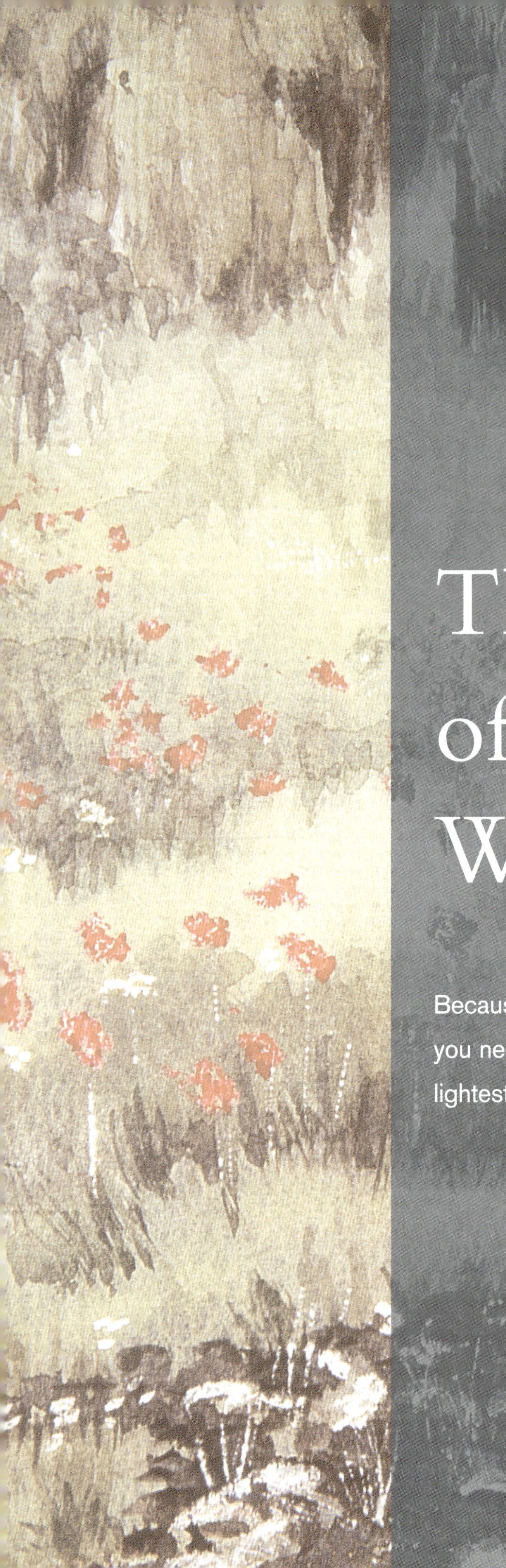

The Use of White in Watercolour

Because of the transparency of watercolour, you need to plan ahead and reserve your lightest areas, especially whites.

Transparency is what differentiates watercolour from other painting mediums. This does create difficulties, as you cannot paint over your mistakes or add white paint if you want to retain this transparency, but the wonderful effects and techniques which are exclusive to watercolour more than compensate.

With opaque mediums – such as oil, acrylic and gouache – you can work from dark to light, adding the lights last over the top of the dark colours. But with watercolour painting the white of the paper serves as your white, so you need to keep these areas reserved and fresh.

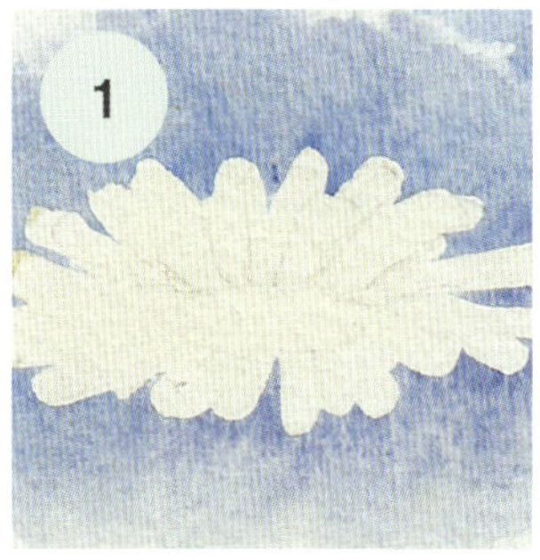 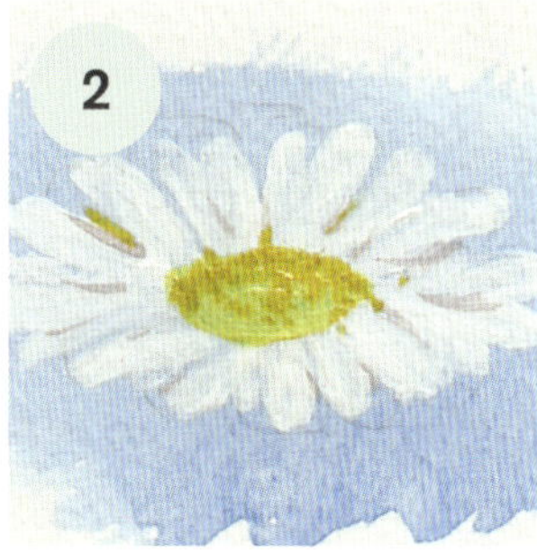 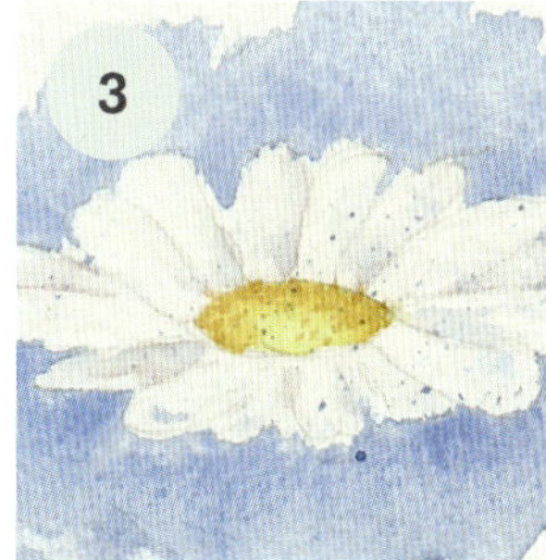 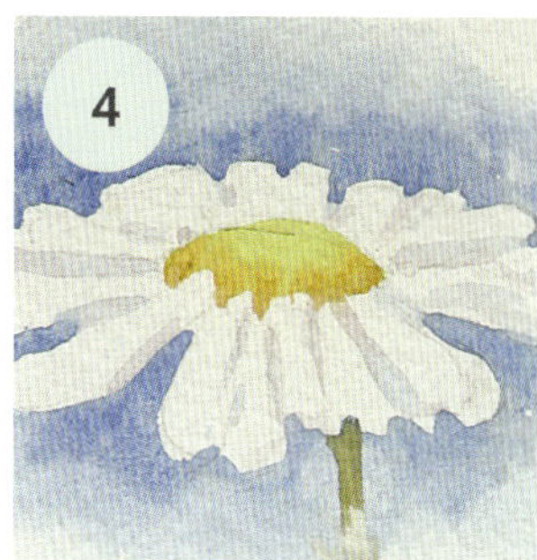

Painting in white

You have various basic options for a white area:

 **Leave the white of the paper and paint around it**
This needs advanced planning because, once you have painted an area, you cannot get the fresh white of the paper back (you could try 'lifting out' the paint after it has been applied, but this will leave a 'ghost' on the paper). I therefore recommend that you draw the object in pencil so that you can paint around it carefully.

 **You can use white body colour (gouache)**
Gouache is watercolour blended with body colour to make it opaque, which allows you to paint white over the top of other colours. It won't have the freshness of the virgin white paper, but is useful if you need a small area of white and don't want to mask it out, or you have decided you want white later in your picture, when masking out is no longer an option.

 **'Mask out' areas by repelling paint with a wax crayon or candle**
If using a candle, I recommend pulling out the wick and sharpening the candle to a point to give you control over it. A wax crayon is useful too, but you get a 'colour' with it instead of the transparency of wax. Both give softer edges than masking fluid but, unlike masking fluid which can be peeled off, this is a permanent block. If you require a small area of colour (like the middle of the daisy above), you need to put it in beforehand, underneath the wax.

 **You can reserve an area by painting over it with masking fluid**
Paint your shape in masking fluid, allow it to dry, paint the background over it, then peel it off. You can fill in the shadows and middle of your flower afterwards.

Now let's look at a couple of these options in more depth

Masking fluid

When this liquid latex is painted onto a picture, it dries to a watertight finish and you can paint around and on it, without the paint seeping through to your 'white' area. You must use the correct solution, though: the white fluid used to paint over typing errors is definitely not suitable. Do not remove the masking fluid until it is dry and has turned rubbery and opaque in colour.

You can also paint an area, such as green for leaves, and then mask off shapes of leaves with masking fluid, to preserve the base colour while you add a deeper colour on top. As long as you allow the layers to dry each time, you can do this repeatedly.

Masking fluid has two disadvantages: it can give very hard, unnatural edges which tend to 'scream' off the page, so be prepared to use it carefully and to soften edges with a damp brush or a tissue; it will also ruin your brushes: to prevent this, dip the brush in washing-up liquid before use, to create a protective film, and wash the brush thoroughly – and very quickly – after you have painted. Alternatively, buy cheap brushes to use specially for it.

Adding lights with gouache

Like watercolour, gouache is diluted with water before application, and contains the same dry pigments as those in transparent watercolour. However, the pigments in gouache are not ground as finely, because it is not intended for fine washes. Because gouache has a greater proportion of binder mixed in with it than watercolour, it is opaque rather than transparent and gains its brilliance from the surface of the paint, not from the luminosity of the paper shining through, as with watercolours. Because of this, you can use gouache to paint light colours over dark ones. This makes highlights easier to add at the last minute, rather than planning ahead and reserving white areas.

In fact you can add any colour of gouache – not just white – but this is liable to give your picture a chalky opacity, because you lose the transparency of that area. This is an advantage if you are specifically aiming for an opaque effect – milky washes to give atmosphere, for example – but it is debatable whether it is still 'pure watercolour' if such white body colour is used.

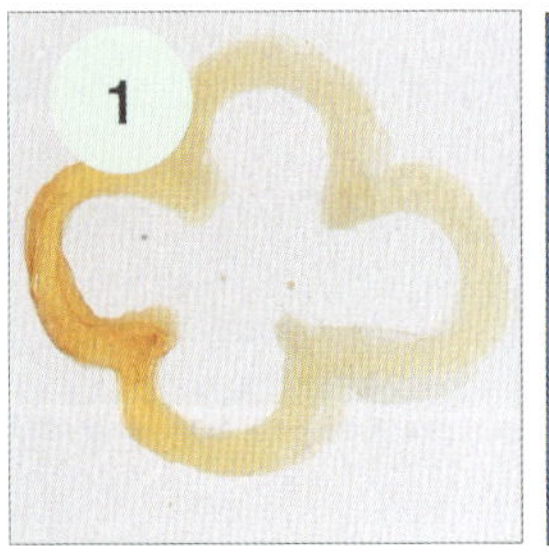
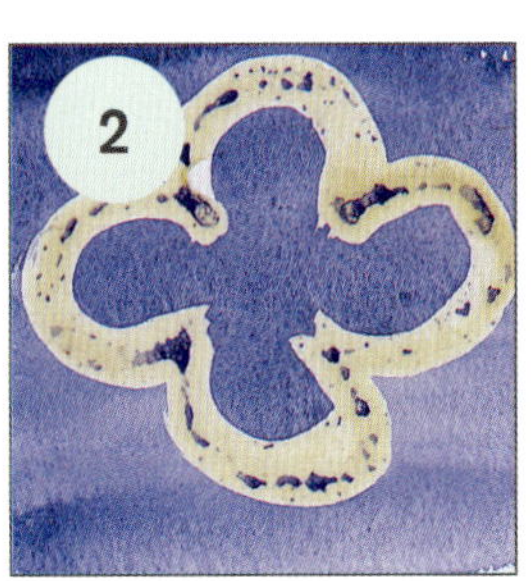

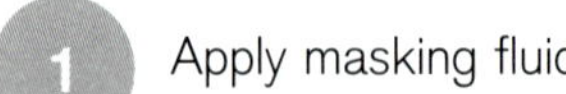

1 Apply masking fluid

2 Paint over it

3 Peel off to reveal the reserved paper

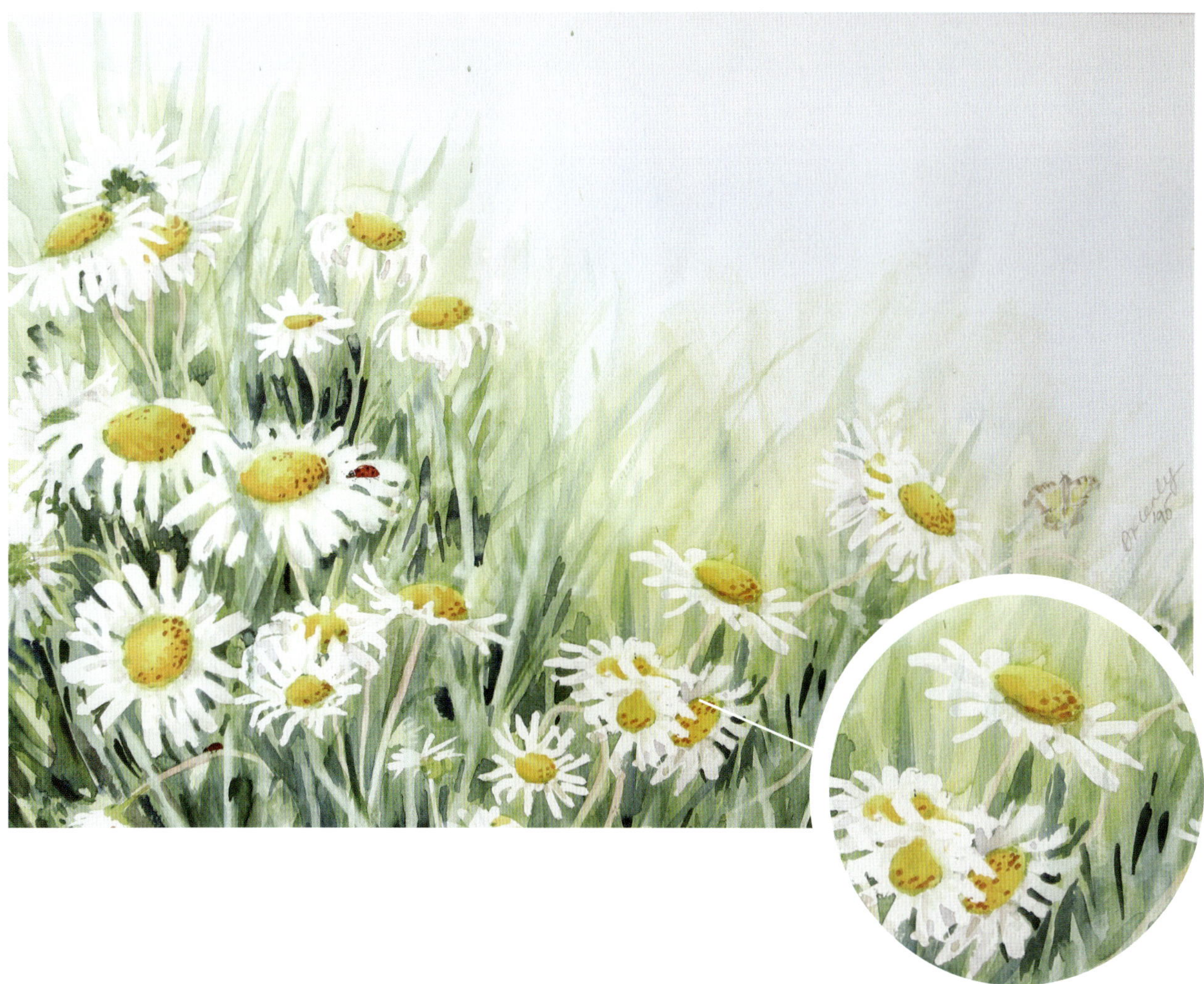

- Paint the background in watercolour first, then paint the daisy over the top in gouache. You can mix your gouache, and tint it with other colours from your watercolour palette to create a different colour, or for the areas of shade.

- Draw your daisy, then paint around it with the background colour, leaving the paper white. The background needs to be strong enough in colour and tone to make your daisy stand out – if it is too pale, your flower will be lost to sight.

- Use a white wax crayon or a candle to draw the daisy in first, then paint watercolour over the top and the wax will resist the paint. Note, if you are doing this you must fill in the yellow centre and any shading required first, as you can't alter it once the wax is on.

- Paint your background in, allow it to dry, then 'lift out' the daisy shapes with a damp, stiff, paint brush and blot with a tissue. Make sure your background is not a staining colour, or it won't wash out. If you want more definite edges cut a template out of card.

To give a sense of depth to your picture, you can 'lift out' smaller daisy shapes in the distance. These will be slightly blurred, so will seem far away and give a sense of depth to your work.

Your flowers don't have to be a circle or an elipse. Notice here how they bend, droop and turn and try to capture these qualities for a more realistic effect

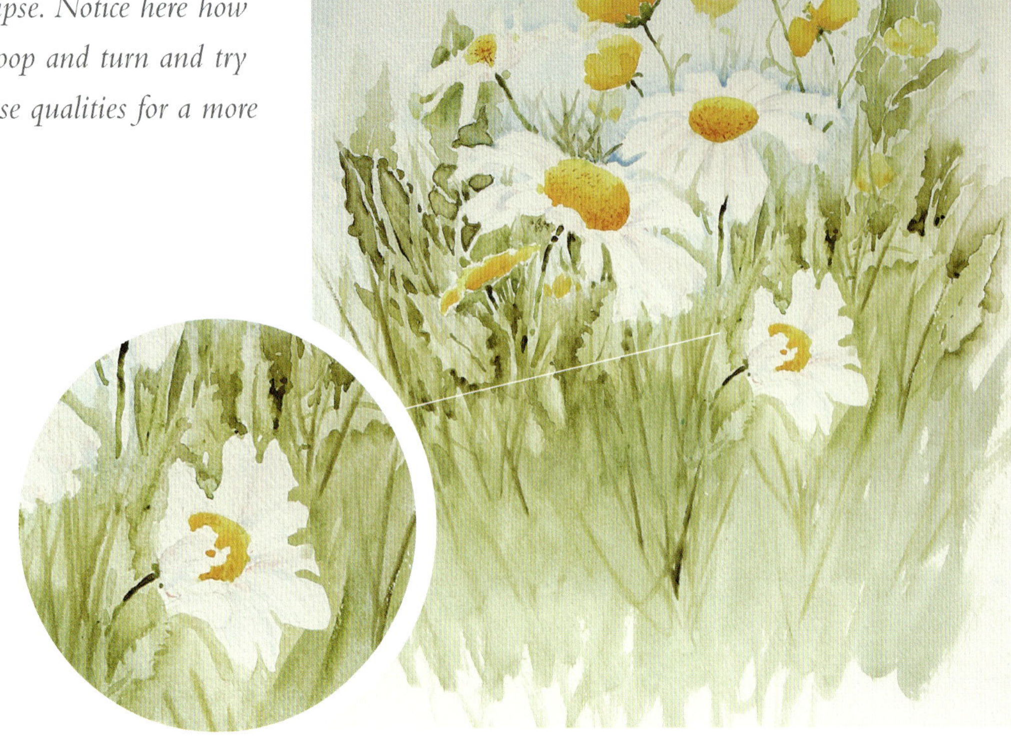

✱ **Project:** Whites, using masking fluid

1. Sketch a simple daisy, remembering that, unless it will be face on, the shape will be elliptical, and the optical effect of this causes the petals to be longer at the edges on the side and shorter in the middle. Don't make the petals a uniform shape – vary them, allowing them to bend and curve. Add a simple stem and a leaf and again, make sure the leaf curves naturally.

2. Fill in the flower and the shape of each petal with masking fluid. Use a brush that is good enough to allow you to manipulate the paint carefully into each petal but cheap enough to throw away, as it is may be ruined by the end of the exercise.

3. Allow the masking fluid to dry (it will turn to an opaque yellow colour). You can speed the process with a hairdryer if you need to.

When the masking fluid is completely dry, wash over the top half of the background with blue paint.

4. Make sure the paint is mixed with plenty of water, to allow it to flow, but remember it will dry much lighter, so don't allow the water to dilute the strength of the paint too much. As you paint your last few strokes at the bottom of the sky area, add more water to lighten it near the horizon (this will make it easier to start your next layer without a visible line showing through).

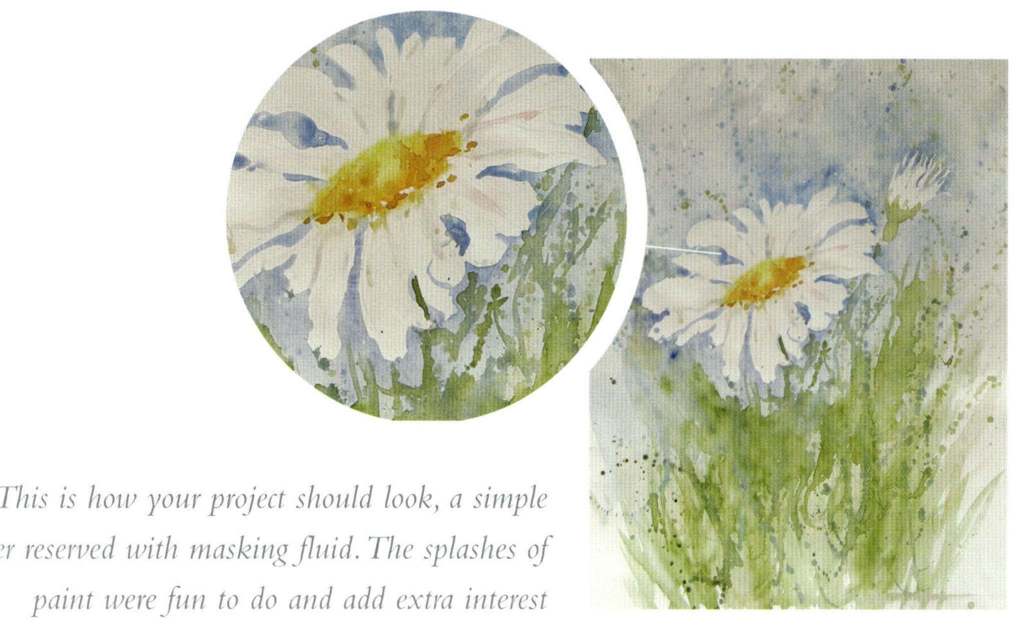

This is how your project should look, a simple flower reserved with masking fluid. The splashes of paint were fun to do and add extra interest

5   When the sky wash is dry, add the grass. Use upward strokes in the direction the grass would grow, and overlap the bottom of the sky. Add more grass stokes in deeper colours if you wish – experiment.

6   When the paint is dry, you could add impact with some splashes of paint by loading and then flicking your brush. Be aware of the direction of your flicks, they have to enhance the picture by going in the direction of the grass and flower growing upwards, they mustn't detract from your focal point and they need to be subtle.

7   Peel off the masking fluid (the best fun ever!).

8   Finish by painting any detail needed onto the flower – for example some of the petals may need a little shade if they are under another petal. Finally, paint the centre of the flower yellow while the paint is still damp, adding some darker yellow round the bottom to give the effect of it being raised in the middle.

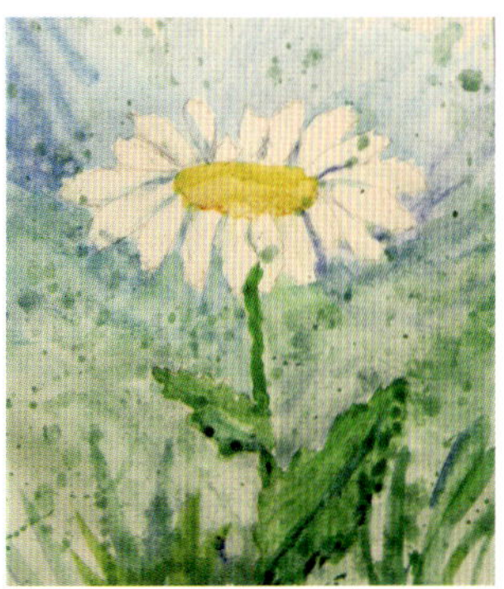

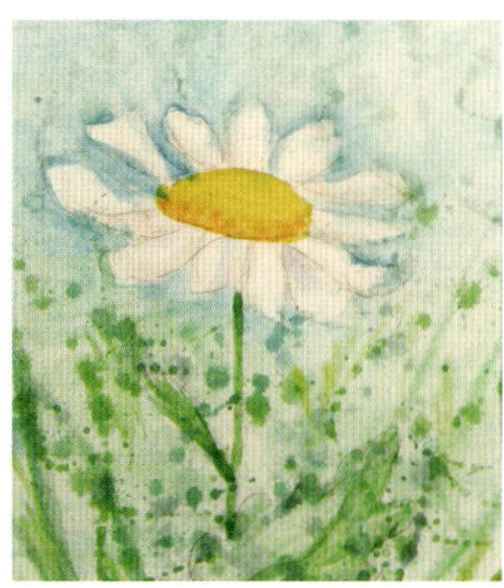

On holiday I persuaded two non-painting friends to buy some cheap watercolours, paper and frames and complete the Demonstration overleaf using masking fluid. These are their end products – not bad for a first attempt and, if they can do it, you certainly can

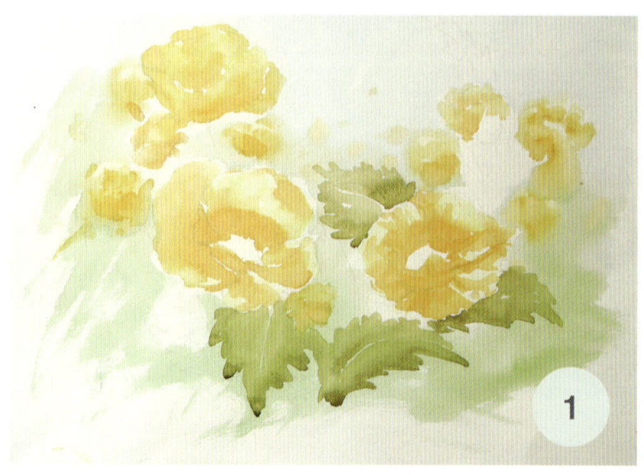

★ **Demonstration:** Flower paintings

The following demonstrations show how I approached
two paintings.

1 First I sketched in the general shape of the
flowers and the leaves. I then flooded in general
colour for the flowers: first a cool lemon yellow
and, whilst it was wet-in-wet, I added deeper
colours to create the form – aureolin, a mid-
tone yellow, and finally gamboge, a deeper,
warmer yellow.

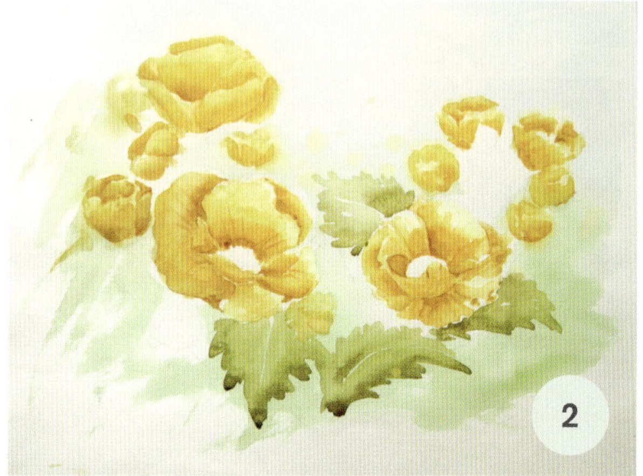

2 When the paint was dry I started to work into
the shape of the flowers, adding darks where
needed and tidying up where the paint had
run, by lifting off any unwanted areas.
Darkening yellow can be difficult as, once you
are using the stronger, warmer yellows you
can't just use a darker version, as there isn't
one. To overcome this, I added a touch of
yellow ochre, then a tiny bit of purple – its
complementary colour – to darken it.

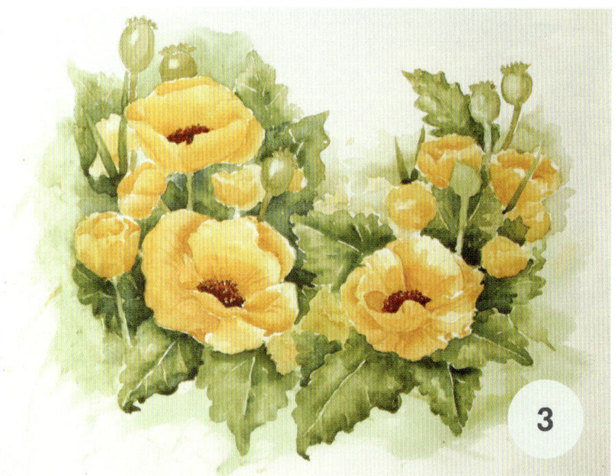

3 I then darkened the leaves where necessary –
where they are in shade, or around the edge
to offset the yellow of the flower. Similarly,
where the leaves need to be lightened, say
for highlights, I lifted off small areas.

4 Once I was completely happy with the general
construction, I did the the 'fiddly' bits and
tightened up where necessary.

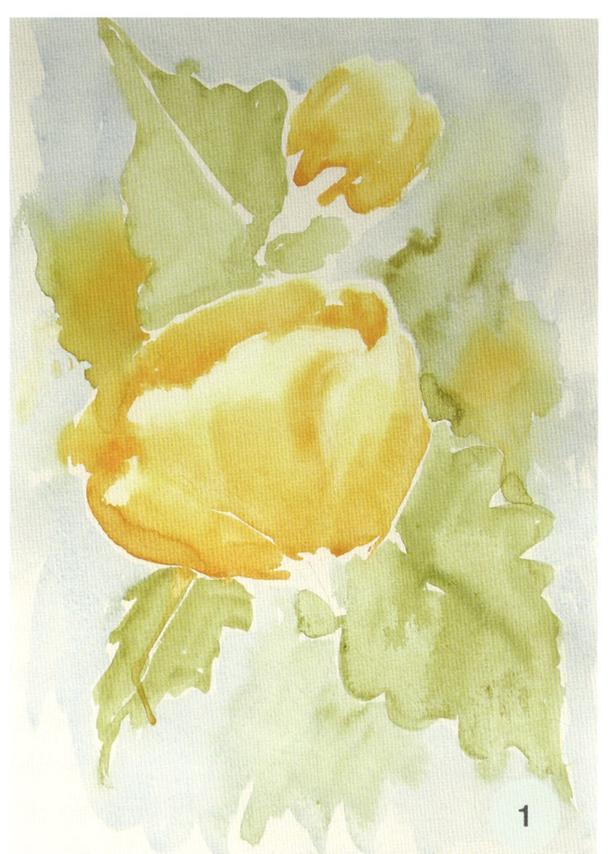

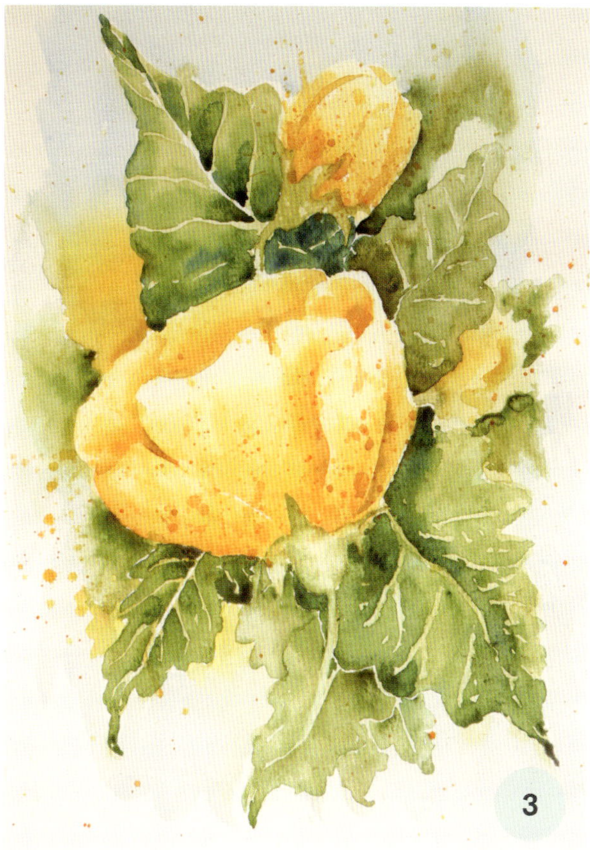

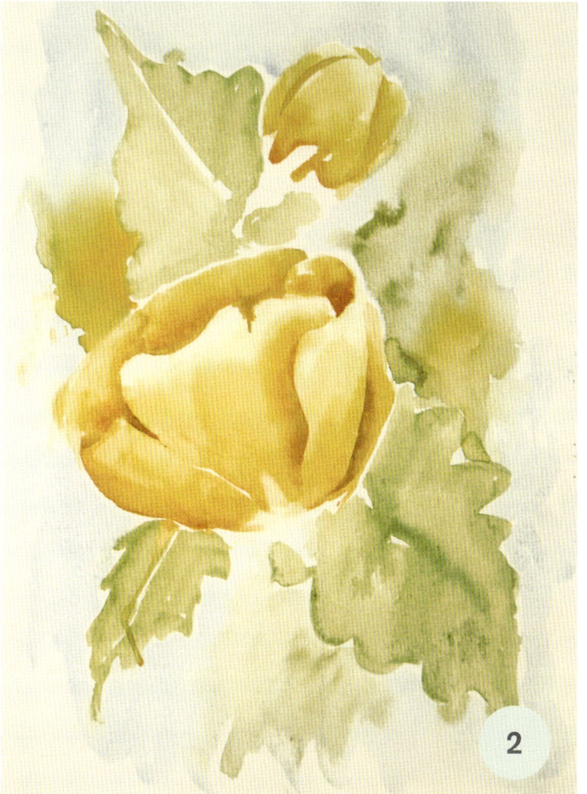

Tip: before you finish a painting, pause and take stock. Walk away from the picture and leave it standing, so that you will see it in a new light on your return.

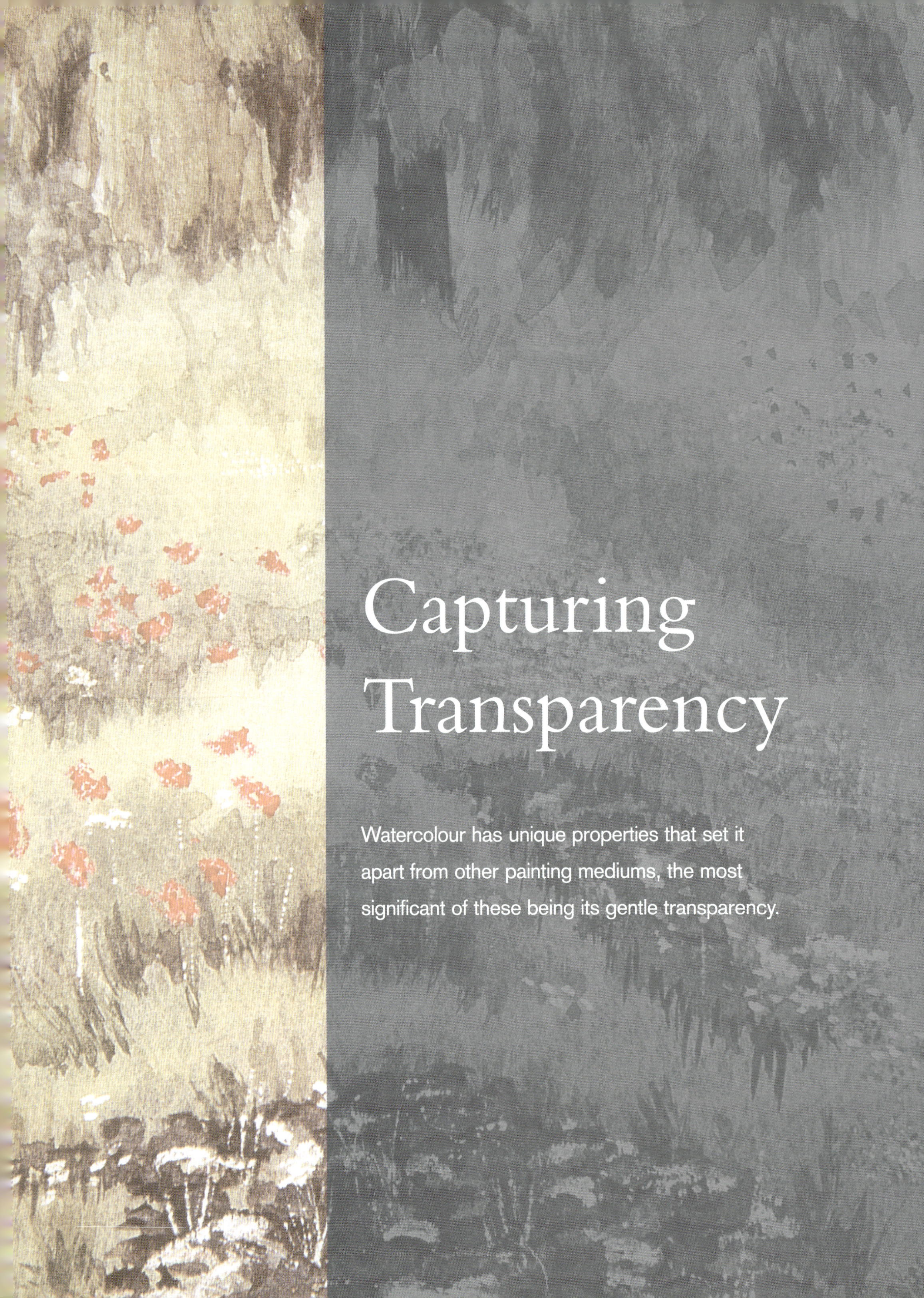

Capturing Transparency

Watercolour has unique properties that set it apart from other painting mediums, the most significant of these being its gentle transparency.

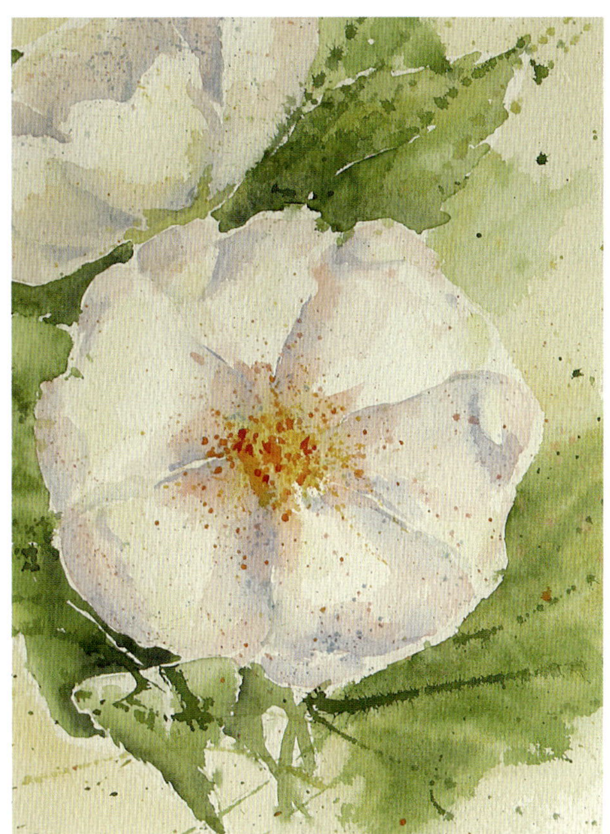

Watercolour should be laid in thin, transparent washes so that you can still see the paper shining through. When you have plenty of water, the washes lay more confidently and clearly on the paper, and other colours can then freely be mixed in wet-in-wet.

Retain as much light as possible in your painting: think about your light source before you start and aim to capture the light – reflected lights and highlights, even odd little flickers of light where the paper speckles through. All these factors help create the luminosity that is so unique to watercolour.

● Allow different tones to do the defining not lines around the edges

A light sketch is fine showing through the paint, but you don't want hard lines outlining an object which are then filled in with paint. With this flower (above left) its edges are defined only by the tone of the paint behind them and by the shadows on the petals.

● Edges should be 'lost and found'

Not all edges need to be depicted. Sometimes it is more interesting to merely suggest something is happening and leave it for the viewer to imagine. If you try depicting half a vase, or only part of a flower, you'll be surprised how little information you actually need to give and how much more interesting it can be. Notice how the edges of the flowers overleaf are not definite, in fact they don't exist at all in some areas, and this adds to the 'light/gentleness' of the piece.

If the transparency of watercolour is not retained, because too much paint is applied too heavily and not enough water used to dilute it, the beauty of watercolour can be lost and the results be 'muddy' and heavy. Here we will look at how to capture the light, how to keep the transparency, and arm you with the knowledge of how your paints behave so you can avoid and control any 'muddiness' in your painting.

For most of us, our first experience of paints came with the thick school paints that would dry and crack up when our mother displayed them on the refrigerator. That may have been a suitable education for oils and acrylics, which can be built up in opaque layers, but watercolour is a completely different matter and you are not looking at covering a surface with an opaque medium.

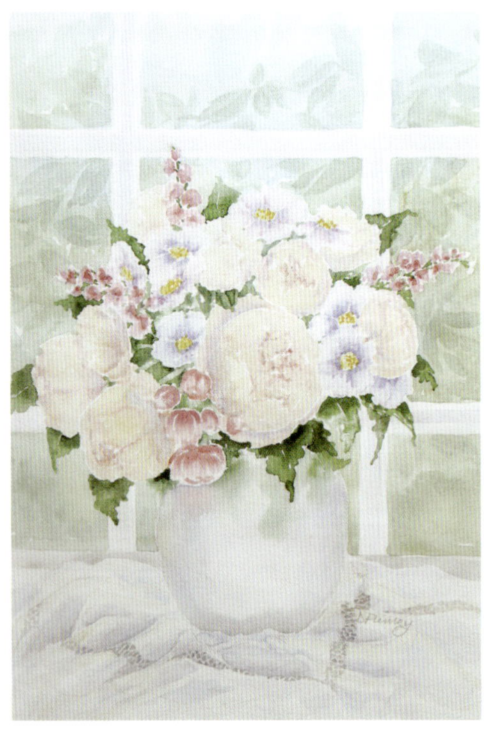

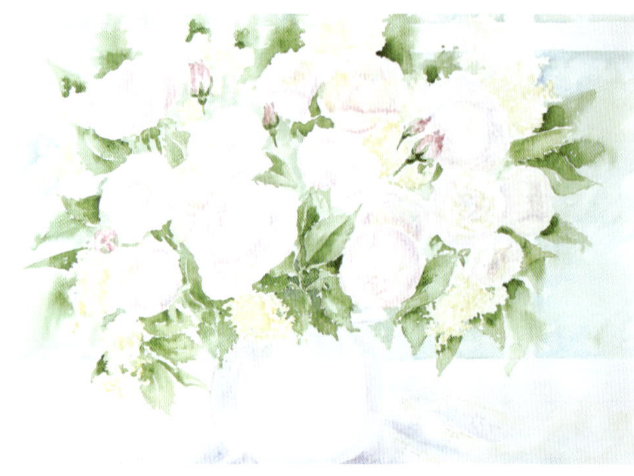

Left: Edges can be lost and found: in some parts non-existent, whilst in others defined by colour and tone.
Above: Sometimes areas can be bleached of all colour and the edges can be highlighted

● Observe how the light hits areas

Sometimes areas can be bleached of all colour (see above right) and edges can be highlighted, whilst others can be lost in the shadows. Exaggerate this when you can, as it makes for more interesting portrayals. When the light bleaches something it may not be necessary to paint it at all – have the confidence to leave your paper completely white at times, as the effect can be quite bold and dramatic.

● Not everything needs to be depicted

Try 'hinting' that something is there, or leave it out for a piece of 'breathing space' in a busy scene (see above left). Remember that what you leave out is as important as what you put in. It is easier on the eye to leave spaces – if too much is happening the viewer doesn't know quite what to take in.

Avoiding 'mud': keeping it transparent

● If you are struggling with muddiness, stick to transparent colours for a while. When you are confident, you can gradually re-acquaint yourself with the tertiary and opaque colours, knowing not to overlay them too often.

● Remember colours dry lighter, so allow for this when mixing.

● If you struggle to get your darks 'dark enough' without them becoming muddy, try using transparent darks, such as sepia or Prussian blue.

'Muddiness' has to be up there in the 'top ten' of common watercolour problems, but it doesn't reveal itself as a problem until you've been painting for a while.

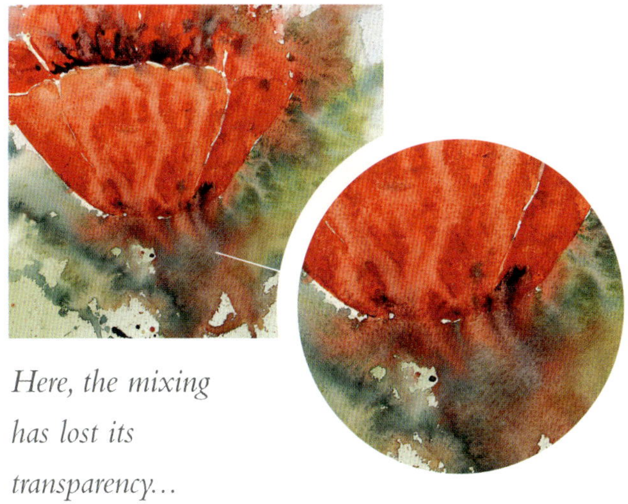

*Here, the mixing
has lost its
transparency...*

You gradually notice your paintings are not as light and fresh as they could be and, the harder you try, adding more colours and mixing more paint, the worse the muddiness gets.

The poppy above is an example of mixing which has lost its transparency, and become too heavy, because there were opaque colours in the mix and too much paint. Notice the difference with the poppies in the picture below, where the necessary darks have been laid, but without being disturbed and overworked, so they have retained their freshness.

*... whereas these darks have
retained their freshness*

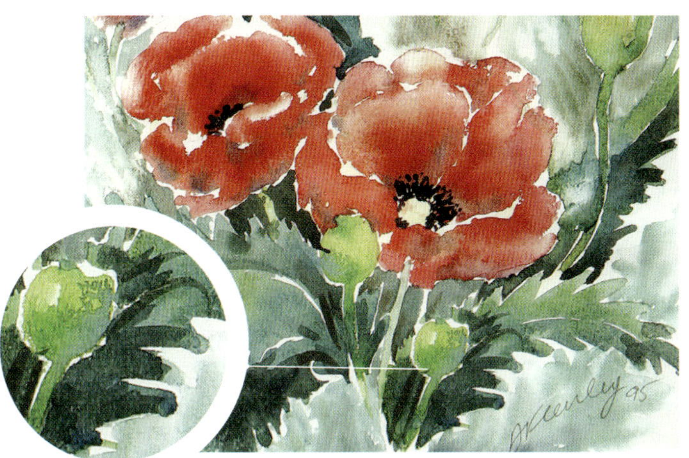

Focus on
Avoiding 'mud'

• Work out your tones and composition in advance. You are then less likely to need to 'go over' bits again and, in the process, mess up the painting.

• Keep everything clean – palette, brushes and water, which needs to be changed regularly. Dirty water is not going to help get a clean wash.

• Get the colour right first time. Have the confidence to lay darker tones, as paints dry up to 50% lighter.

• Use a minimum of brush strokes: going over areas again disturbs the previous washes, ruins the fresh unhindered look of a good wash, and disturbs the pigment in the paint so it will then 'pollute' the next layer of paint laid over it.

• Use a much larger brush than you think you need, but remember that it must have a good tip if you want to paint small areas as well. One made from natural hair (or a natural/ synthetic mix) will hold more paint mix, and allow you to lay a larger area of colour without lots of brushmarks and the need to keep stopping.

• Get to know your paints – avoid using too many opaque or granular colours as these will leave a residue on top of the paper which will turn into mud when disturbed.

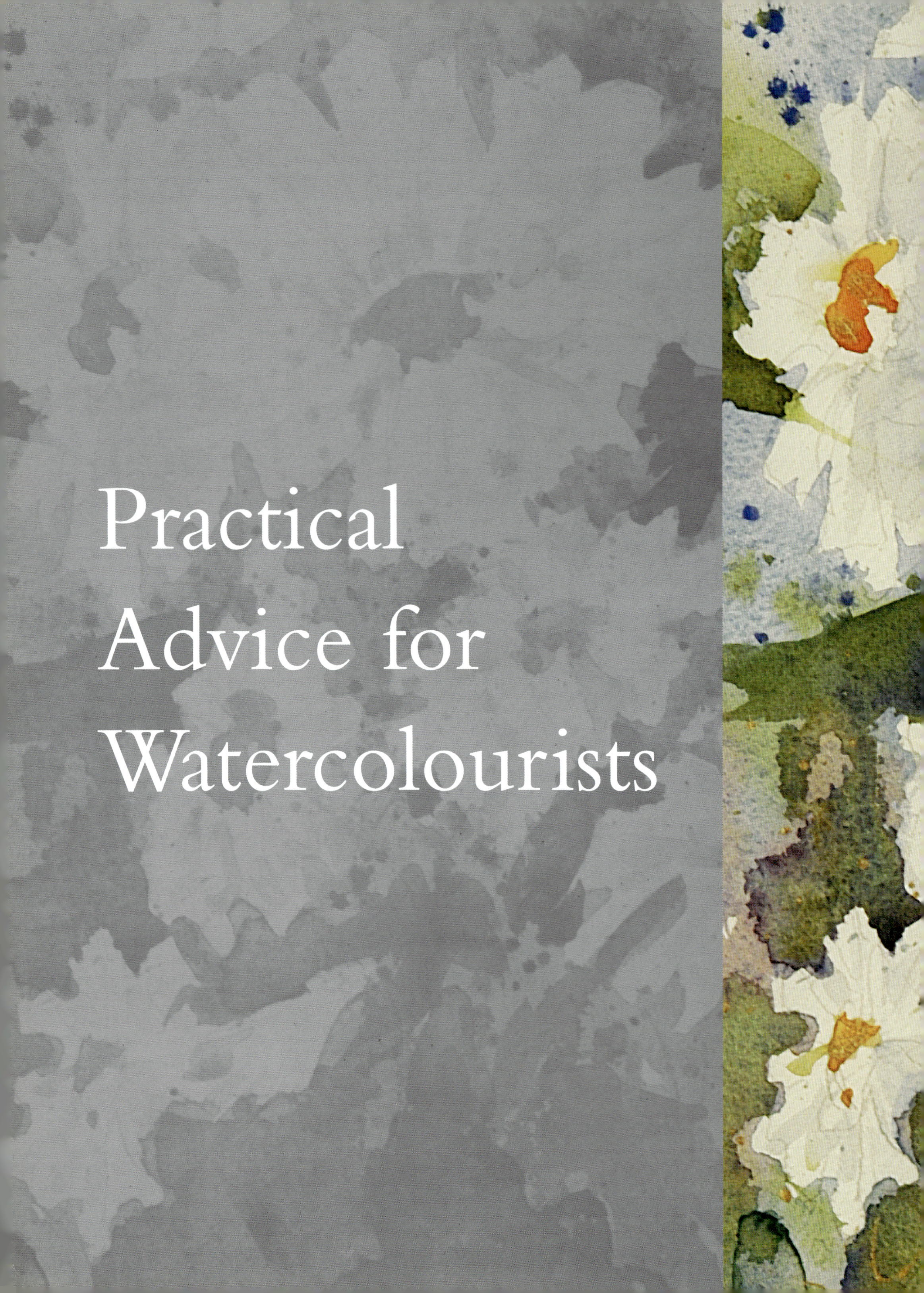

Practical Advice for Watercolourists

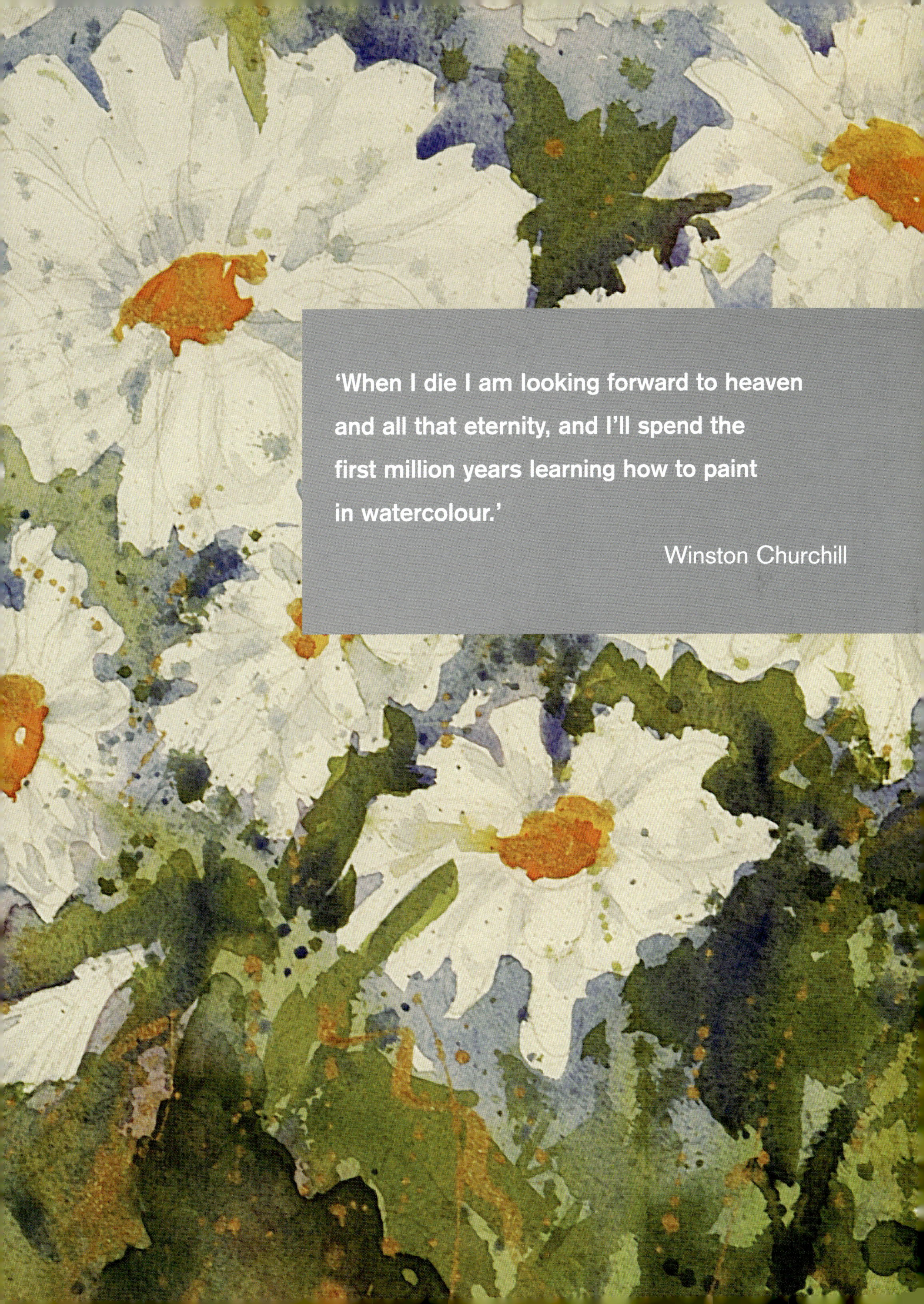

'When I die I am looking forward to heaven
and all that eternity, and I'll spend the
first million years learning how to paint
in watercolour.'

Winston Churchill

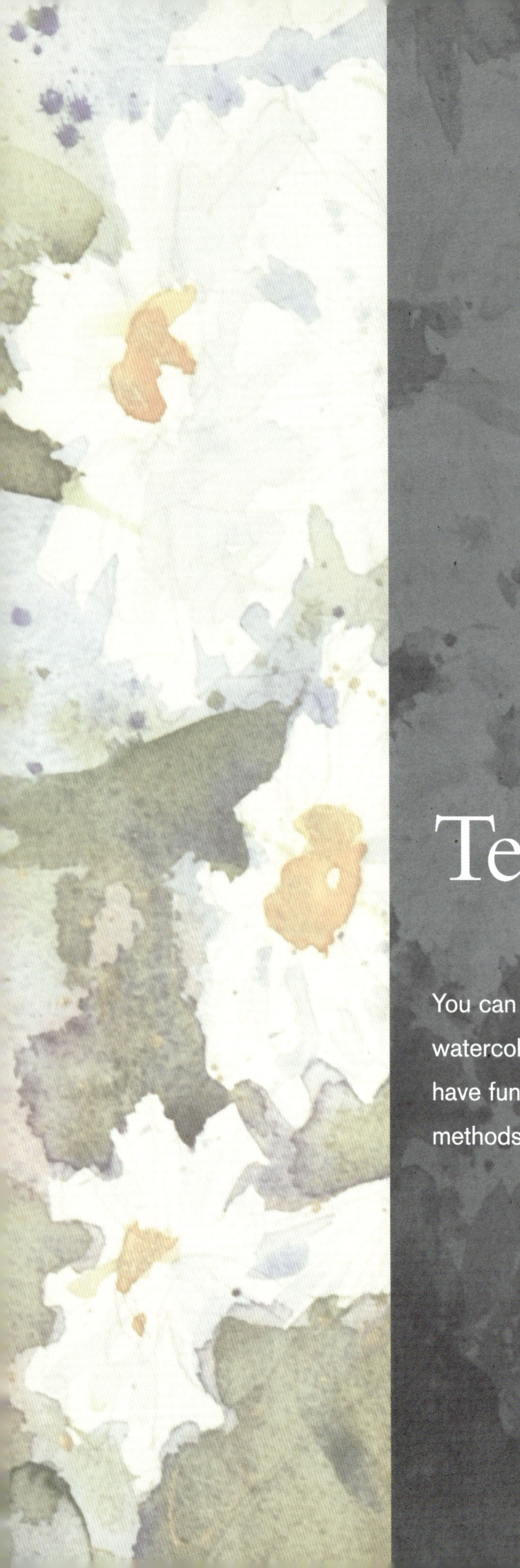

Techniques

You can achieve some lovely effects with watercolour, using different techniques – have fun experimenting with the following methods of applying the paint.

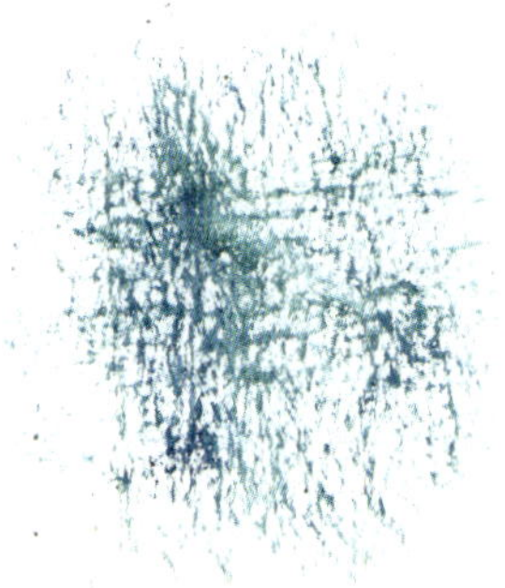

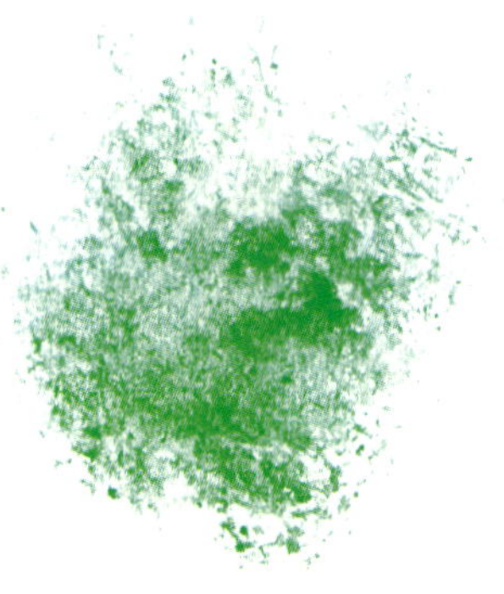

Splattering (toothbrush)

This is a useful technique when you want a loose, speckled effect – for pebbly beaches, distant foliage, and so on. It can be repeated a number of times with different colours, but be careful not to overdo it.

First mask off any areas that you don't want splattered (I keep a pile of old calling cards, some with torn edges, for protecting different shapes and just lay them on the surface to mask the areas I want to save from splattering).

Load your toothbrush with plenty of paint then run your finger across the tufts. Be sure to pull the bristles towards you, so that they rebound away from you and the paint goes onto the paper, rather than onto you.

It is a good idea to practise first with the amount of paint you use, so that you can be sure of achieving the desired effect.

Dry brush

If you use undiluted paint, you will find it is 'dry' and your brush will drag across the paper. This can be used to your advantage to give a sense of texture, for tree bark, for example, or for peeling paint. Different papers, too, render different effects and the more rough or textured the surface of your paper is, the more dramatic the effect will be. And you could paint an area first and then, when it is dry, overpaint with the dry-brush technique in a darker colour.

To achieve the effect, first load a largish brush with paint, then press a tissue around the ferule at the thickest part of the hairs, to squeeze out the moisture but leave the paint. Lay your brush almost parallel to the paper – so the base of the hairs touch the paper instead of the usual tip of the hairs – and lightly drag it along.

Experiment with a few strokes on a test sheet first, until you have the desired effect.

Sponging

This more simple technique is equally effective and very useful where you want a denser, speckled or textured effect, which is ideal for hedges and foliage.

A natural sponge is best, as it holds more water and has a more random texture, but you could rip rough bits off a bathroom sponge, to create an uneven texture.

Dampen the sponge, then dip it into a saucer of paint and gently touch the paper without pressing down hard. Be careful to move it into different positions, so the same shape is not uniformly repeated. To create the effect of occasional bits of foliage catching the light, add spots of highlight using gouache in a colour that is lighter than the object.

Tip: if there is a specific shape you want to emulate, such as a brick, you can cut your sponge to that shape.

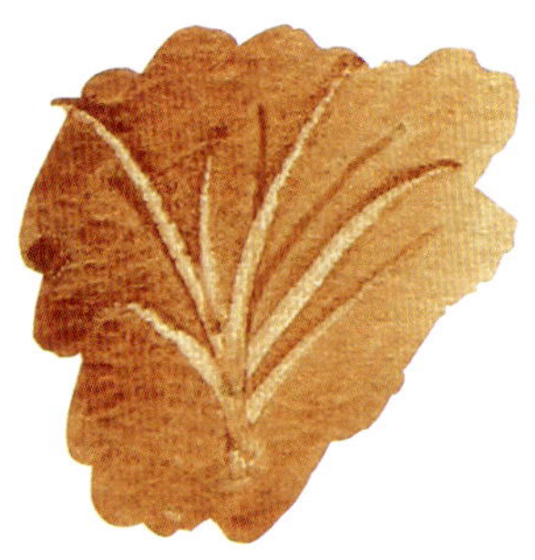

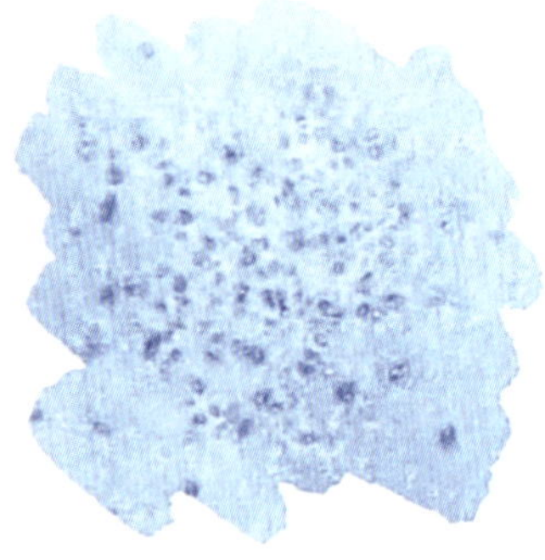

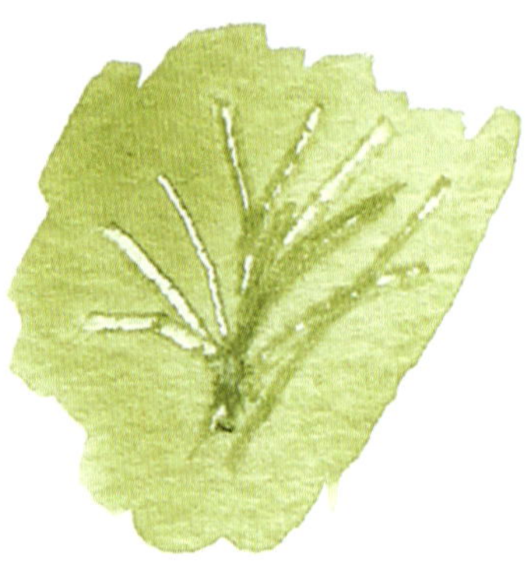

Dragging

Paint doesn't have to be applied with a brush – look around you and you'll be surprised what could be used. I enjoy manipulating the paint with other tools, and this can be done once the paint is already on the paper.

A useful method is to apply a blob of paint onto the paper and then, while it is still pliable, move it to suit you. A good way of creating tufts of grass, for example, is to flick lines from the blob of paint with the handle end of a brush in the natural direction they would grow. This looks more natural than painting them traditionally, with the other (proper) end of the brush.

Tip: the ragged, broken end of a brush handle is a useful tool for scraping into damp paint, dragging, or for applying masking fluid.

Wet-in-wet

Here's the real beauty of watercolour. In nature colours are rarely flat and the same throughout, they vary in tone and colour. This change is rarely a straight line, as colours often naturally merge together and this is the perfect method for capturing that.

Paint an area, making sure you use plenty of water and have the paint quite wet then, while it is still wet, drop in another colour and the two should merge and blend together where they meet.

Practise to find the right time to add your second colour: if you add it too soon, the two colours may completely mix and there will be no differentiation between the two. Alternatively, if you leave it too late, so that the original wash is almost dry, you will get a 'cauliflower' effect as the new wet wash pushes itself into the old, and disperses with harsh lines around the edge.

This technique really does need practice, but it's well worth it.

Scraping

You can create special effects by taking paint off paper, too, by scraping or scratching it with a stick end or penknife. This can be done when the paint is damp or dry, depending on the effect you require. If your paint is still damp it can be manipulated and 'wiped' in a line to give an effect that is lighter than the base – useful for branches on trees, tufts of grass, or hair.

Simply scrape into the paint with a stick, drawing into the lines you want to create. Again, timing is crucial – if the paint is too wet it won't leave the desired mark, as it will simply flow back and fill up the space, and if it is too dry, it will drag rather than 'sliding off' easily. This 'dragging' can be useful if you want a ragged line of white – the effect of the sun hitting the water across a lake, for instance – in which case wait until your surface is dry, then scrape a penknife across in a line to scratch the surface of the paper. The raggedy highlights this creates can be very effective, but it has to be done carefully.

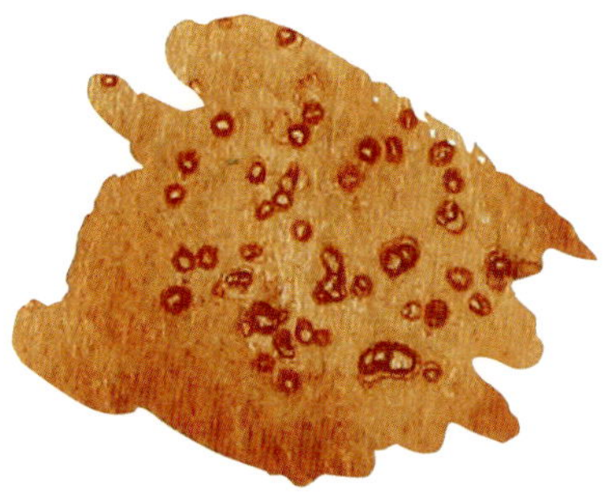

Salt

Lay your wash, then sprinkle salt
onto it. Use ordinary table salt for a
gentle, speckled effect and chunky
rock salt for a more dramatic
effect. As your paint dries, lovely
patterns are created by the grains
– useful for such things as a gravel
path or sandy beach.

Tip: I save sachets of salt from restaurants

and keep them in my art bag. This means

I always have some on hand when I need it.

Art preparations

There are a number of preparations on the market
which can be added to paint, for example gum arabic
'thickens' your paint and ox gall helps it to flow.
There are mixes which render your paint luminous and
others that make it shiny. There are so many on the
market under so many different trade names that it
would be impossible to deal with them all here, so I
suggest you pick up leaflets in art shops and ask if
you can sample any that are of interest to you.

The picture shown below was commissioned by a
brewery. Because of its large size (5 x 3ft/1.5 x 1m)
I had to order the paper especially from Holland.
When it arrived I laid it on the floor and stood over
it for ages too scared to make a start. The interior
designer had sent me some colours but had left the
design up to me and, once I had the confidence
to start, I had great fun. There is always a danger
of going too far, so you need to know when to stop
– which is usually just before you realize it is time –
many a lovely painting has been ruined by its last
stroke of paint.

*I painted this first in traditional
watercolour then, whilst it was
still wet, I added other colours
wet-in-wet. When it had dried,
I added pastels and splattered
more paint on top of that*

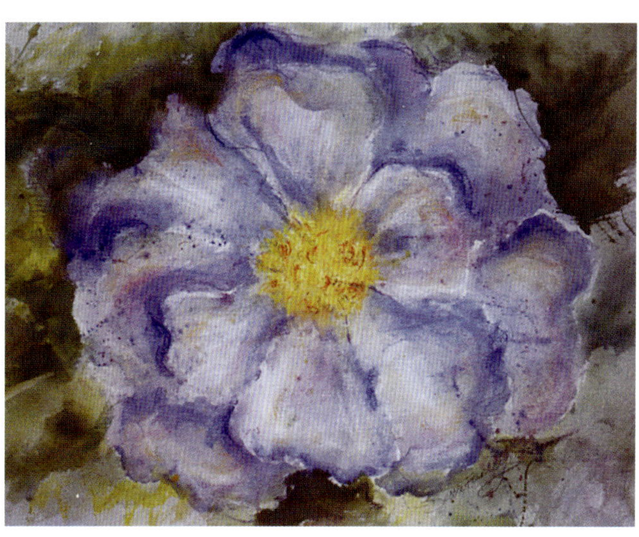

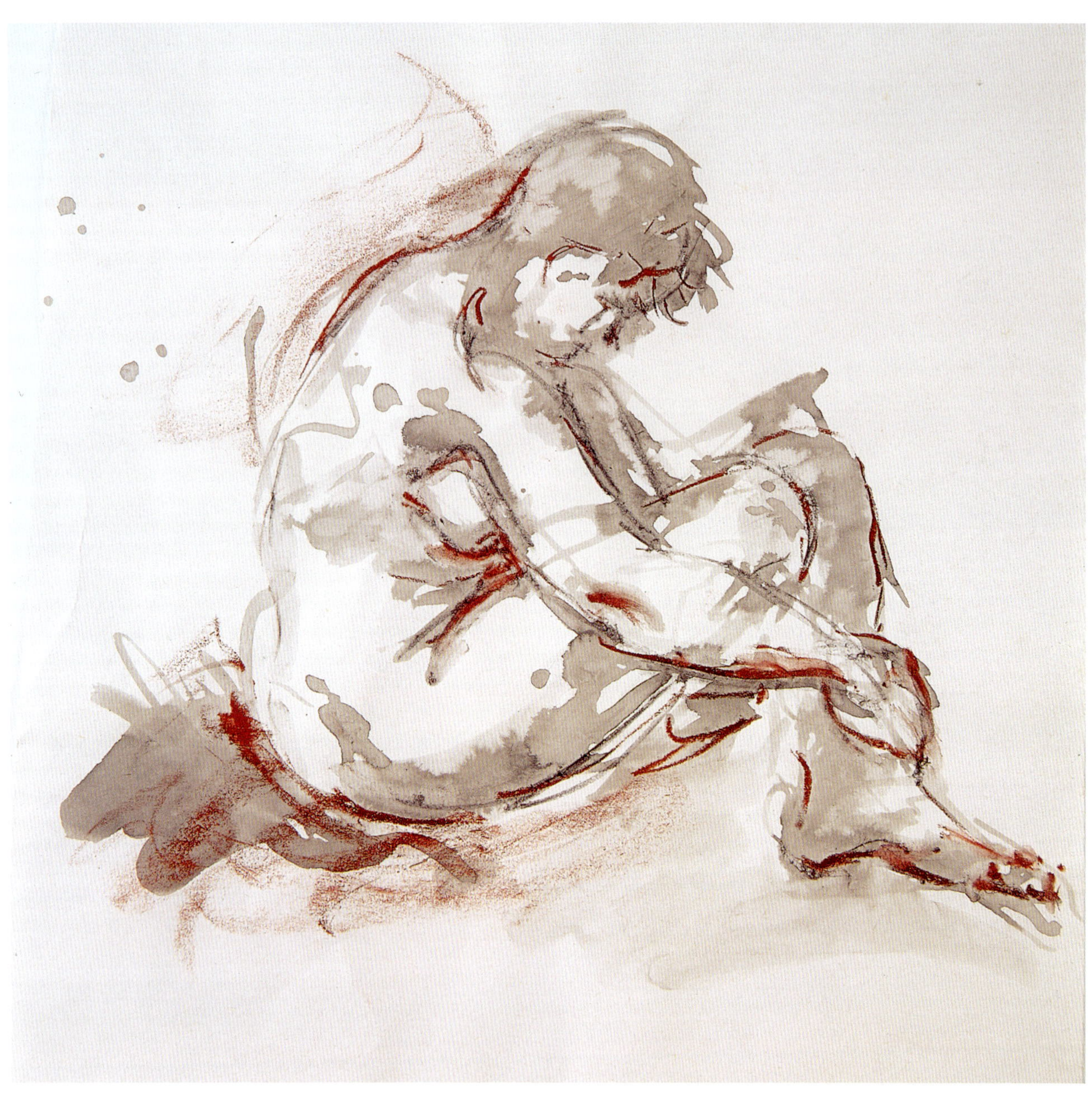

For this study I used ink (applied with long, bendy, willow twigs held at arm's length), conté sticks, charcoal and watercolour (applied with a large brush using my 'wrong' hand to keep it loose). It's easy to worry and be hesitant when using mixed media, so I had a time limit of 30 seconds before I changed medium. This, and the unorthodox methods of application, kept it fluid and exciting. (Further examples can be seen on p. 161)

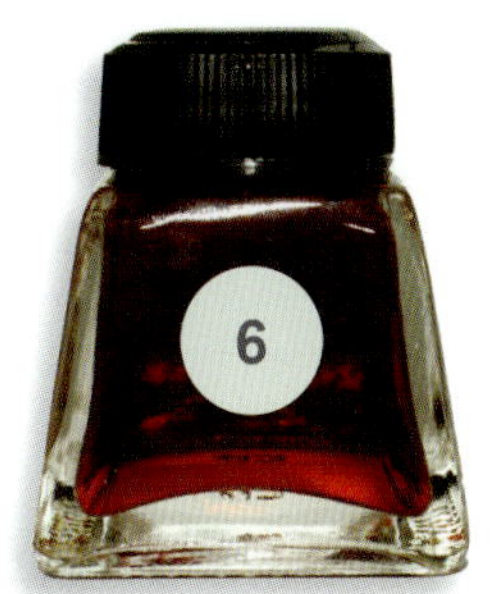

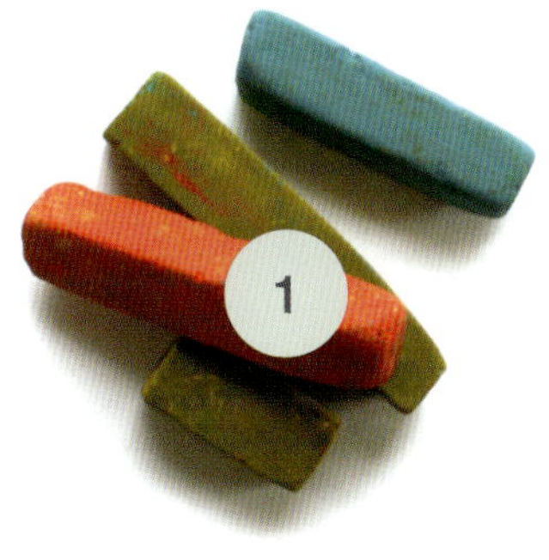

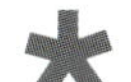

✳ **Project:** Trying mixed media

Try mixing a variety of materials in with, or on top of, your watercolour. Remember, the limitations are only in your imagination: raid the kitchen cupboards, examine the shelves of your art shop, look closely at interesting pictures you may see in galleries and always ask yourself how the effects were achieved.

For the traditionalists who even believe that adding gouache is a crime against watercolour, 'mixed media' is sacrilege. But it can be very exciting to use a variety of different materials along with your watercolours and I favour anything that stretches your creativity, so do consider giving it a go. You could try adding anything you fancy, but the following ideas will give you a start:

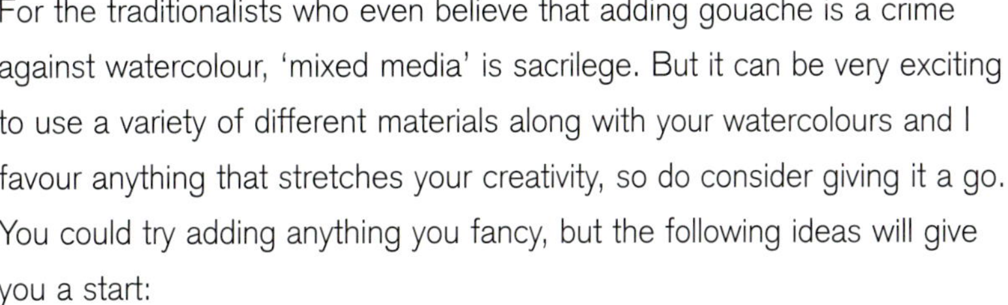

1	Pastel	6	Coloured ink
2	Charcoal	7	Salt
3	Coloured pencils	8	Sand
4	Ink	9	Coffee granules
5	Tissue paper		

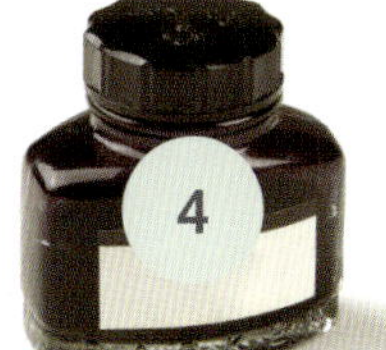

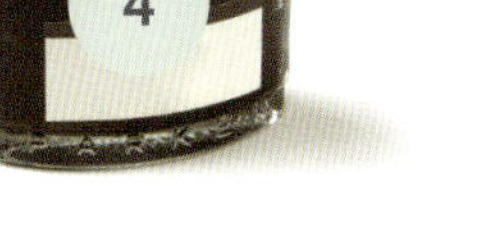

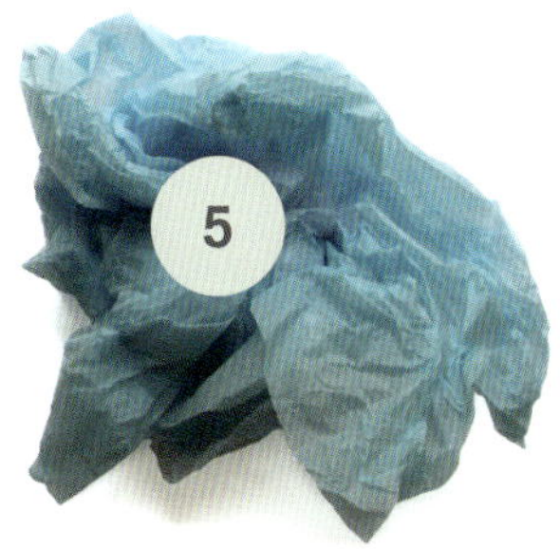

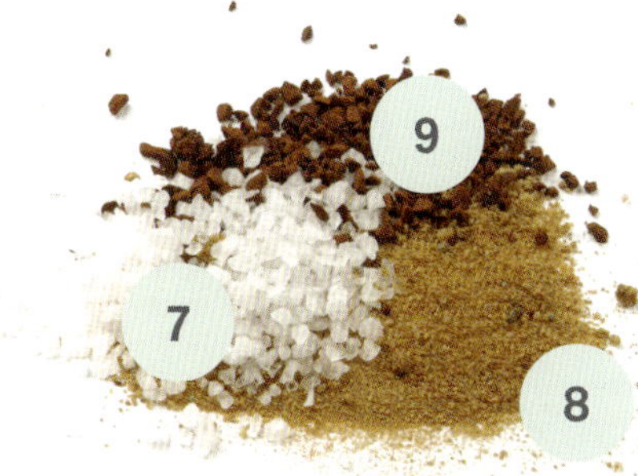

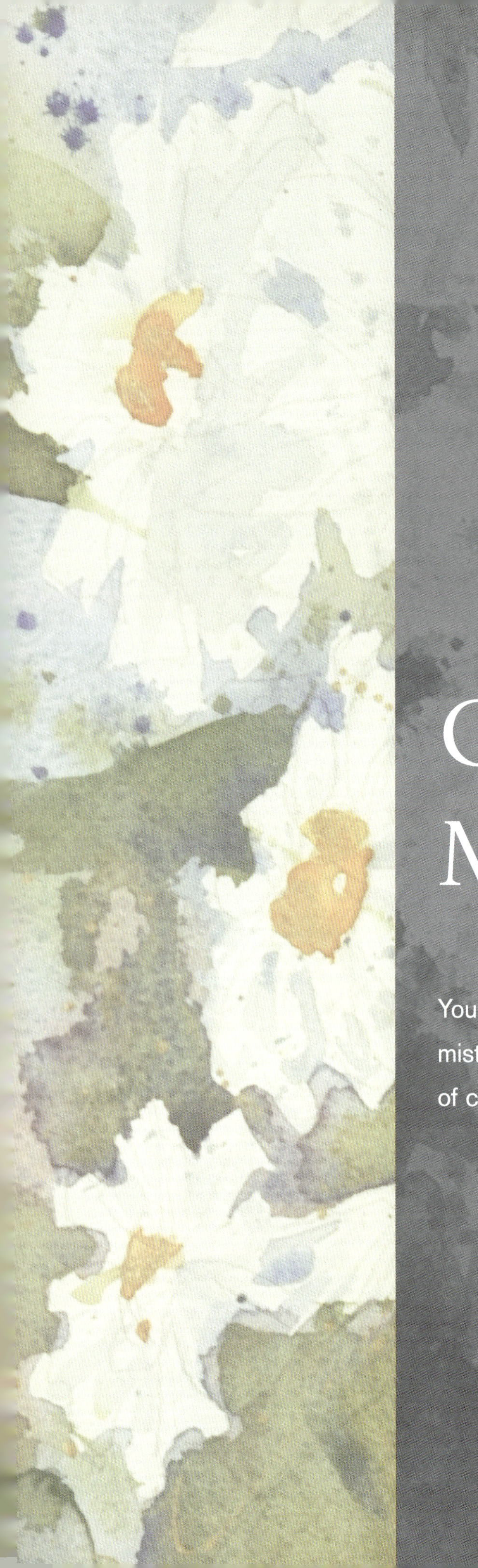

Correcting Mistakes

You can, and almost certainly will, make mistakes – but don't worry, there are ways of correcting them.

It might seem a little defeatist telling you how to correct your mistakes, but any artist can find themselves in this quandary. Here I aim to reassure you, and increase your confidence as you progress.

Some painters are put off using watercolours, as, unlike with oils and acrylics, you cannot paint over your mistakes. But there are a number of ways in which you can tackle this problem.

'Wash off' the whole picture

If a whole painting has become too heavy and muddy, put the complete sheet of paper in the bath (I use the shower head on full power to blast the top surface of paint off). You do, however, need good quality paper for this to work, certainly no less than 140lb (300gsm), and it will need to be stuck down again – as you would for stretching paper – so it doesn't dry all wrinkly.

You will be left with a paler version of your picture, which will allow you to paint over it and continue

without starting out all over again. I also use this method when I want a 'ghostly' effect in the background, or when I want to build up gentle layers.

The effect shown in the painting below was achieved by painting the flowers numerous times, each time washing off the colour – and drying the layers in between – to leave another 'ghostly layer'. Once I had the effect I needed, I lifted out colour on the petals for further effect.

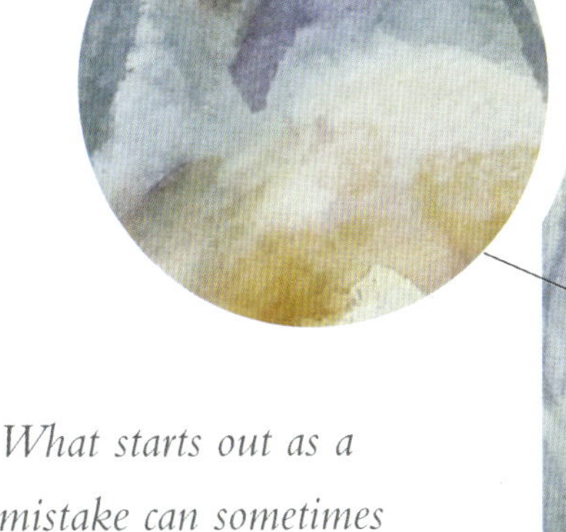

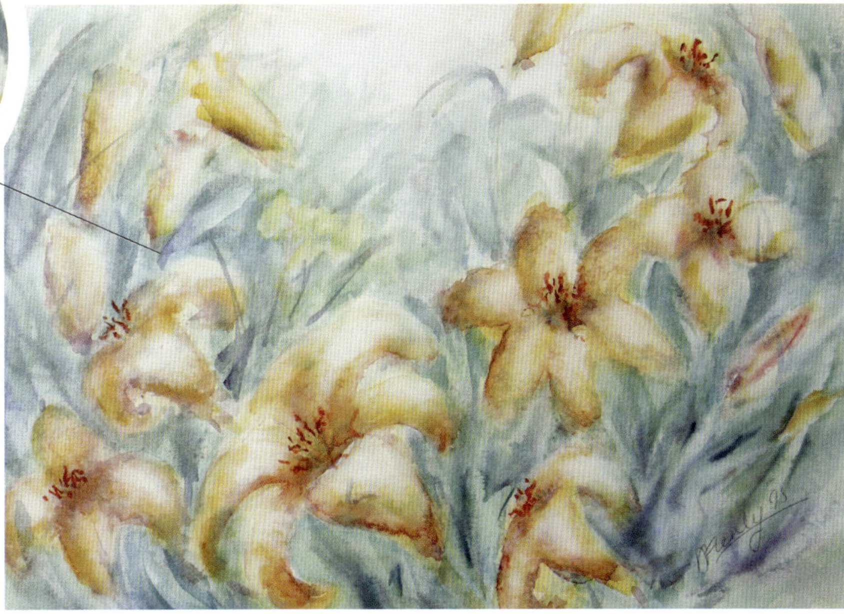

What starts out as a mistake can sometimes become a real advantage. Here, I used lots of water to wash paint off, but this gave a lovely, etherial quality to the painting

'Lift out' the offending area

If it is a small area you want to alter, try lifting the
paint out by brushing the offending area with clean
water, then dabbing it with a tissue. If this doesn't
work, use a stiff hog-hair brush to 'scrub' and remove
the paint. I have a few small brushes I keep specifically
for this purpose. Be careful, though, that you don't
'scruff up' the surface of your paper too much, or
even make a hole in it.

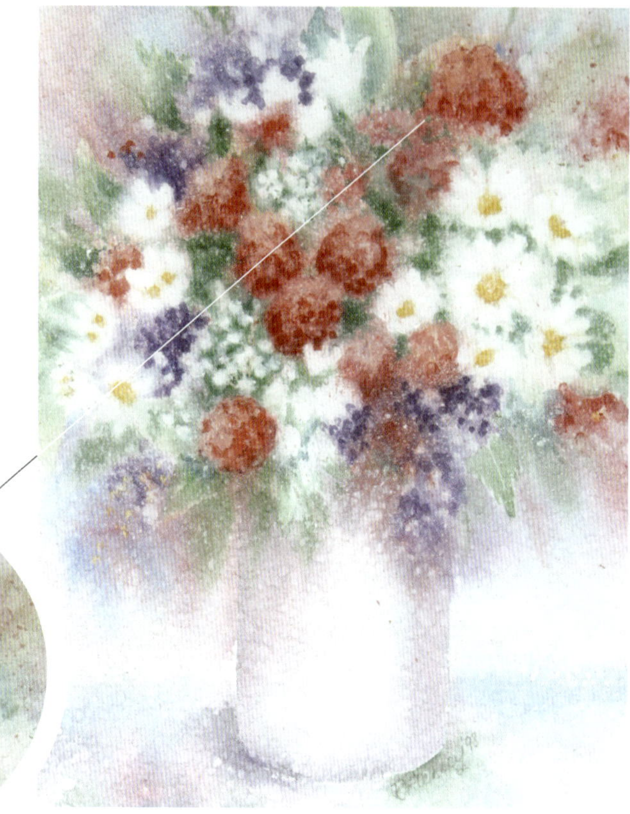

*'Lifting out' isn't only useful for correcting
mistakes – I created the soft edges around these
flowers by 'scrubbing them out' with a soft brush*

Use a template

If you have a specific area or shape that needs lifting
out, make a template – or arrange a few bits of card –
to preserve the surrounding areas, then scrub out just
the area you require. For example, if you forget to
allow a lighter area for a flower stem: make a template
of the shape you need from a couple of pieces of card,
then simply lift the paint out from the relevant area.

Knowing how your paints 'behave' is an invaluable aid.
Some colours will lift out more easily than others so it
is worth learning the 'How your paints behave' chart
(see page 56), so that you are aware which paints are
staining colours, so will leave the paper coloured
when washed off, and which are granular, so will
lift off easily and cleanly. Then, if you know in
advance that you are going to require shapes to be
lifted out – to highlight shapes of leaves from bushes
or distant flowers, for example – this can be done
effectively if you pre-select a non-staining colour,
such as sap green.

If the problem cannot be removed by simply lifting out
with water, you could try adding a little bleach, but you
need to be very careful you don't make a hole in your
paper. However, if a picture has gone irretrievably
wrong, you have nothing to lose!

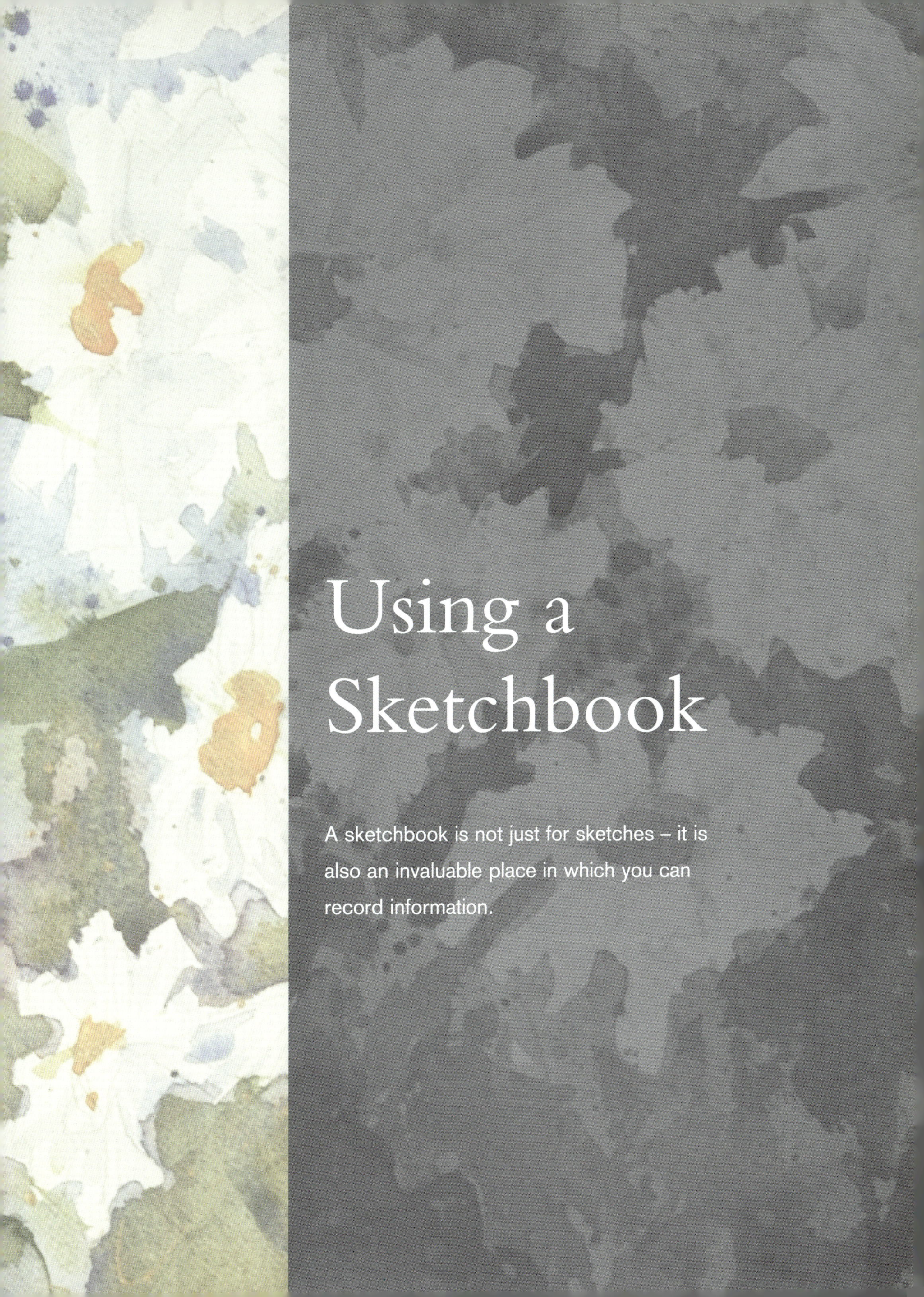

Using a Sketchbook

A sketchbook is not just for sketches – it is also an invaluable place in which you can record information.

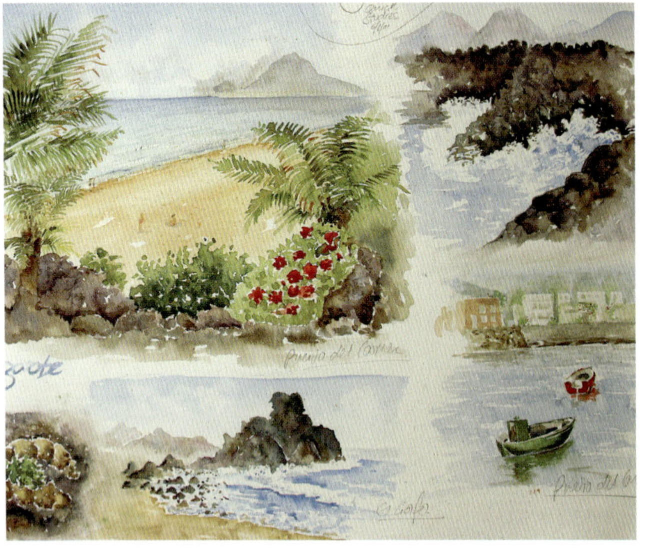

This page from my sketchbook shows some quick studies I did whilst in Lanzarote

Tip: if you don't have the time or the inclination to execute detailed sketches, or to record names of colours, develop your own shorthand so that you can quickly record the information you need in your sketchbook.

There is so much to learn in the world of painting, especially if you are a beginner. I don't believe you will remember everything you are told and this is where a sketchbook will come in useful.

When you see things that interest you, make notes about them and work out ideas, record quotes, preserve samples of colours, stick in cuttings, colour charts and anything else you fancy.

Sketchbooks are essential tools and I stick all sorts of bits in mine – relevant articles, samples of papers, contacts and pictures of other art work that inspires me. If I visit a gallery, I use it to make notes on the pictures and techniques in my sketchbook, too.

Remember, that your sketchbook is for working out ideas, not for impressing people. If it is neat and presentable you have missed the point. I don't like people to even look at mine. Firstly, it would make no sense to them at all, secondly it is deeply personal.

If you are going to take a photograph to work from, it is essential to back it up with sketches and information that can only be captured at the scene and may not show up on a photograph later. I record these factors in my sketchbook at the time, and then clip the photo in with it later, so I can work from both sources.

I would argue that, out of the two, the sketch is your more valuable source because it is a personal reflection of what you felt about a scene and ultimately this is what will make a unique picture. When you are painting out of doors it is crucial to capture the immediacy of a scene. So often things change quickly as the sun moves, or the weather changes, but with a quick sketch you've got the essentials 'captured'.

Try to get as much relevant information down as possible – this takes some practice and you may need to do it a few times and struggle with what is missing before you master this art.

What size sketchbook?

Before purchasing a sketchbook, think about when and where you will use it and what kind will suit you best. I like to keep a tiny one in my handbag at all times. You never know when a scene will strike you, so you are always prepared to record it and make notes if you come across anything interesting. It also means you are never bored, as you can do a quick sketch if you are stuck waiting somewhere – it certainly solves the problem of boring sermons – I sit at the back in church and sketch the backs of people's heads! Small books can cramp your style though, so you will need larger ones to work in, too.

Consider the paper in your sketchbook: cartridge paper is fine for quick watercolour sketches but anything too shiny or too thin won't take paint, so don't be tempted to pick up a cheap one unless the paper is a decent quality. I find spiral-bound books are good, because your working surface isn't bent by the spine when the book is open.

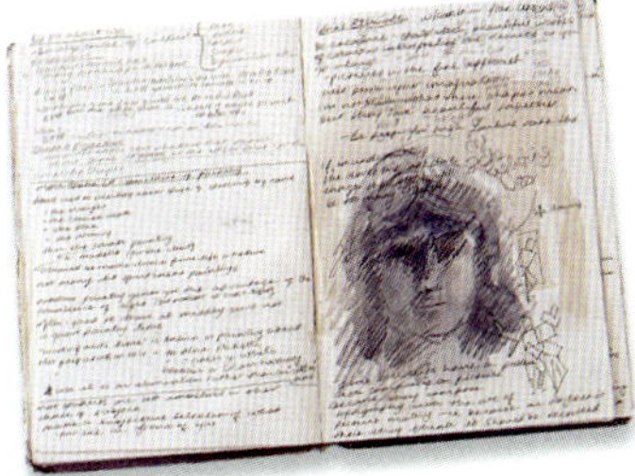

✳ Projects: Using sketchbooks

• Sketch everyday objects, reducing them to simple shapes – sphere, cube, cylinder – first. Plan out a sketch, measuring and mark-making before drawing. Shade it in, keeping light from one source (see pages 31–37).

• Follow lessons from art journals and books – choose ones that helps with any particular issues that you are struggling with at any time.

• Try using different media – from grades of pencils to pens, charcoal, and so on – and keep these in your sketchbook for reference.

• Practise different drawing exercises, using contour, line and shading, for example.

• Draw in your sketchbook every day – from everyday objects to scenes around you. Continually practise and apply the above exercises in it until they are second nature to you.

• If something catches your eye, or you think of an idea, record it immediately, as you may forget later. Note down any ideas in words as well as sketches.

• Collect samples of other artists' drawings – buy postcards, cut out pictures and stick them in. Examine them and the styles used. Copy these and drawings from old masters as a learning exercise.

• When sketching for watercolour, bear in mind that it can be seen under the paint. It must be accurate but without too much detail, so there is allowance for freedom of expression with the paints. You don't want to be 'colouring in', so practise drafting initial sketches for this purpose.

• Sharpen your powers of observation: study some objects, or a scene, then remove yourself (or them) and quickly try to draw what you have seen.

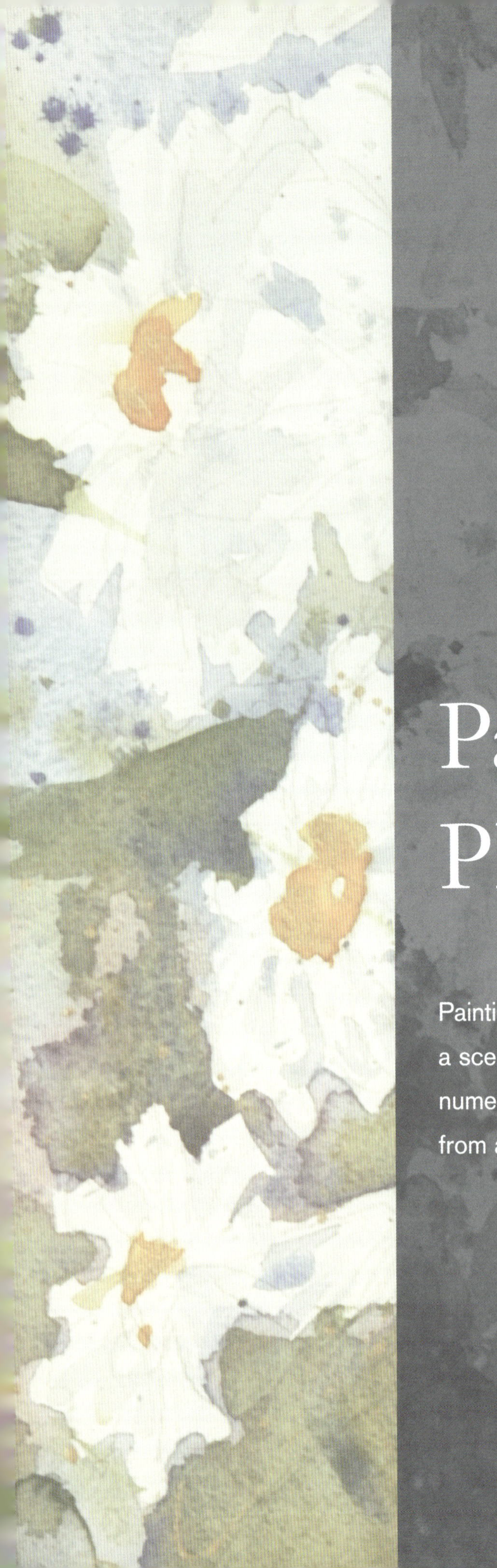

Painting from Photographs

Painting on the spot is the best way to capture a scene, but it isn't always practical so, for numerous reasons, you may need to paint from a photograph.

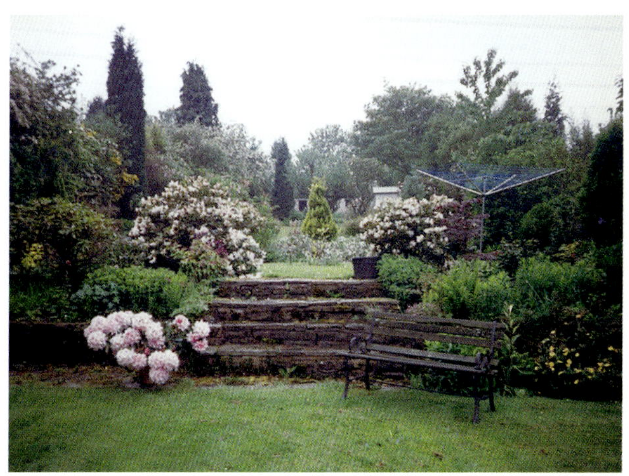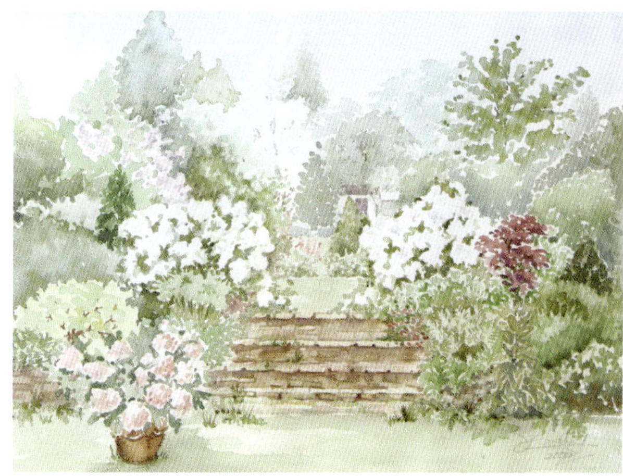

There is no doubt that painting on the spot is the best method of capturing the essence of a scene but it isn't always practical so, for numerous reasons, you may need to paint from a photograph. Obviously, a photograph can never be a substitute for the real thing: as it is a two-dimensional representation, you can't see behind or around objects and, after the event, you can't get another angle or a close-up if you are not sure about something. More importantly, though, you can't capture the 'feel' of a place, the light, the atmosphere in the same way that you can with a painting. These may be abstract ideas but they are the 'X' factor that gives you the feeling for a place.

Therefore, if you visit a place that you want to paint, it is essential that you record details about it in your sketchbook to back up your photograph. If you are just painting 'cold' from a picture, imagine 'being there'.

The same principles apply as they do when working from life, you don't need to repeat exactly what is there, use artistic licence, interpret, eliminate, emphasize.

I keep lots of reference material filed – well, shoved in boxes, actually – under headings such as 'trees', 'flowers', 'clouds', 'hands'. This is very useful, especially when the original is not available.

They can also be used in composite arrangements, but this only works if you bear in mind relative size, light direction and so on, which may be different. I also keep cuttings of other artists' work in each of the areas, as it is interesting to see how other people tackle these subjects.

A family ordered the painting of their garden (top right) for Father's Day. I made a few quick sketches on the spot but, as it was a surprise, I couldn't hang about, so I had to take a photograph and work from that. They didn't want a tightly realistic portrayal but a painting 'in my style', as they had other paintings of mine. I started by using artistic licence to remove the rotary clothes drier, a bucket and a bench, and I then had to simplify some of the plants, especially away from the focal point so that they didn't distract the eye and make the composition look too busy.

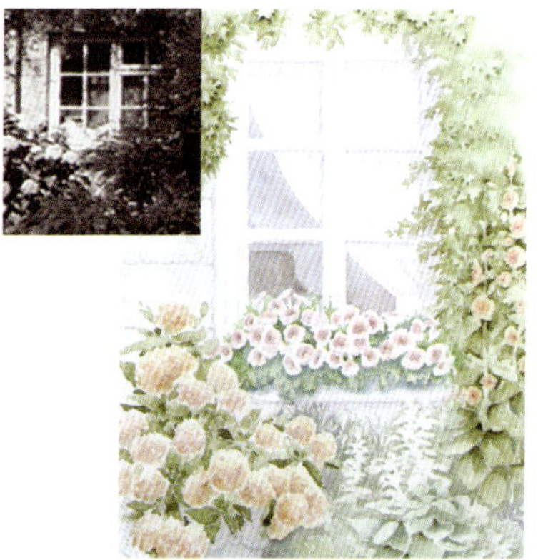

Photographs are very useful for subject matter. I adapted this one in different ways for various pictures, using other reference material for ideas.

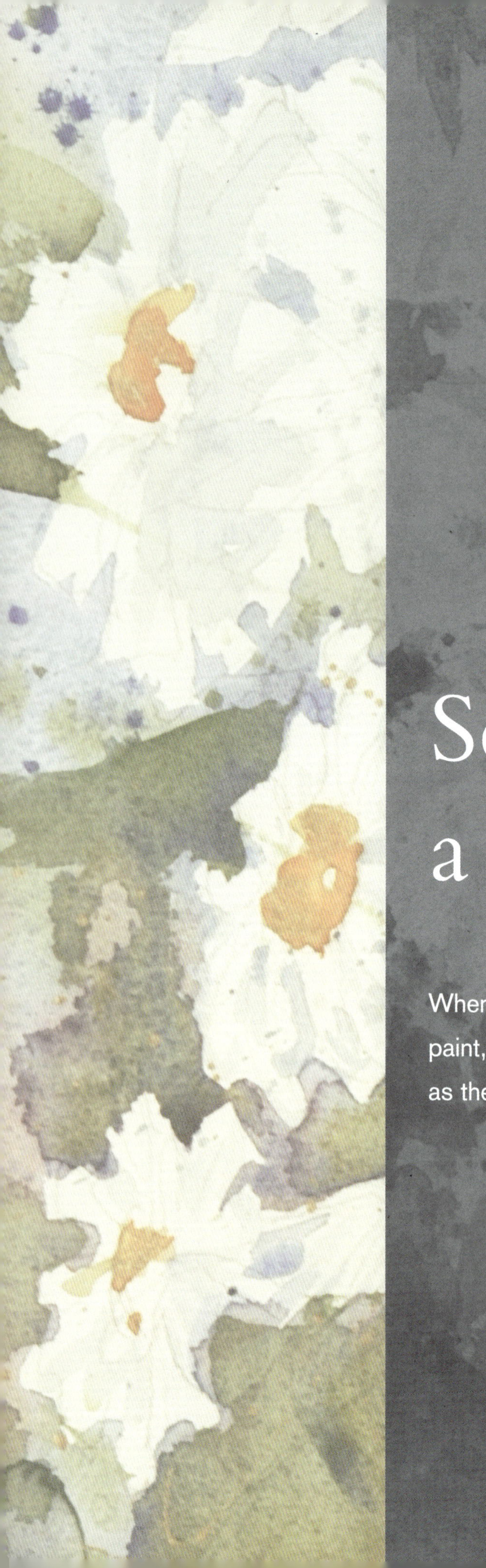

Setting up
a Still Life

When students say they don't know what to
paint, I suggest throwing a few things together,
as there is always stuff around the house.

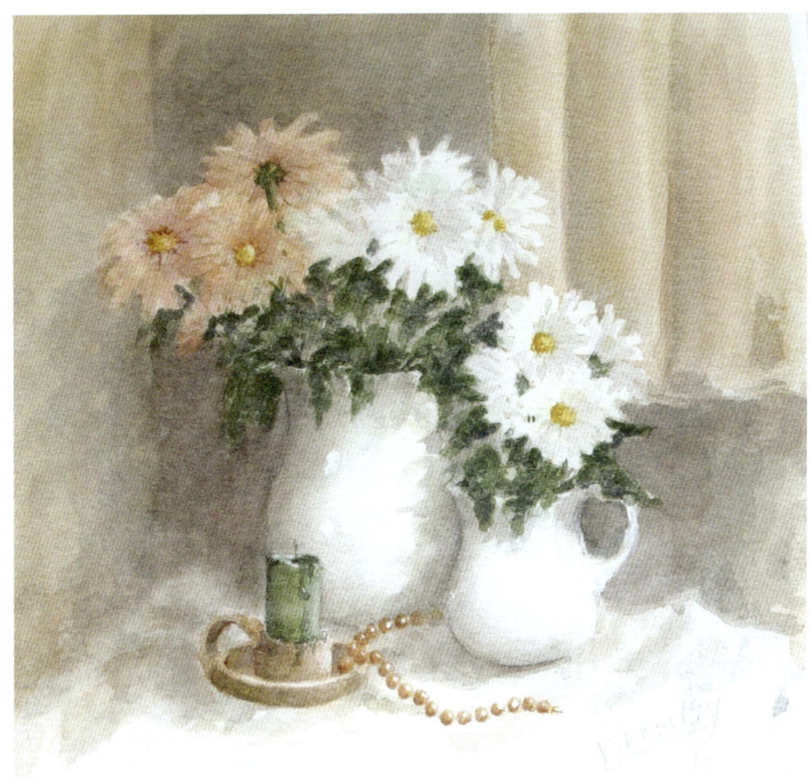

If you cannot think what to paint, and find the idea of setting up a still life daunting and don't know where to start, here are a few tips to set you on your way:

● Choose an area where your still life can be left undisturbed
It will usually take a couple of sessions, so you need to be able to return to it. The middle of the kitchen table, therefore, is not a good idea!

● Consider the light source
Make sure that your main light comes from one direction. This will give you your tones and shadows, so it is important to get this established from the start. If using natural light, bear in mind that it will change as the sun moves in position and will disappear behind clouds. You will also only be able to work during daylight hours.

If you use artificial light, try and set up a spotlight that directs light mainly from one direction. Be warned though, too much light may create a too strong shade and dark tones. You can use white sheets of card to reflect light, or create shade, and I stick these in place with adhesive tape onto whatever furniture happens to be around.

● Have a 'theme' and choose relevant objects
I suggest you use items that have a relationship to one another: for example, flowers may look good with a small gardening fork and gardening gloves, while food may look good with fruit, wine, or kitchen equipment. The pretty flowers in the picture above suit the delicate lace cloth, and the beads tie in with both colour and subject matter. The painting overleaf shows a traditional kitchen jug, so I have used a traditional kitchen gingham table cloth in the same colour.

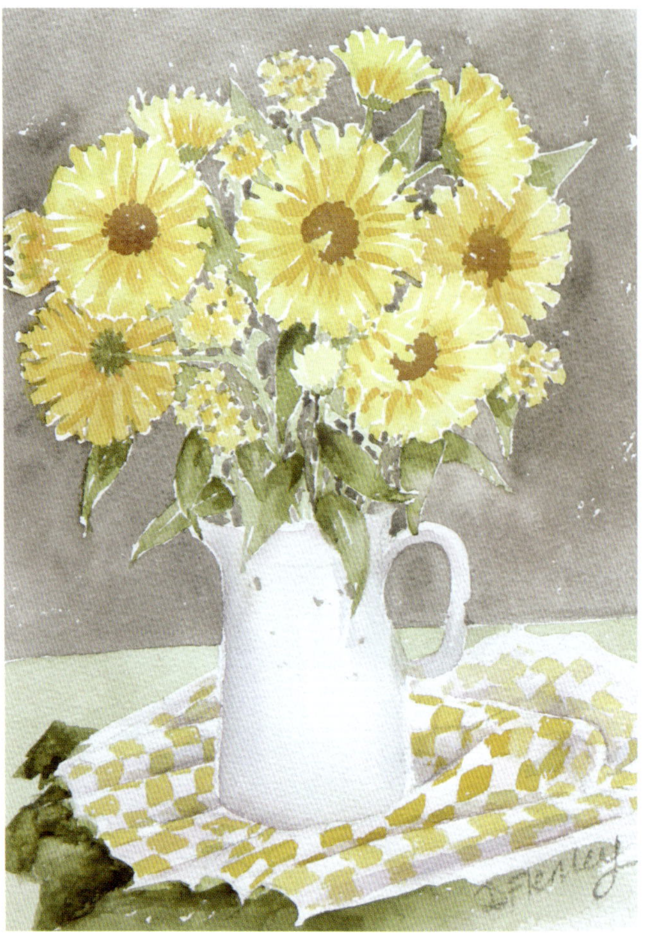

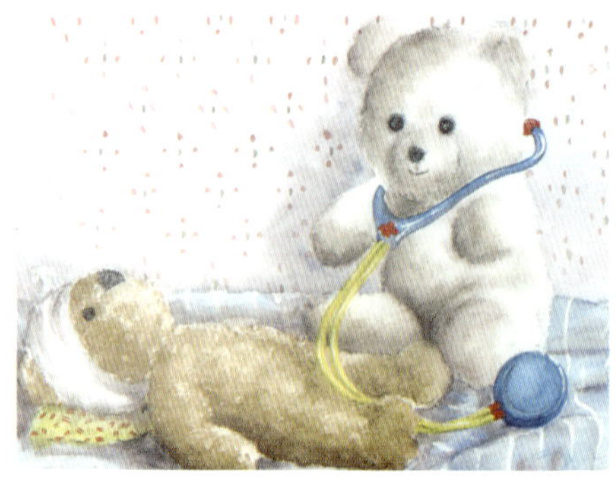

Think it through: one object out of place could ruin the feel of a scene. These teddies (above), for example, were being painted to go in a children's area at my husband's surgery, but I found that his real stethoscope looked scary, so I had to use a toy one, to add to the 'cuteness' of the scene and make it more appealing to children.

● Relate your background to the objects

The supporting items you choose, and where they are placed, can make a big difference. Pretty architectural features help and a window can frame a composition. The kitchen cupboards (left) add to an atmosphere: the colour of the pots echo the colour of the background and the pot in the distance, while the nature of the pots ties in with the kitchen drawers.

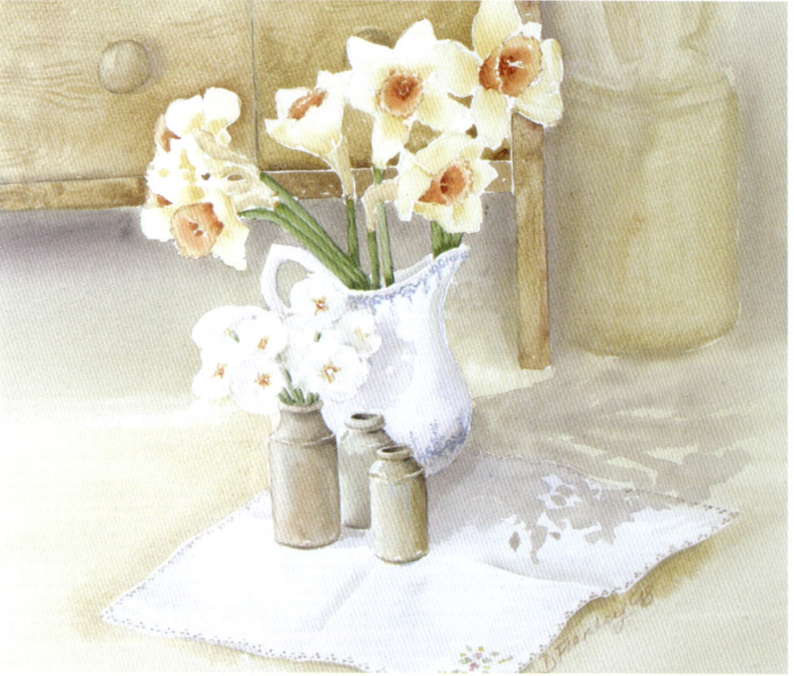

● Think about the composition

Make sure the eye is led around the picture. Try overlapping and balancing the shapes of objects together. Stand back, look and think – does everything work together to enhance the picture? If anything sticks out, move it until all is harmonious and it 'feels right'.

● View your arrangement through a viewfinder

Look at your arrangement through a simple rectangle cut-out of card, and decide how it will fill your frame – remember that the 'negative space' around the objects is important in creating the whole picture, so don't leave too much space around the edges.

● Take photographs

If you are unlikely to finish in the foreseeable future, take photograph as a source to work from later.

I keep a box of suitable bits for still-life arrangements, which is why you see the same pots and cloths appearing in different pictures. Save nice pieces of pottery, candle holders, vases and cloths to stand them on, as it makes life easier when you decide to do a still life.

Focus on
How do I know when a painting is finished?

So many watercolours are ruined by painters not knowing when to stop, so this is an important question. Whilst you can alter small mistakes in watercolour, once you have gone too far you've had it because, unlike with oils and acrylics, you can't paint over your mistakes and there is little chance of retrieving your picture without losing the freshness. My advice, therefore, is to stop BEFORE you think you have finished. Go away and leave it for a while.

When you return you will see it afresh, so then consider the following points.

● Is anything wrong, which you failed to notice before?

● Look at it in a mirror so you see the image reversed – does this show up any problems that you weren't aware of before?

● Does it really need more doing to it and, if so, what does it need?

● If it's flat in its values, so nothing stands out, add 'punch' to it by making one area stronger. likewise, if there is too much going on, lift out some areas and 'quieten' them down.

● Take more 'time out' from the painting. Are there any glaring problems, bits that still just don't 'look right'? If so, now is the time to address these. Finish in style and you will have more chance of success.

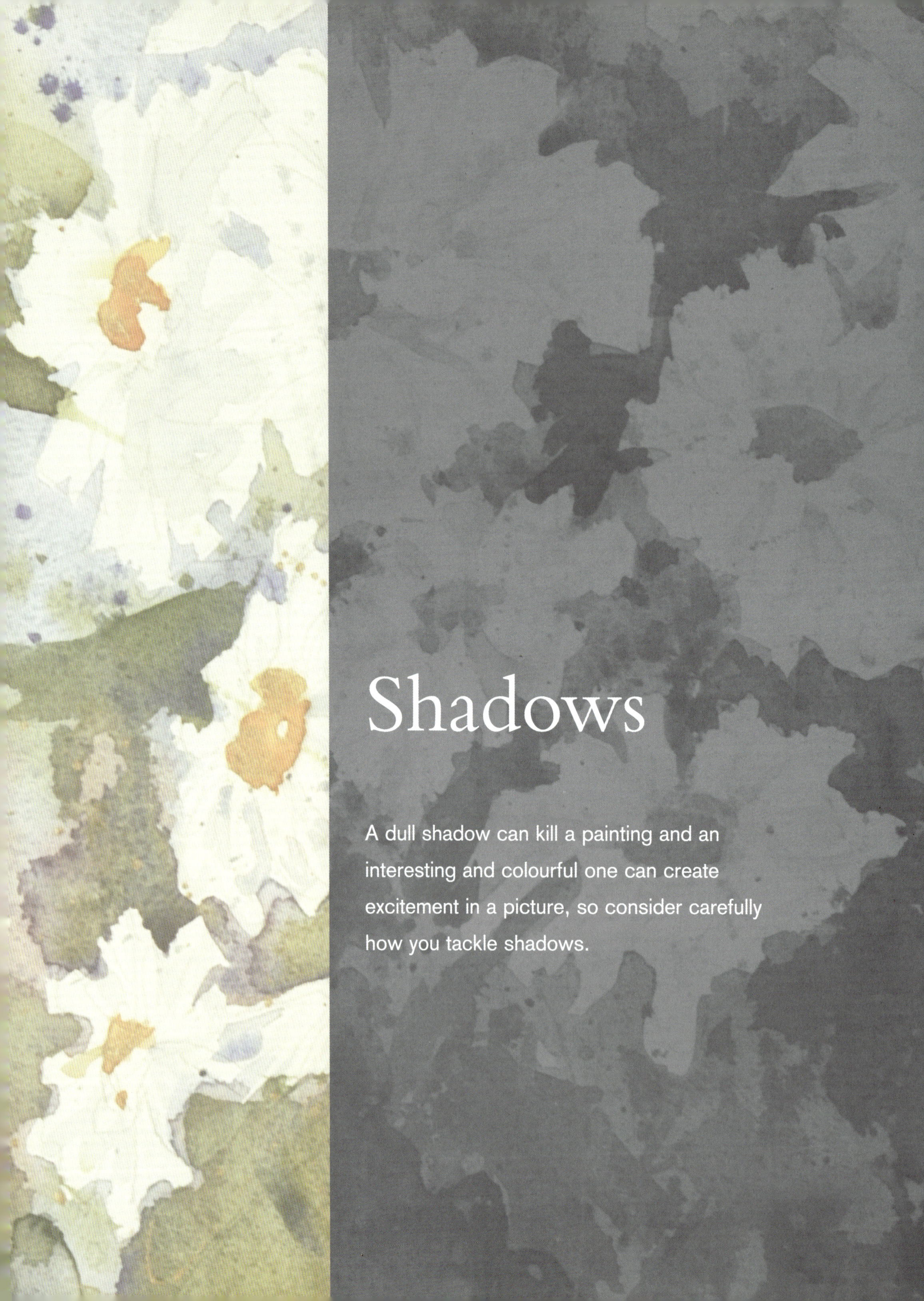

Shadows

A dull shadow can kill a painting and an
interesting and colourful one can create
excitement in a picture, so consider carefully
how you tackle shadows.

A s you will see in the example below, shadows are
not just grey: they are, basically, a darker form
of the local colour, with lots of influences around them
which affect their tone and colour. Some art manuals
claim that all shadows have blue in them – this is an
advance on them being grey, but still stops short of
the full possibilities. If you keep looking and imagining the
possibilities you will start to see lots of colours – capture
them and then exaggerate their portrayal in paint.

If you have used two complementary colours in a
painting, mix and use them in the shadows, but not
so that they both disappear into a neutral – allow
some of the original colours to show through: mixing
them on the paper is one way to achieve this.

Don't fall into the trap of painting different shadow
shapes across each other – one will cancel out the
other, or the two will form a new shape.

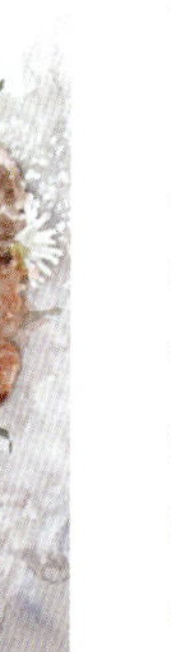

✳ **Project:** Painting shadows

Set up a still life with colourful
objects on a white surface. Look
very carefully – for a long time
if necessary – anticipating colour
in the shadows. Start with a
wash of local colour and drop
in shades of other colours around.
Exaggerate the colours you see,
then try and capture these colours
in the shadows you paint, so
that they harmonize with the
painting and enhance
your composition.

Make the shadows
convincingly dark,
especially at their
edges, but beware of
them looking as if they
have been cut out and

stuck on the paper: even the
darkest shadow should not be
painted black.

Employ different colours and mix
them, Prussian blue and alizarin
crimson, for instance, are ideal for
the very darkest shadows. Consider
not just the immediate shade but
the reflected light that comes from
alternate sources. If there are
several sources of light, each light
affects its area differently, for
example, light may come through
the window, there may also be a
table lamp, an overhead spotlight or
another window through which the
light is more direct and each of
these will have a different offering
to bring to the scenic table.

*These shadows are not plain grey, as you would
expect them to be, but rather a mixture of colours*

Colour

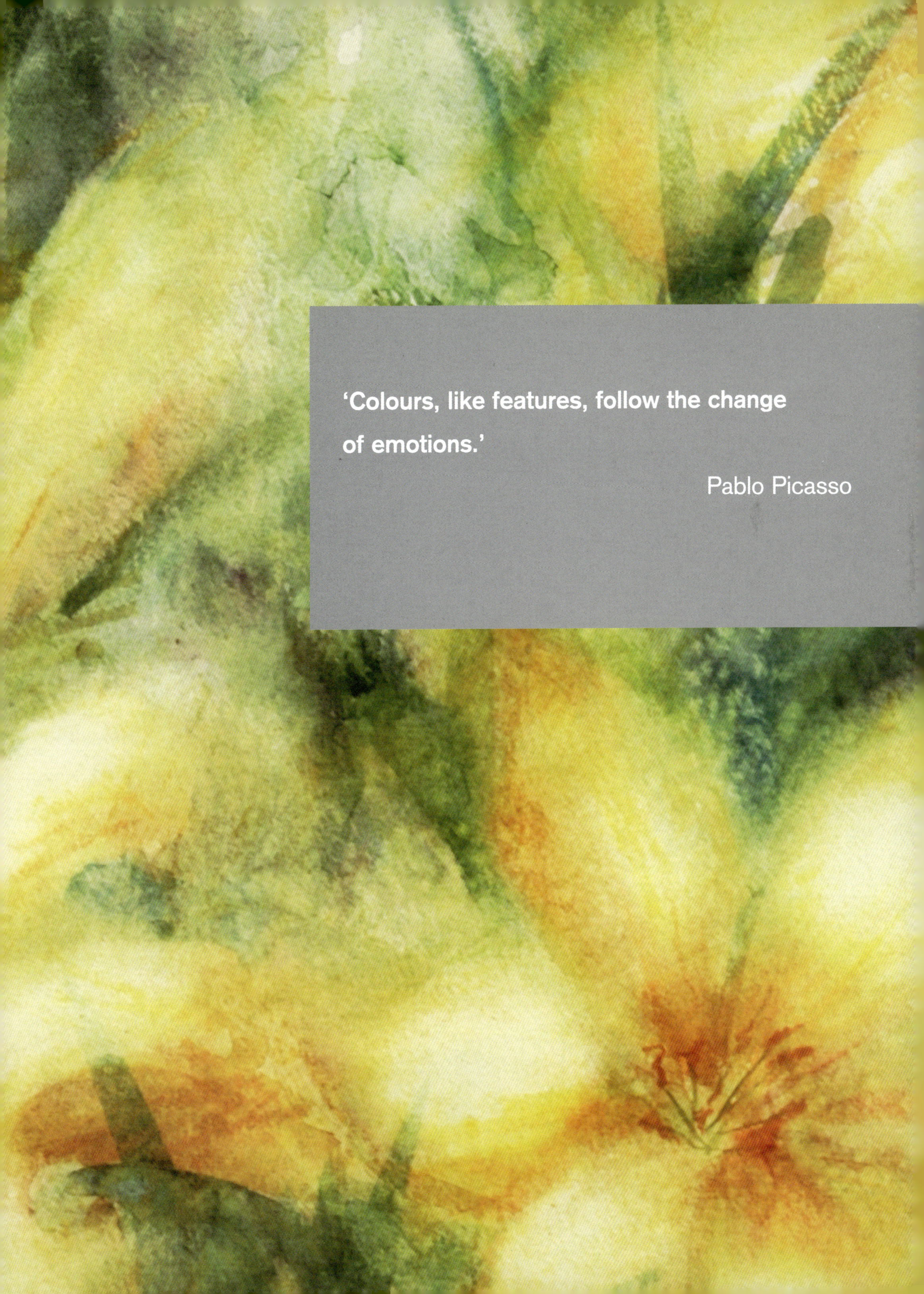
'Colours, like features, follow the change
of emotions.'

Pablo Picasso

The Colour Wheel

In this chapter we cover how colours 'work' individually, how they mix together, and how they work alongside each other.

have already explained that you need to understand how your paints behave to get the best out of them. Similarly, you need to understand your colours and the way they work, so that you can use them to set the scene and mood of your picture. Here I show you how you can achieve this.

Composing the colour wheel

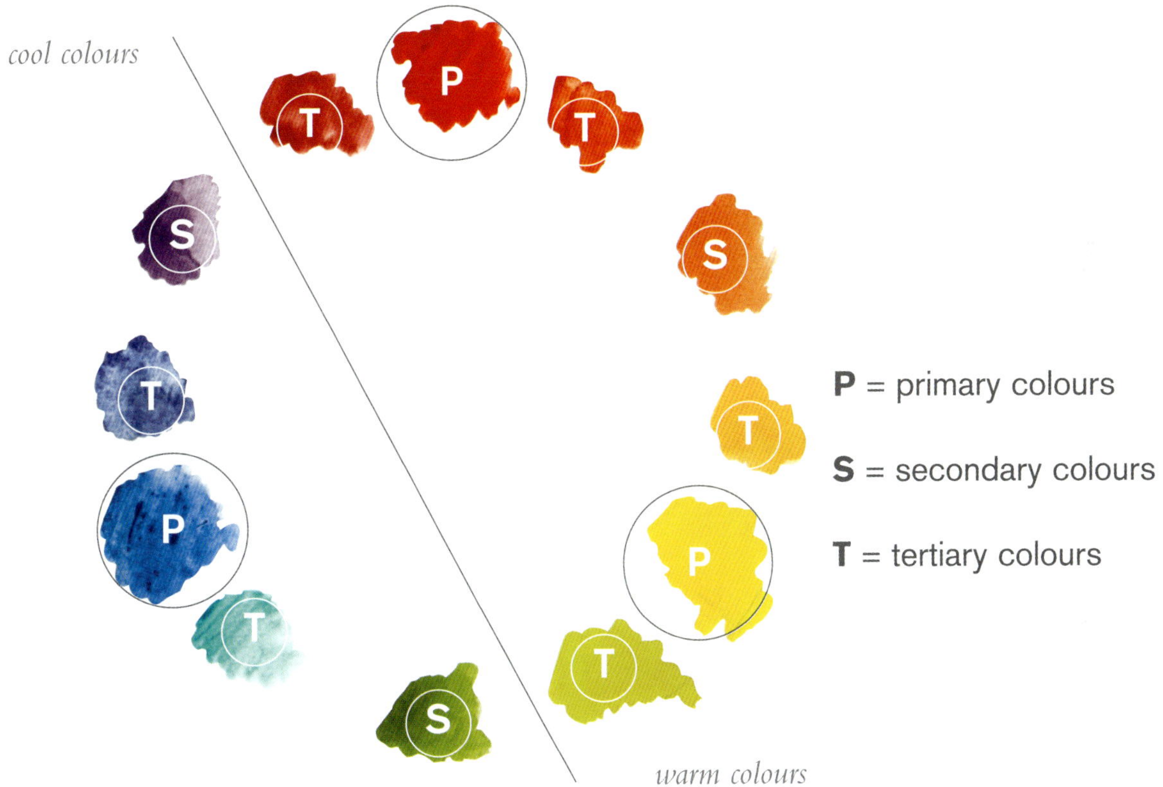

Primary colours

In art, as opposed to physics or printing, the primaries are red, blue and yellow. These can't be mixed from any other colours but an approximation of all other colours can be made by mixing from them. In watercolour, the nearest we have to the three primaries are cadmium yellow, cadmium red and cobalt blue. Two primaries make a secondary.

Secondary colours

These are orange, purple, and green and they are made from mixing two primaries: red and yellow make orange; blue and red make purple; and blue and yellow make green.

Tertiary colours

These are made from mixing two secondaries, or a secondary and a primary, and are subtle colours with similar low tonal values, such as yellow ochre, burnt umber.

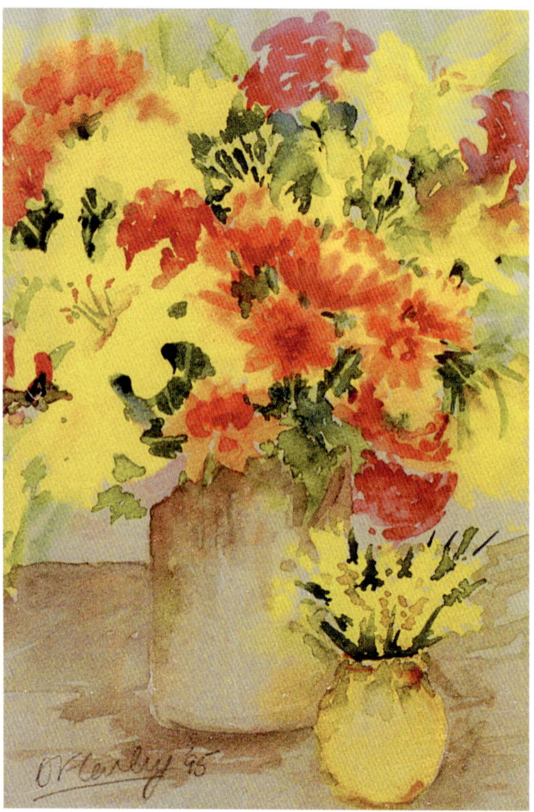

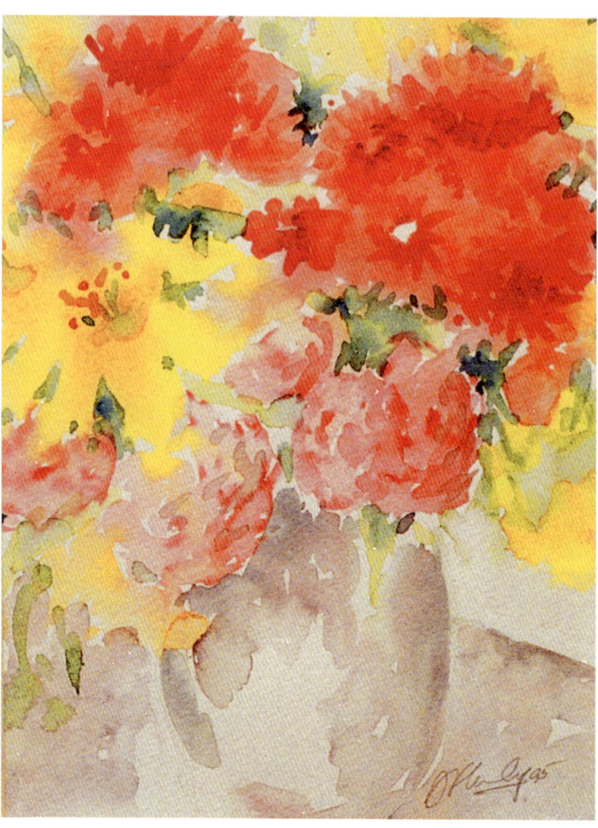

Two examples of warm-coloured flowers

Sides of the wheel:
Warm and cool colours and their uses

I remember having a children's book which showed a 'Hot orangey red fire in front of a red sky', compared to 'Polar bears on a blue-white landscape'. If ever two scenes summed up the difference between warm and cool colours that has to be it!

You can see the difference in the two sides of the colour wheel (previous page), the warmest lying on the orange side and the coolest in the blue/green sector. Warm colours tend to contain red and warm yellow, whereas they are absent in cool colours, which tend to contain blue. Bear in mind that some colours can be warm or cool, depending on their colour bias: notice the difference on the colour wheel between the warm yellow next to the orange, and the a cool yellow next to the greens. It helps to know which colours can be warm and cool, so you can use this to maximum effect.

Generally speaking, the warmer colours (reds, oranges and yellows with a red bias) create a more vibrant, stimulating atmosphere in a painting, whereas cooler blues, greens and cool greys make for a more relaxed and peaceful atmosphere, such as in landscapes.

Cool colours suggest a sense of space, whereas warm colours can be more claustrophobic. For example, we have recently re-painted our dark red lounge in a cream colour, and all the visitors say how much bigger the room looks. Warm colours are seen to 'advance' and cool colours to 'recede', which is why we put warm in the foreground and cool in the distance in a landscape.

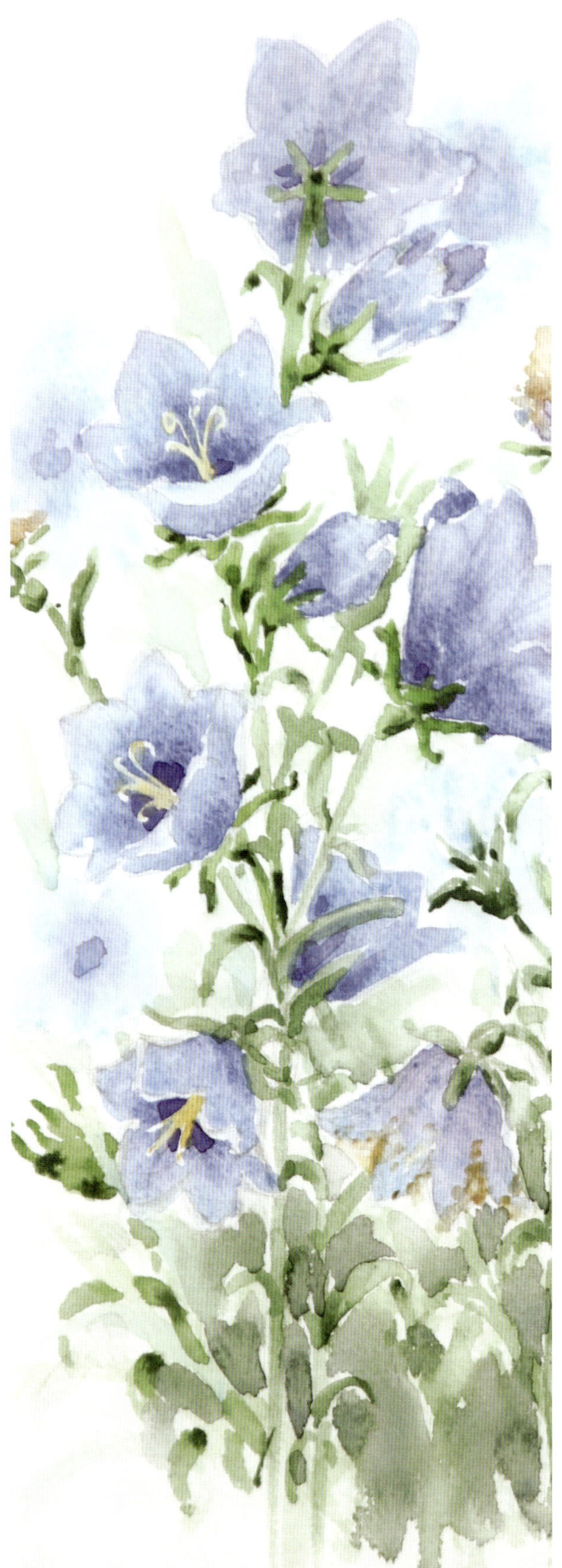

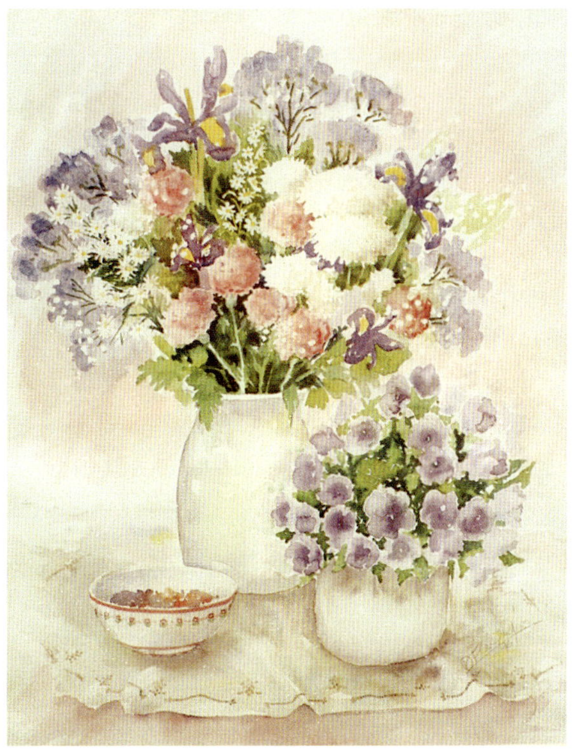

Cool-coloured flowers

I also often put warm and cool colours together, especially within the petals of a flower, as this can add a vibrancy.

For the mixing of greens (see p. 115), this knowledge of warm and cool becomes invaluable but, generally, a painting benefits from predominantly either a warm or cool overall temperature to give it conviction, while a painting with colours that are all warm or all cool tends to be 'wanting' for a splash of the opposite temperature to balance out any monotony. The blue flowers on the left are all right, but uninteresting, whereas the white and grey painting above has a dash of warm in the pink flowers which emphasizes the coolness of the rest.

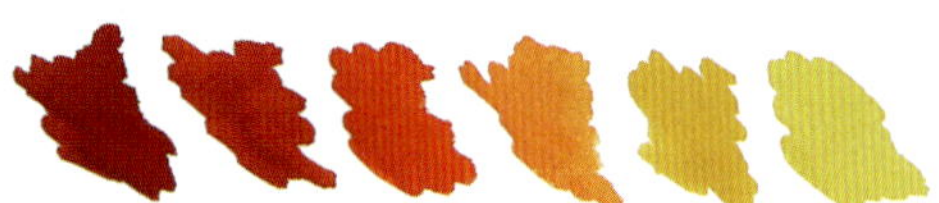

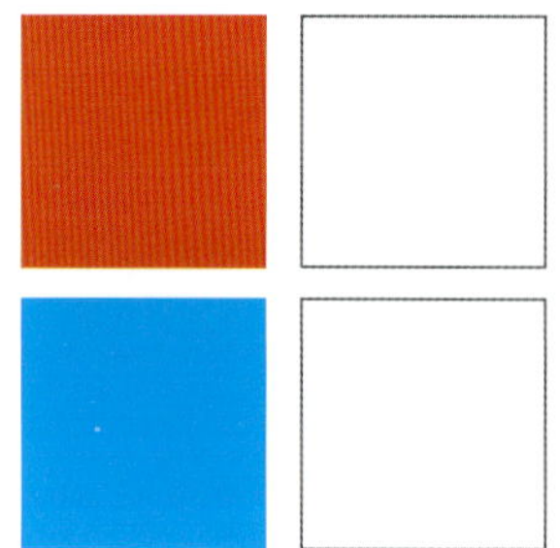

Neighbours on the wheel:
Analagous colours

Colours that are next to each other on the wheel harmonize well together. They relate to each other in a 'kinship', for example red moves easily into orange and then into yellow, giving them compatibility.

When these adjacent colours are from the same side of the wheel the results are the most intense in temperature – all warm or all cool – but if they are used solely in a painting the result is monotonous. Because analagous colours harmonize so well, they can serve a useful purpose in playing a more supportive role in a composition, away from the focal point where the eye needs a restful area, and acting as a foil to the more dominant parts, where contrasting and clashing colours would attract the eye. When used together they make a pleasing/easy-on-the-eye picture.

Analagous colours – left: green and yellow;
right: predominantly yellow, red and orange

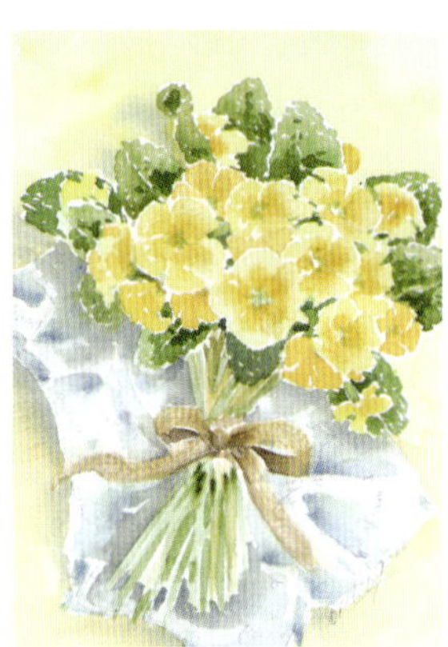
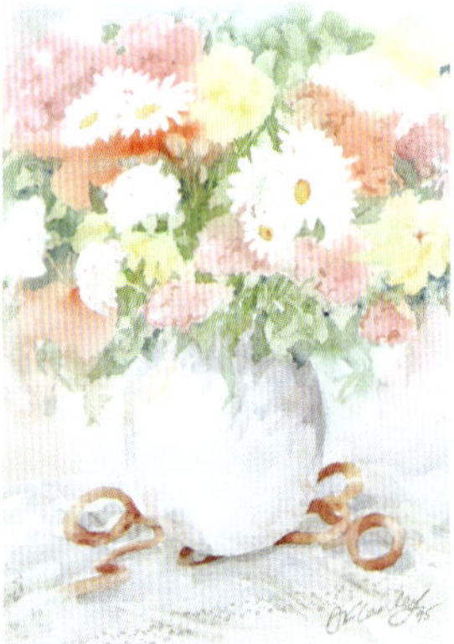

Opposites on the wheel:
Complementary colours and their uses

Stare at one of the squares above for as long as you can manage, then look into the empty box and you will see the complementary colour of your subject. This illustrates the special relationship that colours have with their complementary colour.

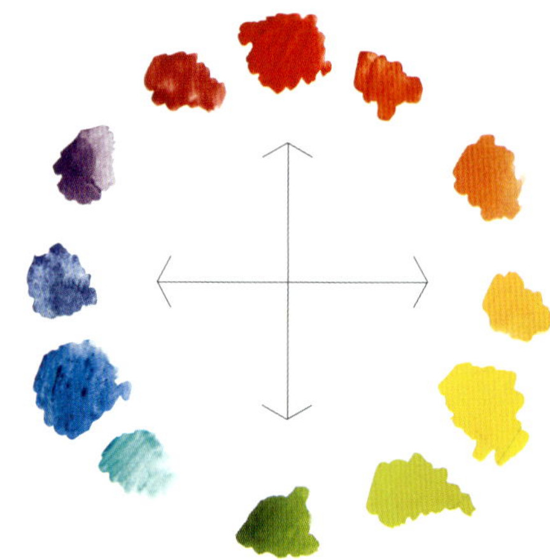

Complementary colours are the 'negative' colour of the other and are opposite each other on the wheel – just track directly across the wheel to find them. Examples of complementary colours include:

Yellow	Purple
Blue	Orange
Red	Green

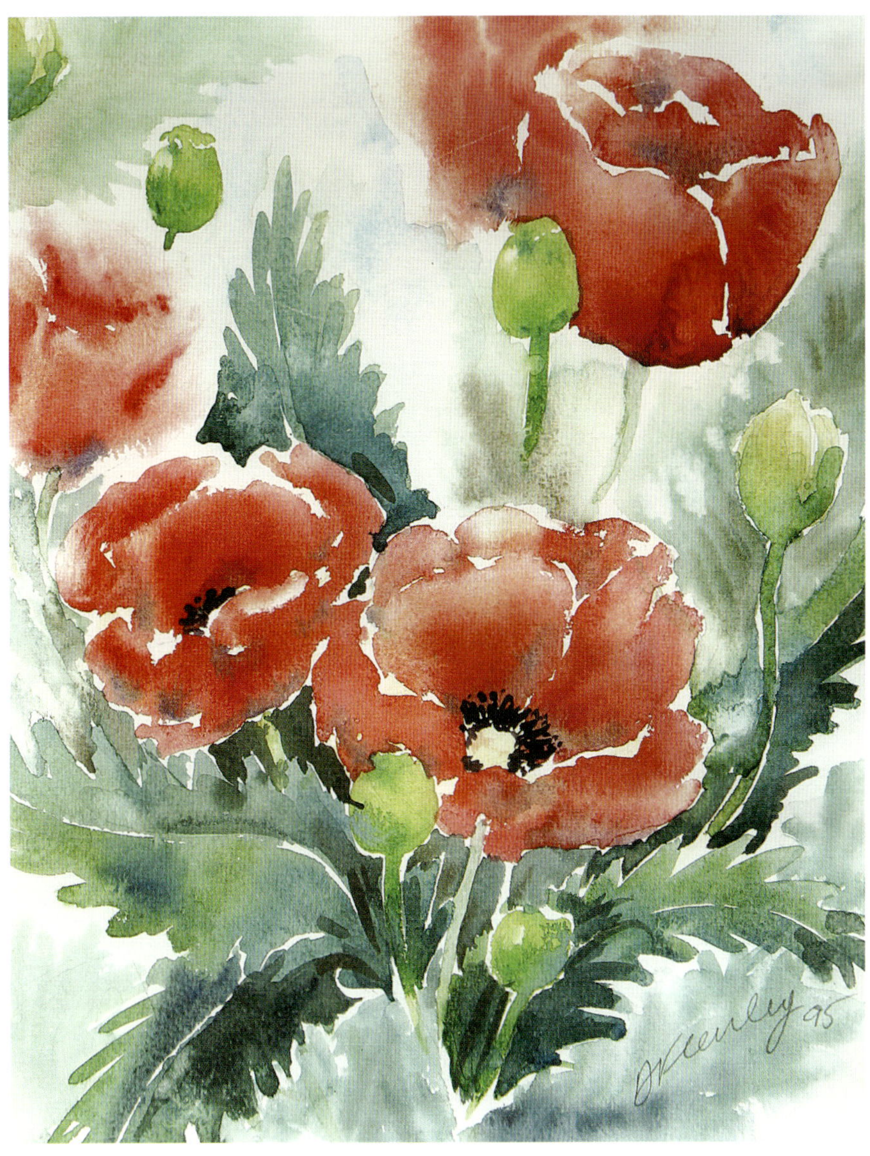

The green and red are complementary colours, so are dramatic when placed together

If analagous colours are like friendly brothers, then complementary colours can only be likened to rival gangs: instead of being harmonious like analogous colours, complementary colours 'argue' with each other visually and, when put together, the two colours 'vibrate' or 'sing', drawing the attention of the eye.

You can use this to your advantage if you want to emphasize an area in your painting, as putting complementaries at the focal point will certainly bring the eye to the main point of interest.

The Impressionists used complementary colours together, so that the colours vibrated together and enhanced the effect of light. Monet's red poppies in a green field, and his purple and yellow in haystacks are examples of this.

You can find complementary colours when nature is at its most striking, for example red poppies in a green field or, as I remember seeing in the Red Sea, a purple fish with yellow spots.

Focus on
Complementaries

Some artists differentiate between 'mixing' complementaries and 'visual' complementaries. The difference is that the former are the theoretical complements, as already described (opposites across the wheel that neutralize when mixed), whereas the latter are colours that visually enhance each other when put side by side – these are usually close to opposites on the wheel, not exact, yet have just as much impact. Purple, for example, is the complementary to yellow but a blue, especially a blue with a purple hint in it, is very effective as a contrast. So, experiment with close neighbours to your complementaries and aim to find contrasting complementary colours that 'zing' and look exciting when they are placed together.

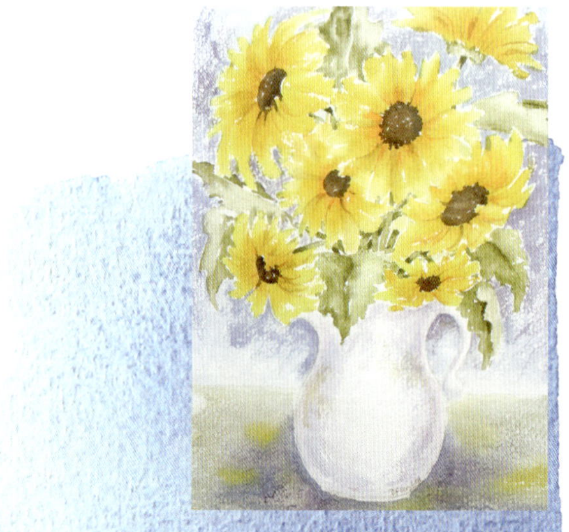

In the picture top right you can a see visual complementary colour working with a blue background behind the yellow flowers.

You can see the blue background works well in these two pictures of gerberas, but the addition of purple in the painting on the right gives it an extra contrast.

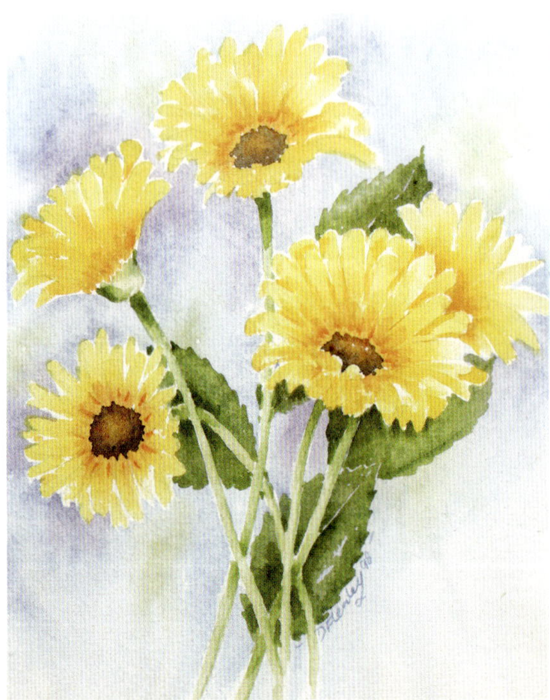

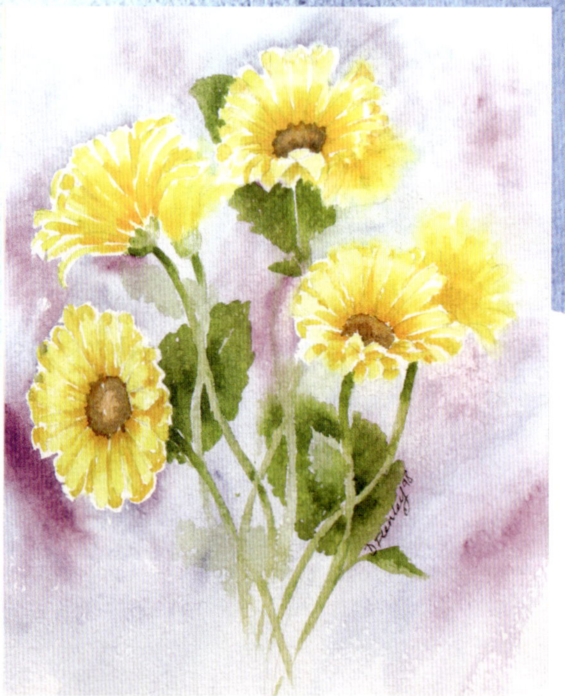

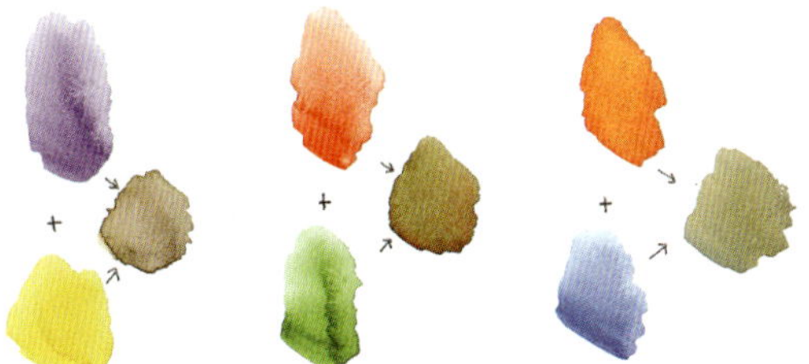

Complementaries mixing to grey:
Purple/Yellow, Red/Green and
Orange/Blue, mixed into neutrals

Meeting in the middle of the wheel:
Using complementaries to mix greys

If you mix two complementary colours together they 'cancel each other out' and you get a neutral greyish tone, as shown above. I've owned up elsewhere in this book to confiscating the occasional tube of green to force students to mix their own, and I have to admit a good few tubes of Paynes grey have found their way into the bin too, because ready-mixed greys produce such a flat, uninteresting, lack of colour.

Grey is not 'a pale black', nor should it ever be. There are warm and cool greys, and greys with different colour biases and, if you can mix your own, then you can adapt the colour and tone of grey to suit your picture (see also p 98, 'Shadows'). The colours don't even need to be mixed on a palette – you can lay them together on the page and let them run into each other, as shown in the example below.

The shadows here are not grey, but blues and pinks standing alongside each other

Tip: if you MUST use a grey go for

a soft Davy's grey and add a gentle hint

 of another colour to blend or contrast

with the surroundings.

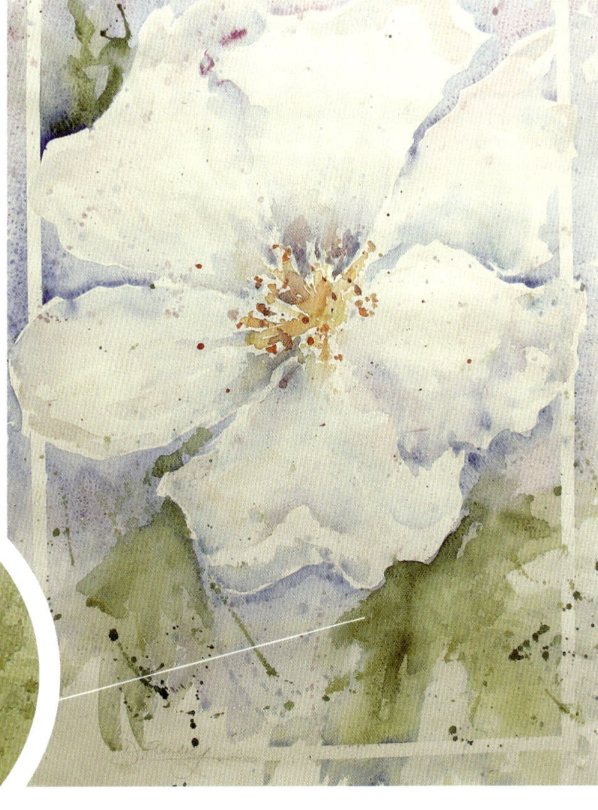

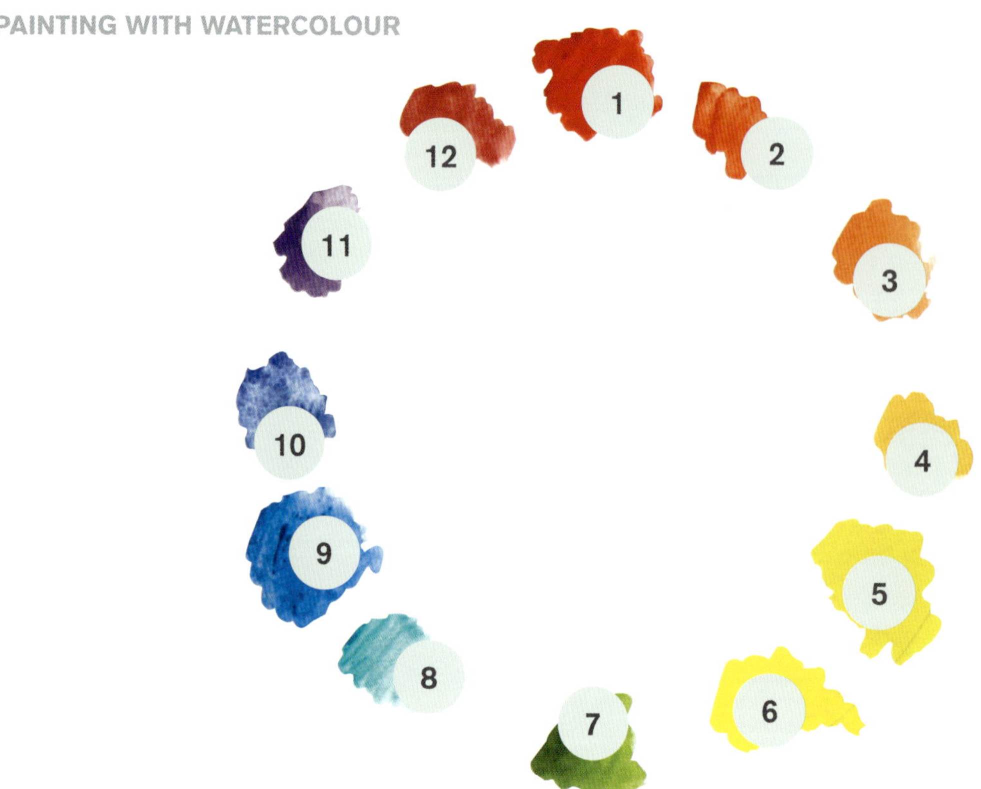

How the named colours fit into the colour
wheel (as opposed to spectrum colours)

1	Winsor red	5	Gamboge	9	Cobalt blue
2	Scarlet lake	6	Lemon yellow	10	French ultramarine
3	Cadmium orange	7	Sap green	11	Windsor violet
4	Indian yellow	8	Cerulean blue	12	Alizarin crimson

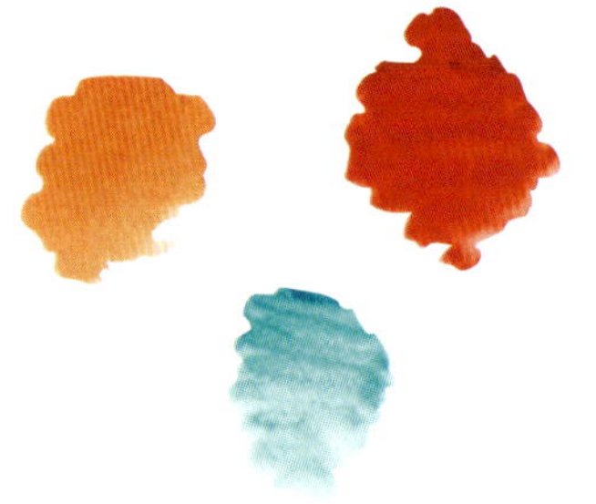

Tip: no matter how tempting it is to have lots of colours,

it is best to stick to a few and get to know them well.

When you know how they react, you are in control,

instead of your paints having the upper hand.

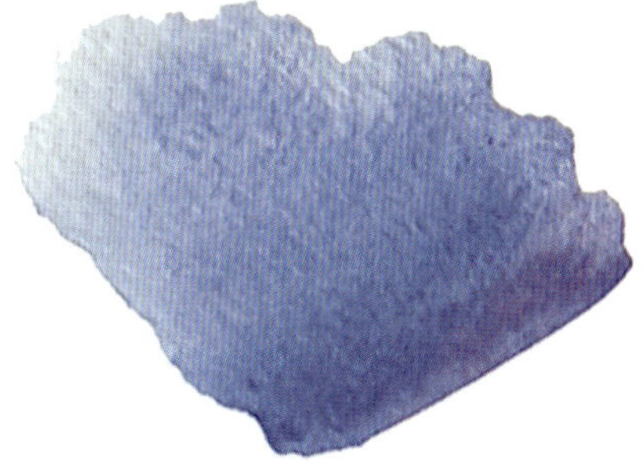

Your paints on the wheel
Understanding their bias

How often have you tried to mix a colour and found you just can't get it right? This is probably because you don't understand exactly where your paints fall on the colour wheel and do not know what their colour bias is. One of the most useful things I ever learnt was an understanding of colour bias and how this can affect mixing colours, and consequently where each of my tubes of colours with their 'trade names' fitted on the colour wheel.

It is simple to think blue and red = purple, blue and yellow = green, and so on, because we are looking at the theoretical spectrum – primary red or blue, or primary yellow which, when mixed together, do give such straightforward results. In reality though, most of our tubes of colours don't fall into that exact 'red' or 'blue' category and consequently you can't identify them simply on the spectrum. Most are blended and mixed with other colours, and so they have a 'bias' towards the colour that is influencing their mix. Alizarin crimson, for example, can't be placed exactly in the red triangle as it has a hint of blue in it, so it goes somewhere nearer to the blue triangle, whereas cadmium red has a hint of yellow in it, so can be placed nearer the yellow section.

Likewise with yellows: gamboge or Indian yellow, for example, have a hint of red in them and are warmer (have a red bias), so they are nearer to the red section on the wheel, whereas lemon yellow or Winsor yellow are much cooler (have a blue bias) and so go nearer the blue section.

Once you understand where your colours fall on the colour wheel, you can use and mix them with confidence, knowing how they will 'behave'.

It takes a lot of hard groundwork to get to know your colours and to be aware of how they all look, work and behave, but this knowledge will be invaluable in enabling you to manipulate and use colour to your advantage, so it's well worth putting in the effort.

Your sketchbook should be the place where much of your learning is centred, it should also be your reference guide, where you have samples of colours and mixes stored. I regret the number of times I have taken samples of colours from shops or from other artists, worked out mixes, or made notes about another artist's colour palette, and so on, all on scraps of paper which I subsequently lost. If all that information had been kept in one place it would be invaluable.

My advice to you, therefore, is to have a sketchbook especially for colour, and try out the Project overleaf.

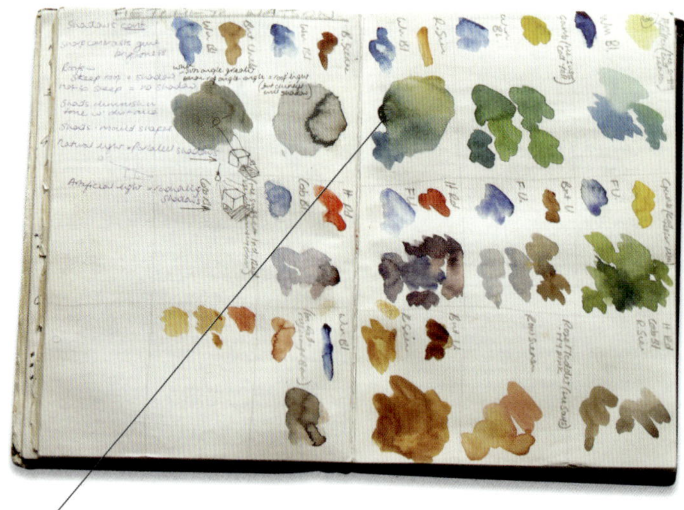

Mixtures of colours in my sketchbook, tried out to see what 'feel' they would give

✱ **Project:** Colour your sketchbook

For this I recommend using your largest sketchbook, as there is so much information to record. A sketchbook made of watercolour paper is best, so you can see how colours react to their surface (granulation for example doesn't show on cartridge paper). Alternatively you could try colour mixes on watercolour paper and stick them in.

1. Draw a colour wheel and put your paints onto it, working out where they go – for example, cool yellows will go nearer blue, warmer yellows nearer red, and so on – and refer to it repeatedly.

2. Include 'sample' colours from art shops (unscrew the end of a tube and dab it onto your paper – but never in hot weather, as you'll get an almighty mess and nasty looks!).

3. Stick in colour charts from main watercolour manufacturers (available free from art shops).

4. Practise mixes and record the results.

5. Record information from articles and from other artists: their colour palette, their favourite mixes, information about how colours react together, and so on.

6. Add previous exercises where you experimented with granulation, staining qualities and so on to this collection, so you have all your colour references in one place.

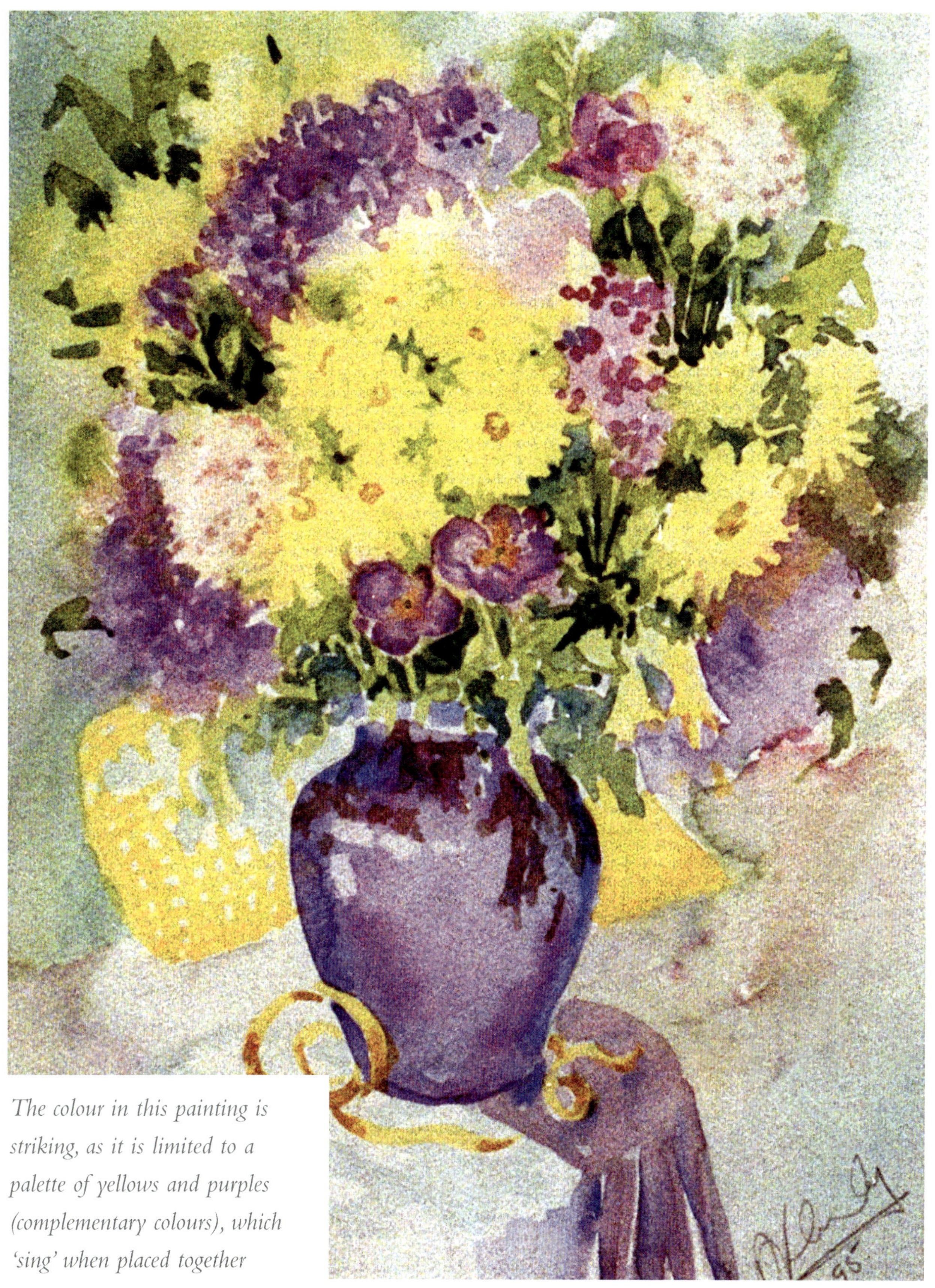

The colour in this painting is striking, as it is limited to a palette of yellows and purples (complementary colours), which 'sing' when placed together

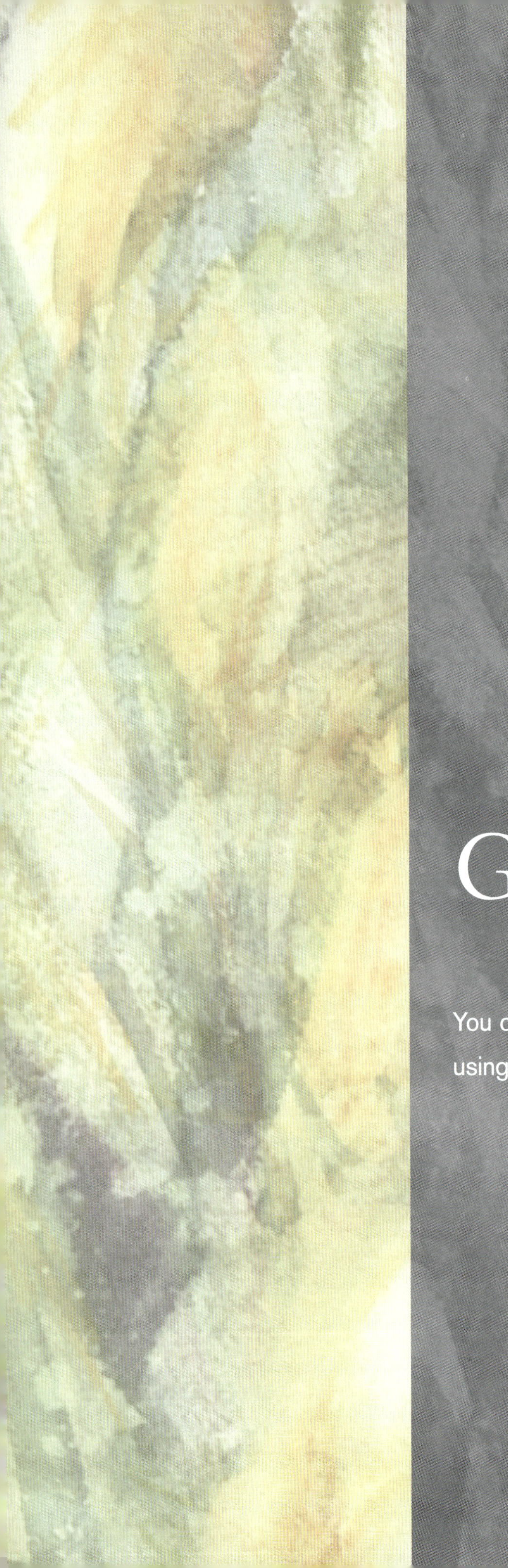

Greens

You cannot portray the subtleties of nature
using greens straight from the tubes.

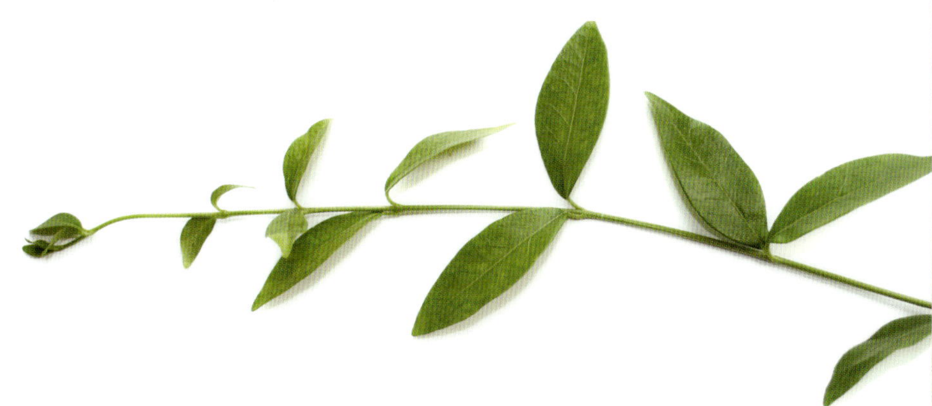

Mixing realistic greens

One of the most common questions I am asked, as a tutor must be, 'How do I get my greens to look realistic?' and 'How do I mix my greens?' It's actually a pleasure to be asked this, because I know that the alternative is the student who thinks you don't need to mix greens, because they're already in the tube.

Colour in nature is rarely flat and uniform, like the colour from a tube: it is constantly changing, with objects varying in tone and colour temperature as the light catches them. This needs to be captured and echoed in a varied use of greens throughout a picture, as the colour can very dramatically, even in one small leaf.

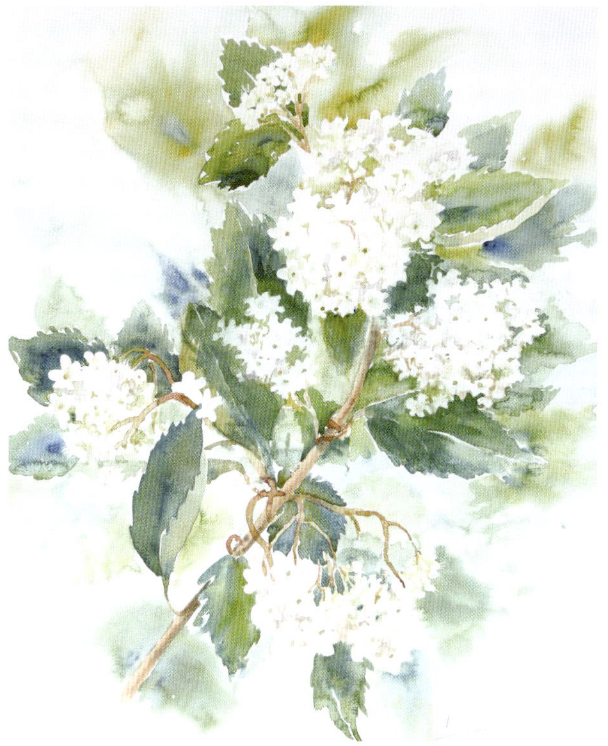

✳ Project: Mixing realistic greens

If you aren't quite ready to make your own greens, the easiest way to achieve variety is by altering the tone or colour of your existing green.

- **Darker** – add a deep blue, e.g. Prussian blue

- **More 'autumnal'** – add a light brown, e.g. yellow ochre

- **Fresh and spring-like** – add a cool yellow, e.g. lemon yellow

- **Brighter and more vibrant** – add a strong yellow, e.g. gamboge

- **More neutral** – add a red, its complementary colour

Mixing your own greens

I recommend that you start mixing your own greens
from blues and yellows, and then, when you get more
confident, from other colours too, so it's worth hiding
your tubes of greens for a while and becoming used
to mixing. The advantage with mixing greens is that
the colour is never uniform, as it varies with the
amounts of blue or yellow in the mix. When you are
keeping to the same basic colours, no matter how
much you vary the mix and produce different results,
these will always harmonize together, because they are
from the same original colours, but if you put totally
different greens together, they can be discordant and
have no relation to each other.

Mixing greens becomes easy when you understand
which blues and yellows you are using and how they
behave. It would be easy if it was just a case of mixing
a blue and yellow and making green, which is probably
what you thought at primary school. The problem arises
when you realize that you rarely get a simple blue or
simple yellow. There are lots of different variations in
colour and in reality some yellows have a hint of blue or
red in them and this hint – or bias – of another colour
affects the outcome of the mix. Whole books have
been written on this theory but to try and simplify it:

Yellow can have a bias towards blue (cool),
e.g. lemon yellow, Winsor yellow, aureolin

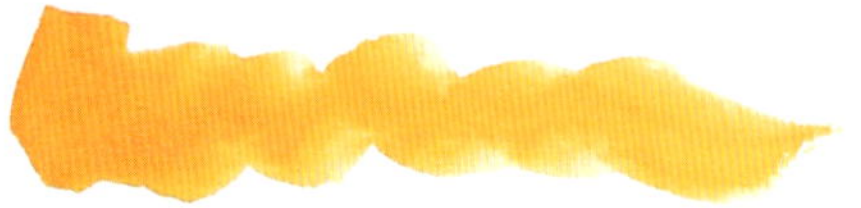

Or towards red (warm),
e.g. cadmium yellow, gamboge, Indian yellow

Blue can have a bias towards red (warm),
e.g. French ultramarine

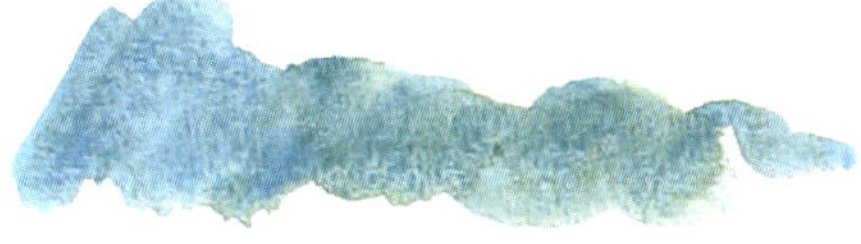

Or towards yellow (cool),
e.g. cerulean, Prussian blue

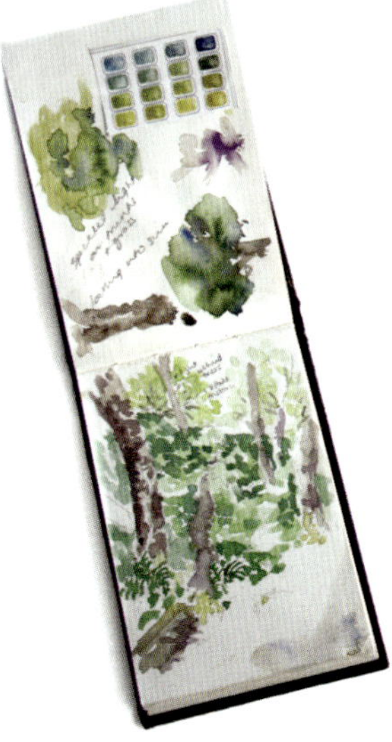

Tip: make up names to remind you of favourite mixes

e.g. cobalt blue and sap green = 'sapalt', aureolin yellow

and Prussian blue = 'auprush'. It helps you remember

and is useful when recording colours in your sketchbook.

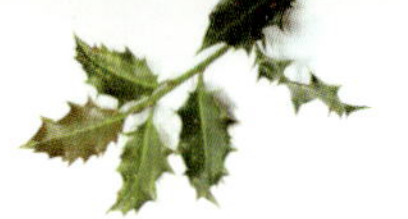

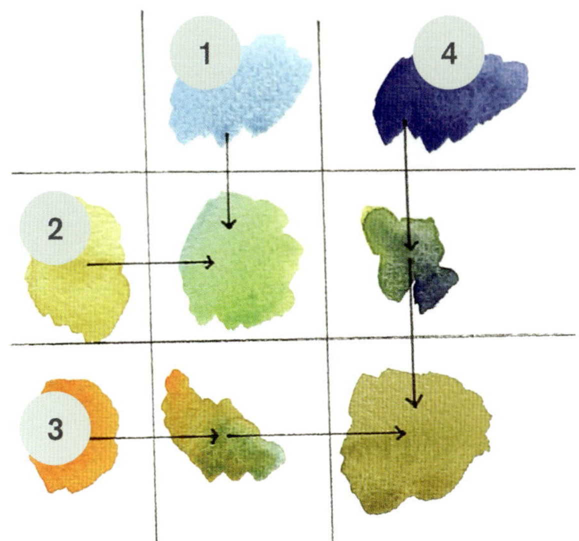

Tip: when you find a particularly useful mix always record it. Ask or read about other artists' mixes and record these results too.

1. Cool blue e.g. cerulean

2. Cool yellow, e.g. lemon

3. Warm yellow e.g. gamboge

4. Warm blue e.g. ultramarine

Cool blue + cool yellow = a cool, fresh spring green
This is because you are mixing a yellow (that has a hint/bias of blue) with a blue (that has a hint/bias of yellow).

Warm yellow + warm blue = a warm, autumnal green
The red-bias in this mixture – red being the opposite (complementary) of green – 'dulls' the green, creating a muted colour.

★ **Project:** Greens

- Collect a variety of leaves and greenery from the garden or park – as many different greens as possible. You will be surprised how many there are.

- Try mixing greens to match them, bearing in mind that our paint will dry lighter, so you need to anticipate the match for when the paint is dry.

- Match the natural variations in colour and tone, adding more or less of the blue or yellow as you go along.

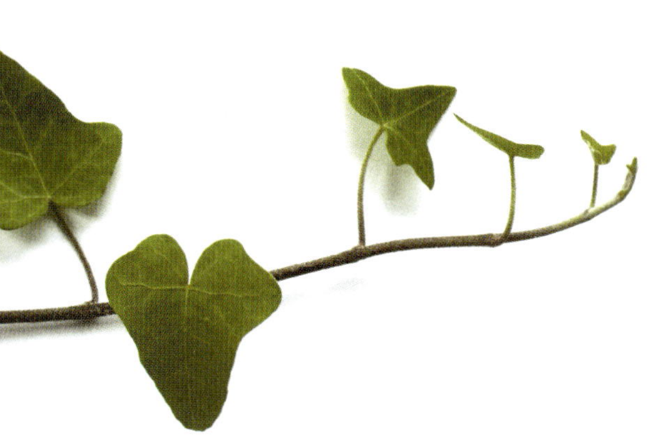

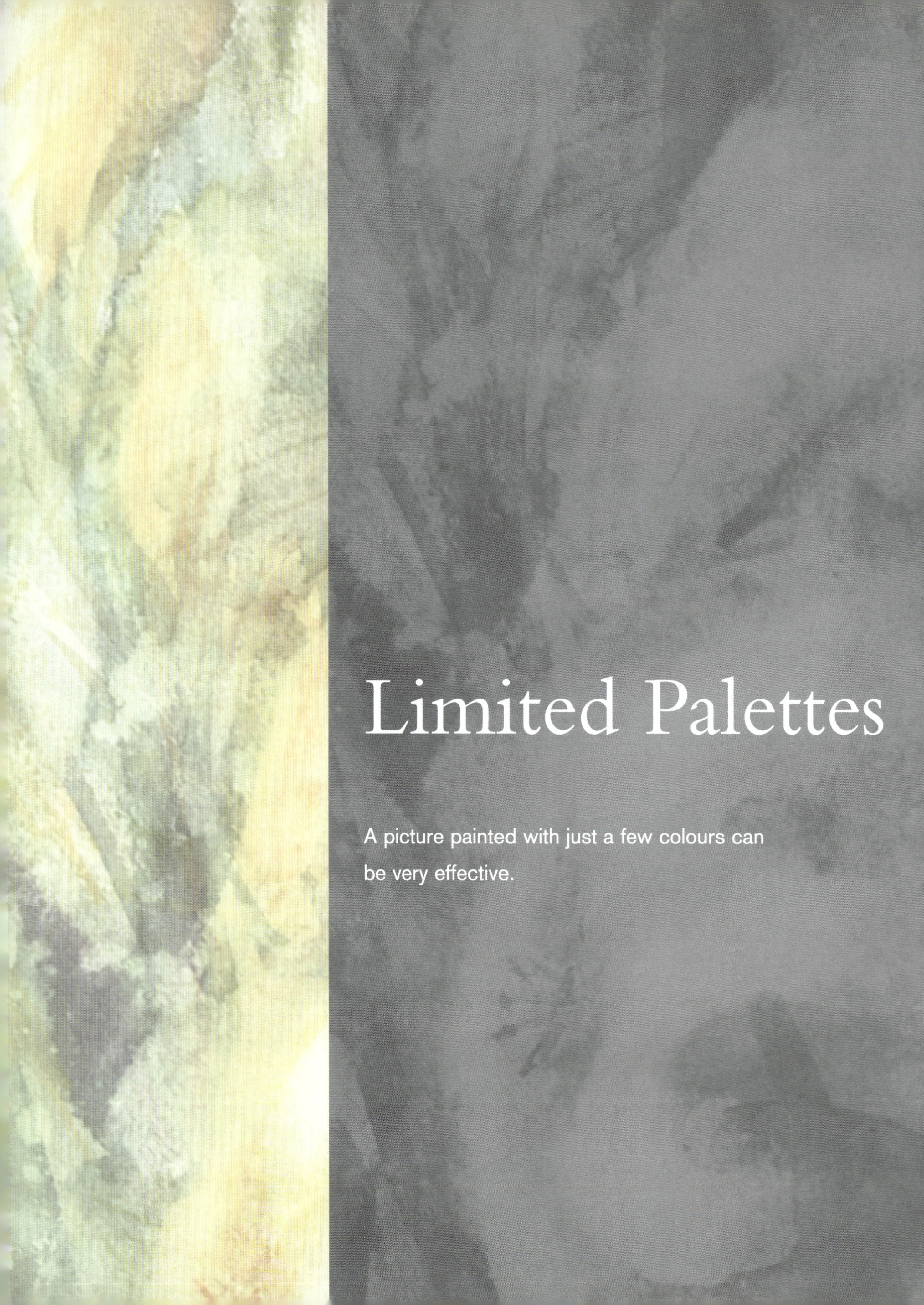

Limited Palettes
A picture painted with just a few colours can
be very effective.

You may have noticed how effective a painting in just a few colours can be. This is known as a 'limited palette' and, as there aren't a mad variety of colours to clash with each other, the results can be harmonious and quite atmospheric.

It takes a conscious decision not to use a full palette of colours, especially where a specific colour is needed – or believed to be needed – such as green for leaves. You have to choose the colours that are going to be in your mix, stick with what they can offer you and resist the temptation to try and match your local colour exactly.

Sticking to this principle that 'less is more' can be hard to accept, as we are often tempted into thinking that having more of anything is better.

The advantages of using fewer colours include:

- Your painting will be more harmonious, because there will be less opportunity to use flat, ready-made colours. The limited source of colours will need to be mixed into each other, and this will give a sense of unity throughout the picture.

- You will be able to handle them more effectively and consequently get better results from mixing and the effects that they create.

- You can become familiar with the behaviour of your colours.

The negatives of having too many colours include:

- For beginners, you can't familiarize yourself with the qualities/behaviour of each colour of paint.

- Your picture becomes 'discordant' as too many colours are used.

- Picture has no unifying colour factors, or specific colour reactions.

- There's no chance for colour to indicate mood: if the correct 'local colour' is always used, it reduces artistic interpretation of the objects or scene.

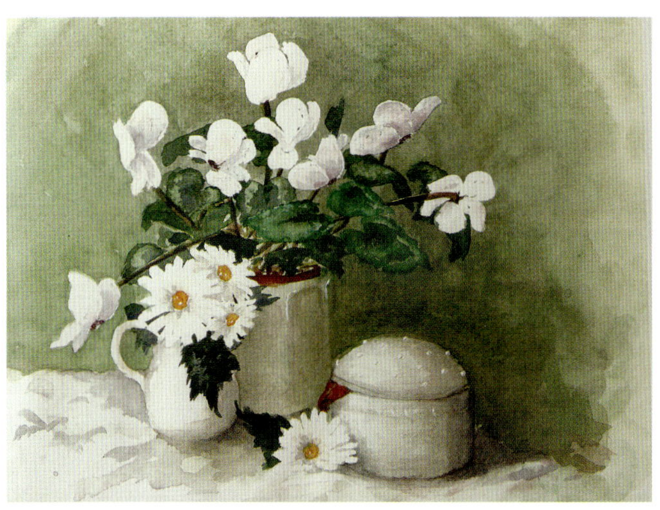

The colours here are limited in their palette to greens and whites, giving a harmonious feel to the painting. The splash of yellow and brown prevents it being too bland or monotonous

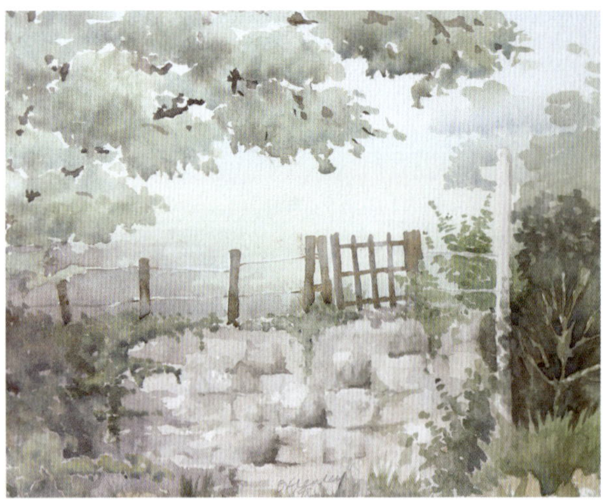

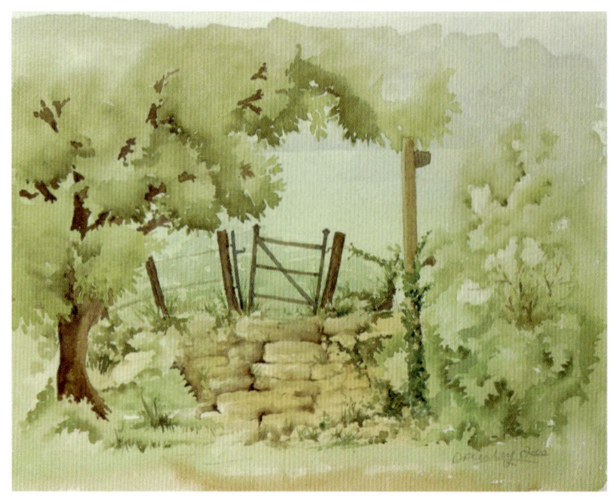

Paintings of the same scene, using different limited palette mixes

The two pictures above – of the coast road from Barnouth to Harlech in North Wales – have been given two different interpretations simply by using two different limited palettes of colours. When the sea mist is down and it's early morning, it has a different feel and atmosphere compared with when it is a warm sunny day, and that difference is reflected here, one in a warm and one in a cool palette. One painting was done on site and the other is an interpretation from it later, and these show that you don't need to reproduce the local colour at all. Your interpretation is what counts and, by using a limited palette of a few 'key' colours, you can give a place a 'feel' and create atmosphere in a painting.

By using just three colours in each of the paintings shown below, each picture has its own 'feel' and mood: the first has a light, fresh feel because cool colours were used, whereas the second, using earthy colours, has a heavier autumnal feel to it, determined by the choice of warmer colours of paint. If more than three colours had been used in each picture, the effect would have been diluted.

So, if you want to get a unified feeling to your painting, mix just three colours. It usually needs to be one from each of the primaries in order for you to achieve a full range to your picture, but your choice can vary enormously, depending on the mood and feel that you want to achieve.

Try a quick study like these, see how using three different mixes gives you a different feel

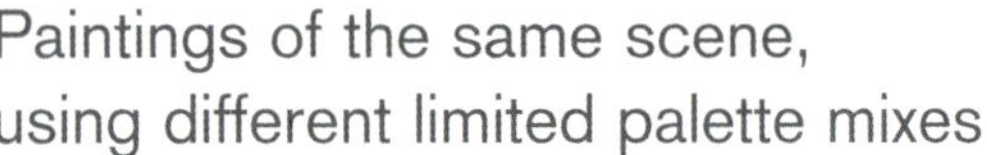

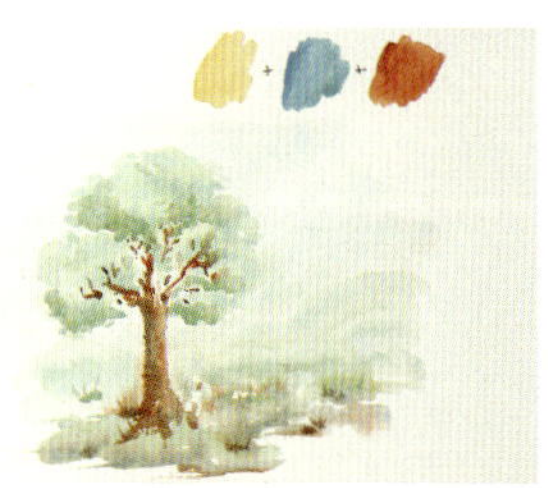

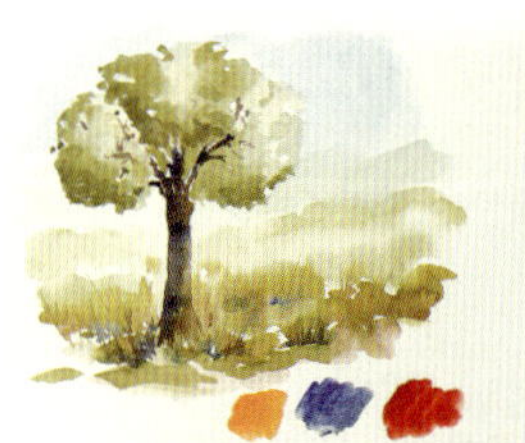

Tip: you don't have to stick to the original 'local' colours – grass doesn't have to be traditional green, and think of the impact of a red sky!

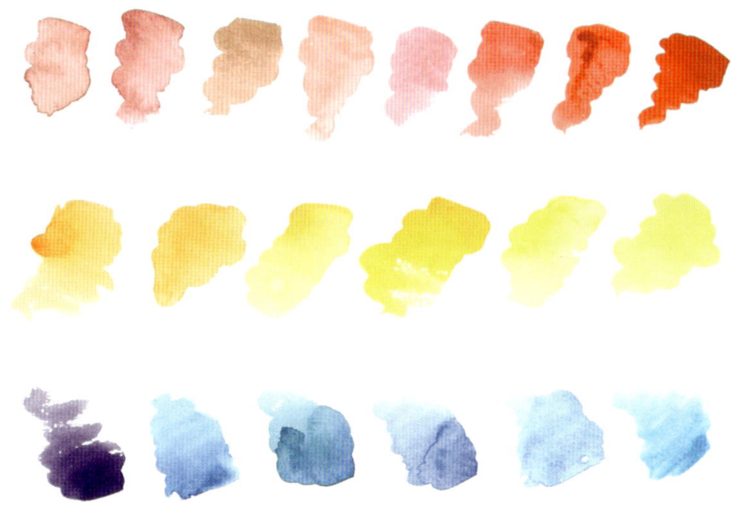

*'Red' can be anything from
burnt sienna to vermilion*

*'Yellow' can be anything from
yellow ochre to lemon*

*'Blue' can be anything from
indigo to cerulean*

Remember, you won't be able to recreate the exact local colour of your subject, but that is the whole point. Each colour and combination will add a different feel to the mix and the end result. Just keep experimenting with different colours and find mixes that suit the mood of your painting. For example:

For a soft, light, feel	Lemon yellow + cerulean blue + permanent rose
For a grainy, earthy, heavier atmosphere	Yellow ochre + burnt sienna + ultramarine

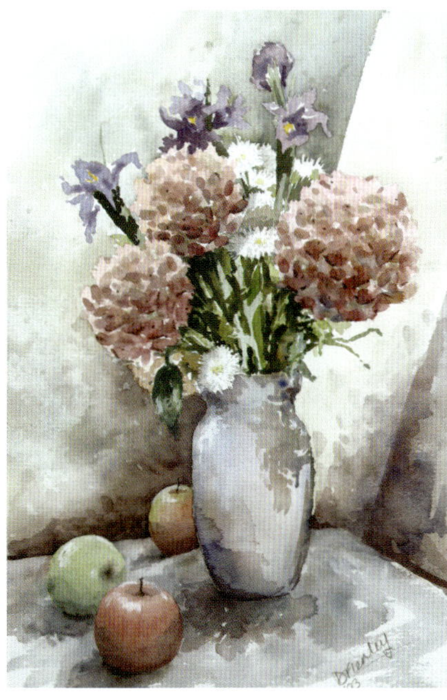

*This painting has
impact because the
colours all harmonize
in a limited palette of
greys and crimsons*

Tip: if you cut down

to a limited palette you

will be more in control

and your pictures will

have more impact.

✳ Projects: Limited palettes

1. Mix a variety of limited palettes from reds, blues and yellows, then keep the results for reference. Notice how each mix will lend itself to a different subject.

2. Try out a simple scene using the different palettes in your sketchbook, identifying which mix of colours will suit each scene.

3. For a sunny day on the continent: try a warm yellow like gamboge, a bright blue like cobalt and a warm red like cadmium red, which together would create the warm, strong colours reminiscent of a sunny day.

4. To depict an overcast day on the Yorkshire moors: use cooler colours, for example yellow ochre, which is a dull tertiary colour, French ultramarine, again because it is the least bright of the blues, and a browny-dull red such as burnt umber or burnt sienna. Together these will create a cool, muted, effect that would echo the bleakness of the scene.

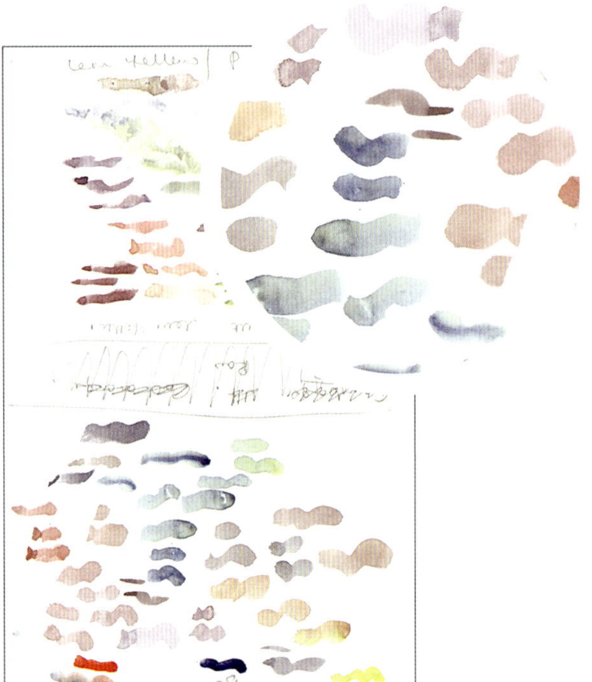

Focus on
Using Colour

- Have you planned out your use of colour and does it make a statement?

- Does it fit the 'feel' of the scene you want to convey (the mood and the subject matter)?

- Have you selected colours that will serve to enhance the colour scheme (rather than dip into any colour to match the local colour of what you are seeing)?

- Have you chosen a predominantly warm or cool palette?

- Whichever temperature palette you have chosen, have you included a small amount of the opposite temperature and then placed warm against cool, or vice versa, for impact?

- Are your most dramatic contrasting colours near, or emphasizing, the focal point?

- Are there any dramatic areas of colour that distract from the focal point? If so remove them or dull them down.

- Do you have a range of colour values?

- Have you used colour to make your shadows instead of using grey?

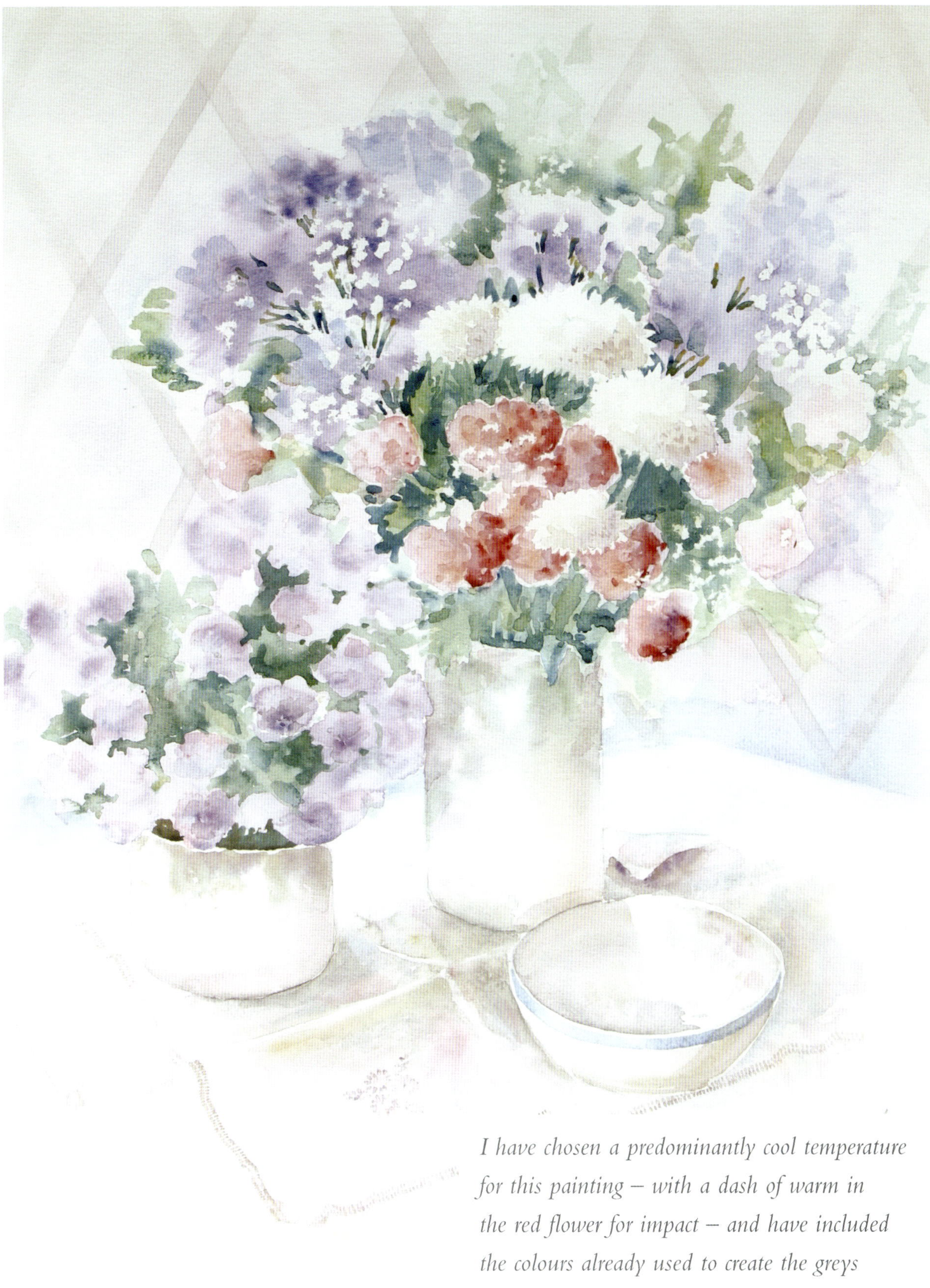

*I have chosen a predominantly cool temperature
for this painting – with a dash of warm in
the red flower for impact – and have included
the colours already used to create the greys*

Theory of Painting

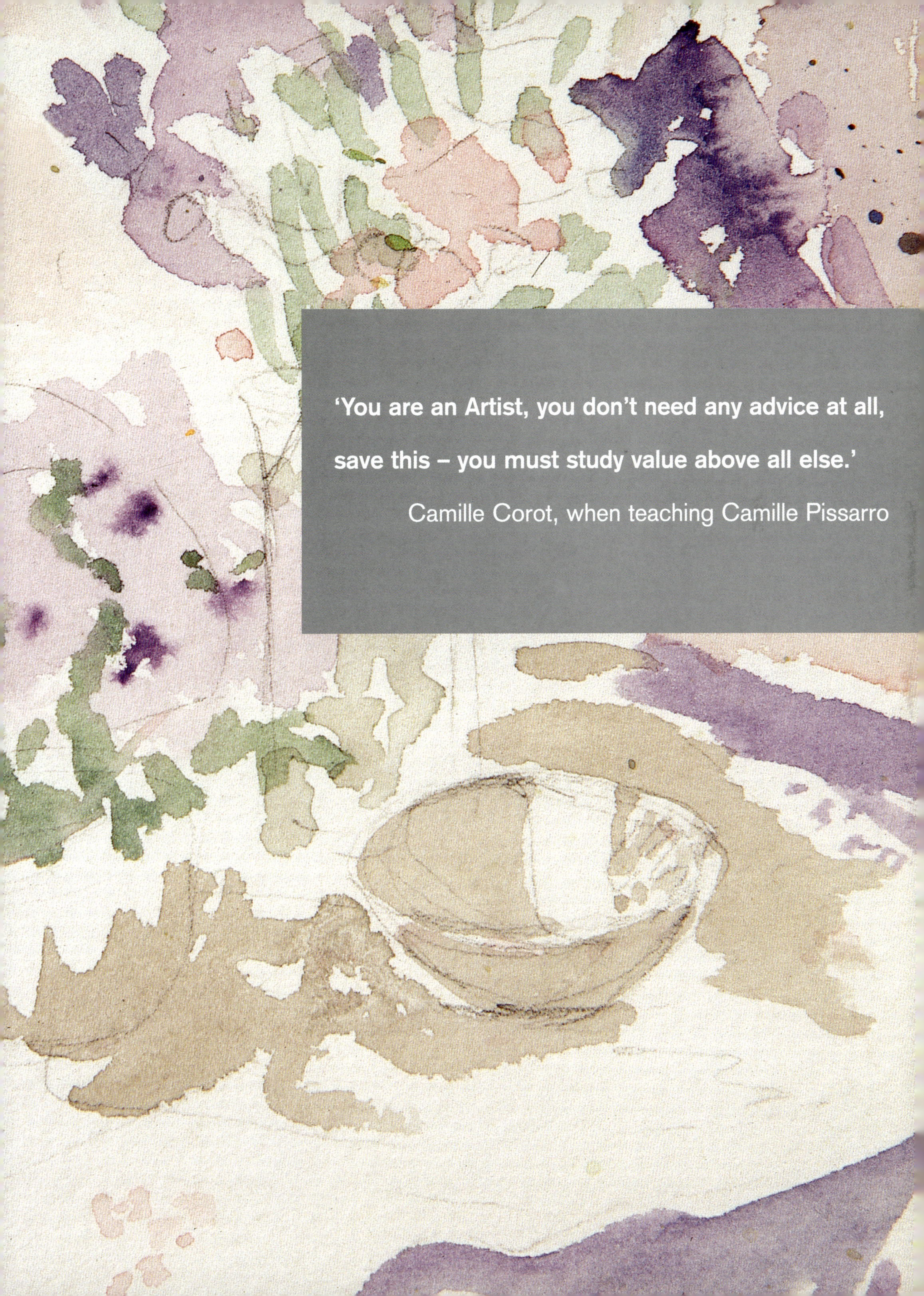

'You are an Artist, you don't need any advice at all, save this – you must study value above all else.'
Camille Corot, when teaching Camille Pissarro

The Importance of Tone

When looking at a scene try to ignore the colour and analyse the tones, as if switching the colour television down to black and white.

Tone describes the lightness or darkness of a shade or colour and the 'tonal scale' runs from black to white, with infinite shades of grey in between.

While line drawing is appropriate for diagrams, plans and so on, to transform the two-dimensional surface of the paper into a three-dimensional image with depth and form, tones must be used (what children call 'shading in'). In nature forms do not have 'outlines', they are distinguished by their tones. Tone, for example, turns the circle below into a sphere.

The work of beginners sometimes lacks depth and looks too 'bland'. This is because they are too frightened to apply a full range of tones, so their darks are not dark enough and lights are not light enough. Even the most brightly coloured picture will look flat if the tones are not varied enough to give the image some contrast.

Always notice where the light falls. In the sphere below, for example, where the top catches the light there are lighter tones, but where the shape curves away into shade it becomes progressively darker. Think of this image simply in terms of light, medium and dark, then apply this approach to your work.

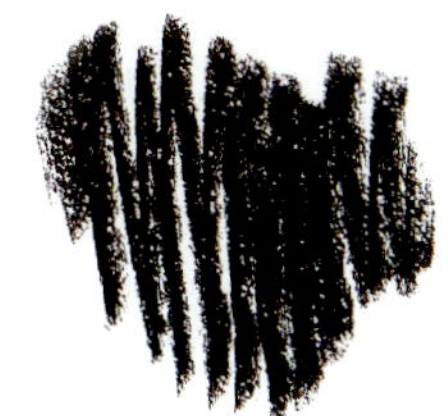

Focus on
Making contrasts strong enough

- Watercolour dries up to 50% lighter, so what seems too dark when you put it on may end up too pale. Bear in mind also that you are probably concentrating on one small area, rather than the picture as a whole. Once the subsequent 'dark bits' are in place it won't be so noticeable.

- Do not allow what you know to interfere with what you can see. You might know that something is white, but against a certain background it could appear dark. Conversely, a black coat worn in the sunlight may appear to be lighter in tone than the shady white wall behind it.

- Each colour is only light or dark in relation to the adjacent colour/tone, so don't just look at the area of tone on its own, analyse each area in relation to its surroundings.

- In nature there are infinite tones, but you have to reproduce your scene, as far as possible, within the limitations of your paint: the brightest sunlight and the darkest shade could never be matched, and it would be impossible to note every stage of tone in between, so limit yourself to what is available.

It takes a keenly trained eye to achieve the right tones, so painting a tonal scale similar to the one below will be time well spent. You need to 'learn' tones as you would notes on a piano, and this is the equivalent to practising your scales, and the foundation of a good performance.

Everything you paint will fall somewhere between black (5) and white (1, not shown here) on a value scale. It helps if you can reduce tones to a range of five, as it is then easier to ascertain what tonal value an area is.

✴ Demonstration: Tonal scale

Establish black, white and mid-grey first, then insert dark grey and light grey relative to their neighbouring tones.

You could now have a go at the nine-point scale, including tones in between.

Tip: Keep a set of solid graphite sticks that already have different tones, so the hard work is done for you. Do a tonal sketch with these.

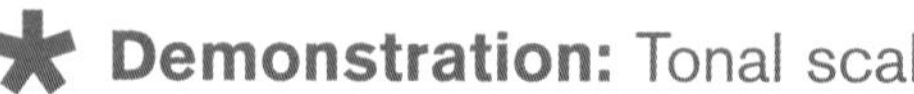

✴ Projects: On tone

• Take some black-and-white pictures and divide each area up into different tones, purely in terms of light and dark. Identify what each tone is on a five-point or nine-point scale.

• Make a 'tone card' with holes in: paint a range of tones in a scale, then punch holes in each tone. Look through the holes to match the tone and identify which particular tonal value an area is.

• Screw your eyes up and peer at your subject. This will eliminate much of the detail and emphasize areas of light and dark where the main tonal contrasts are, so you can concentrate on those.

Alternatively, view your subject through a coloured Cellophane sweet wrapper, or sunglasses. This will eliminate slight variations in tone, so you can easily see the more distinct variations.

• Create a picture with tones: take five different tones of paper (white, light, medium and dark greys and black, to match your five-point scale) and make a picture with collage using these five tones. Because you are restricted to the five shades, you have to think about your picture in just five tonal values.

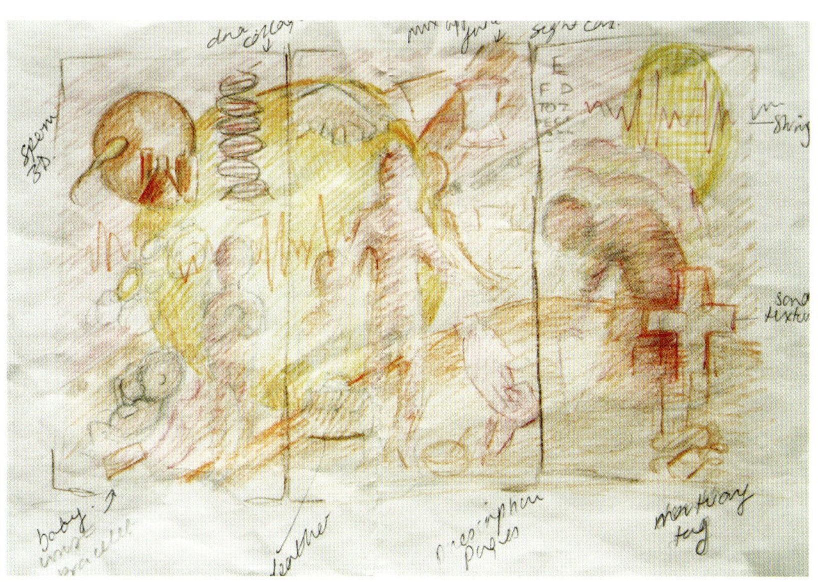

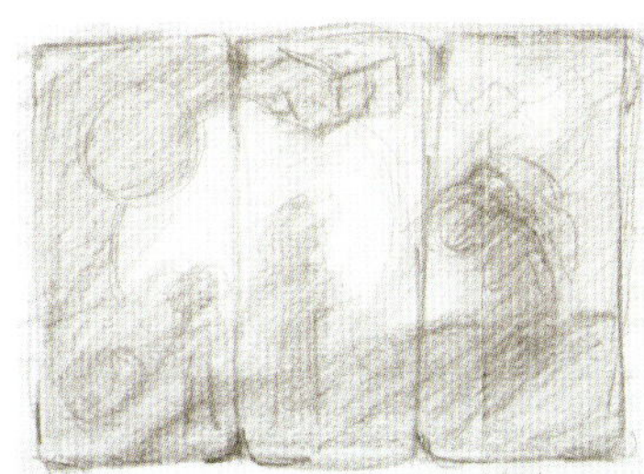

Tonal sketches

As we've seen, the tonal balance is very important and a quick tonal and compositional sketch is an essential step before commencing painting. I always do one and I'm a 'bull at a gate/never stop and plan anything' sort of person so, if I recommend it, there has to be something in it.

A tonal sketch needn't take long – think in terms of just light, medium and dark. The sketch above was done quickly, to plan out a large work for a doctor's surgery. For the benefit of the doctors who were commissioning it, it only needed to show the images that were to be included – but for my own benefit I needed to do the additional sketch (top right), so I could plan how the painting would balance out tonally.

In the medical-commission sketch there's a lot going on – it needed to be 'busy' with lots of images to entertain patients while they were waiting, but it could have been far too busy and have lost any overall impact. To prevent this, I arranged areas together in similar tones, and this breaks up the bittiness and unifies the picture.

The final painting can be seen from the road through a big picture window. Passers-by cannot register all the little images in the scene so – from a distance – it could be a mess, but they will notice the strong tonal values that compose the picture, so it appears interesting from both near and far.

Creating harmony or impact

The pattern of lights and darks in a composition form the foundation on which the rest of the picture comes to life. So, when you are planning a picture, distribute these visual weights carefully, as you would the objects in a still life or the composition in a landscape.

The use of too many colours or disparate tones in a composition can make a painting appear disjointed. So, avoid too much 'busyness' and give your painting harmony by blending and linking together areas of similar tones. This will create some areas which are 'quieter', so the whole composition is easier on the eye.

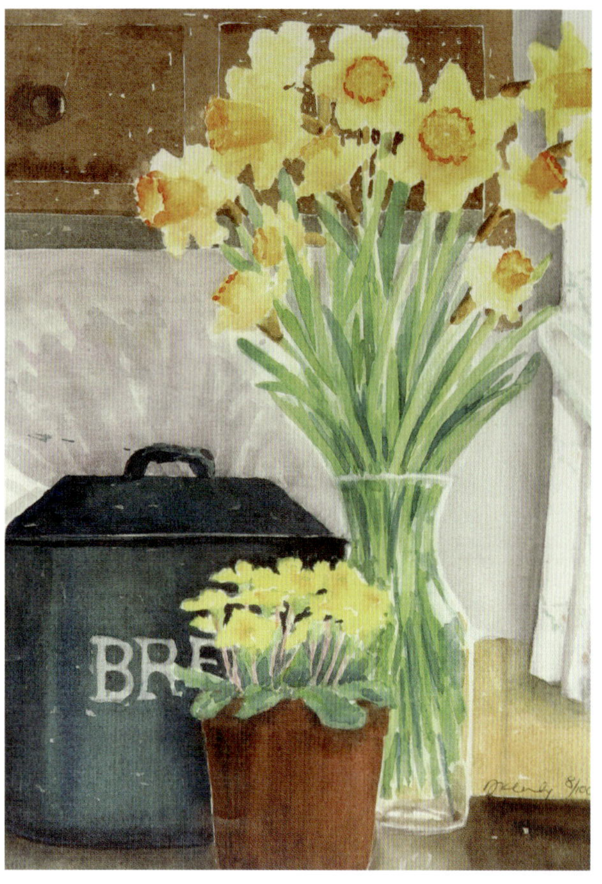

This principle is effective in the picture above, as both light areas of flowers are emphasized by placing dark areas (the cupboard and the bread bin) behind them

Conversely, if you want to make an impact and attract the eye – say to where your focal point is – have the greatest contrast of tones at that point, with your darkest darks next to your lightest lights (this is known as 'counterchange'). For maximum impact, a small splash of light in a mass of dark – or vice versa – provides a dramatic accent.

The two pictures below were painted from the same garden. The composition of the painting on the right works, as the tones are unified into a 'U' pattern, but the one on the left is not a success. Although I worked to a similar U-shape – with the birdbath and foliage leading around the window – there are too many competing areas of different tones. The patio at the front is in strong contrast to the rest of the picture, so draws your eye to that area away from the focal point, while the brickwork is the same tone as the foliage, so there is not enough contrast there either. It would have worked better if I had darkened the tones on the patio so that they blended with the foliage, and kept similar tones all through the U-shape, so creating a unified area that the eye could follow around the picture.

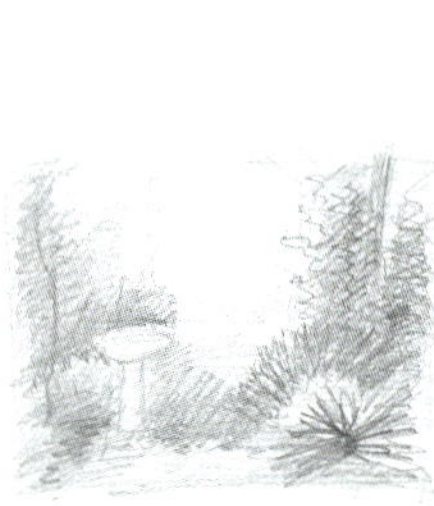

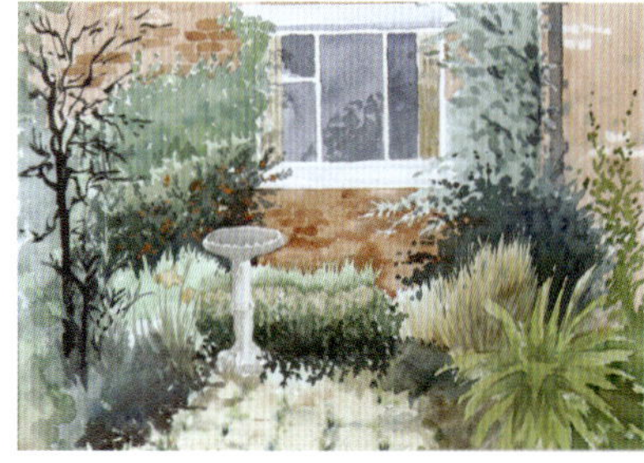

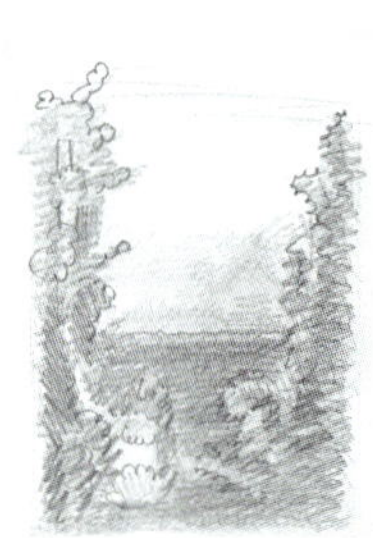

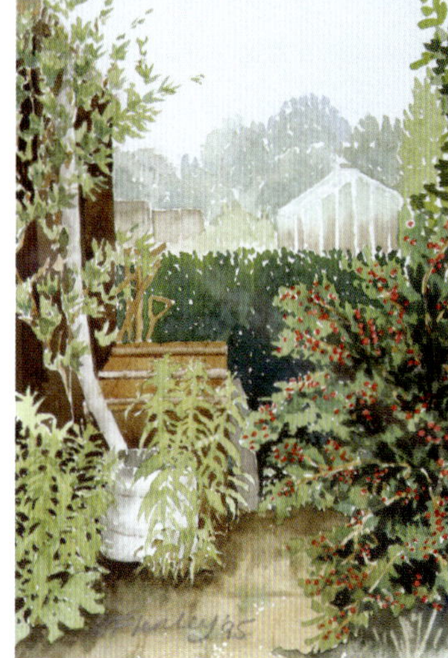

Creating mood and atmosphere

As an artist, your role is to introduce feeling and atmosphere into a piece – not simply to reproduce the scene as seen by others – and tone is a useful tool to use.

A high tonal key (light tones) can suggest an airy, sunny and bright mood, whereas a low tonal key (dark tones) can give a moody, atmospheric feel, so the same scene can be presented differently, just by altering the tones. This doesn't simply mean making the whole picture lighter or darker, which would just create an insipid or too dark version of the same picture. It means altering the tones, lightening in some areas but countering that with some dark in others to balance out the composition.

Creating a balance with tones

Don't go for equal amounts of light and dark: they will compete and neither will be important enough to create a mood of its own, or to support a focal point. It's the same principle as not having the horizon in the middle: go for approximately one third and two thirds, or three quarters and one quarter light to dark, which will enable one overall mood to prevail. Consider how the viewer's eye will be led and how the layout of the tones can enhance – as opposed to interfere with – that. A sudden change in tone in the middle of a passage would cause a break in the rhythm and interrupt the journey.

Creating consistency with light source

Your source of light 'creates' your tones so, when setting up a still life, or painting any objects, always consider your lighting and keep to one light source only. A simple angled lamp aimed at objects will highlight the tonal values and make it easier to do tonal drawings.

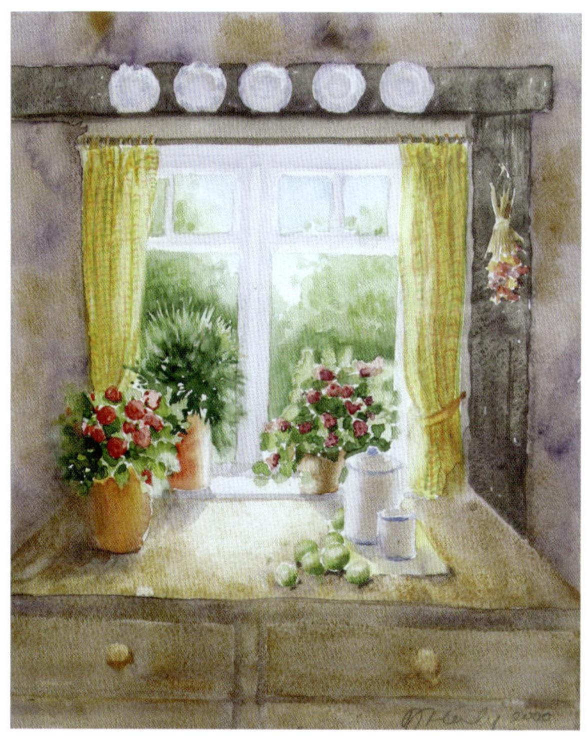

This painting works because it is two-thirds dark and one-third light, but as important is the direction of light and the impact is has on the pots

Bear in mind that direct, strong light creates interesting shadows, whereas hazy, overhead lighting – or indirect light – creates shadows that are softer. Be careful that you do not mistake shadows for tone.

Colour and pattern can confuse matters too. You should still be able to see the colour and the texture of an object – for instance, the bark on the tree or the grain on the wood – but it will be darker on the side away from where the light is hitting it, or where it is in shade. Sometimes, when the light hits something, it will 'bleach out' all the details, giving you an area of 'white' without details discernable in that area.

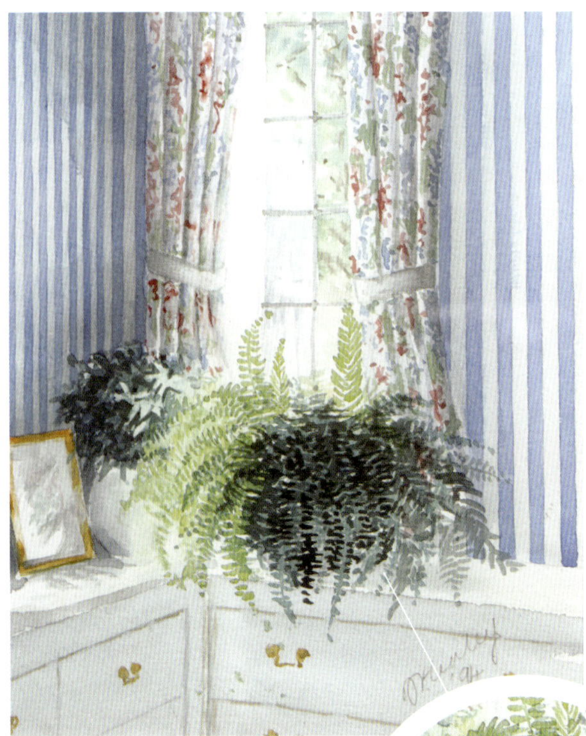

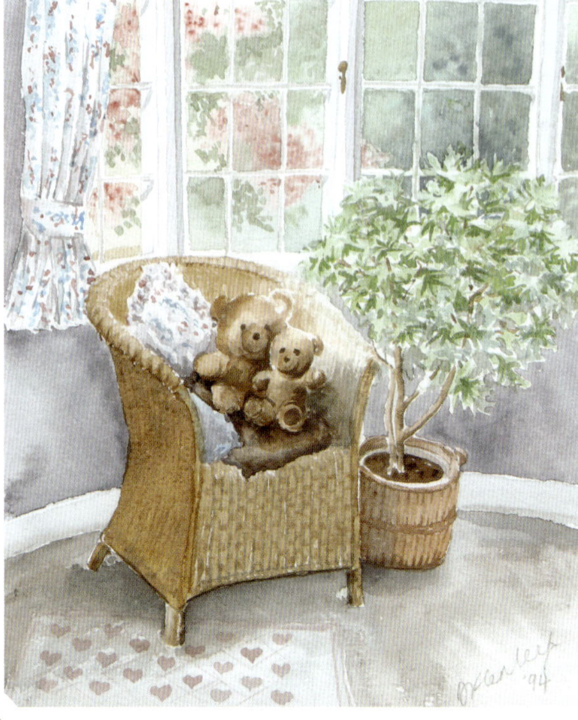

In this painting the light is channelled through a small window and the highlights from it have such an impact on the plant that the tones are changed drastically

Whereas, here, the bay window is larger and has light coming from more directions, so it has a less dramatic impact

Tone and colour

It is easy to understand tone in terms of black and white, but once colour becomes part of the equation it can become confusing.

We tend to assume that some colours are particular tones – yellow a high tone and brown a low tone, for example – but the intensity and hue of some colours and the way they can change when light falls on them means that it is never as simple as that. Colours are affected by what is around them, so a yellow flower (which we assume = a light tone) against a navy pot (which we assume = dark tone) seems straightforward but, once the flower is in shade and the pot is in the sun, it could be the reverse. So, it is important that we learn to see colours in terms of their tone (lightness or darkness) as opposed to just their hue (colour, for example red or blue).

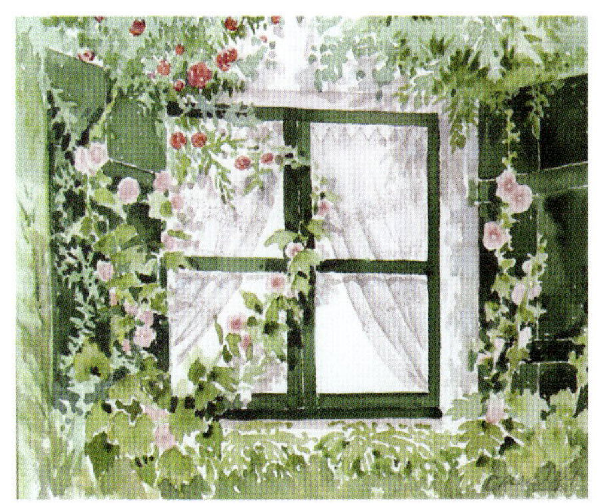

In the picture above both the paintwork and the foliage are green, but what differentiates one from the other is the tone of green, which makes the leaves stand out against the paintwork background.

Similarly, below, the colour of the green foliage and the blue shutter are the same tone, so it has been darkened where the two meet around the top of the window, to create a contrast between the two areas.

By planning the tones in advance you can work out your criteria beforehand, produce a more successful painting. You can also avoid some common problems, such as using up your darkest tones, then coming to an area of deep shadow where you can't go any darker, or losing your highest (whitest) tone, because you have painted over it.

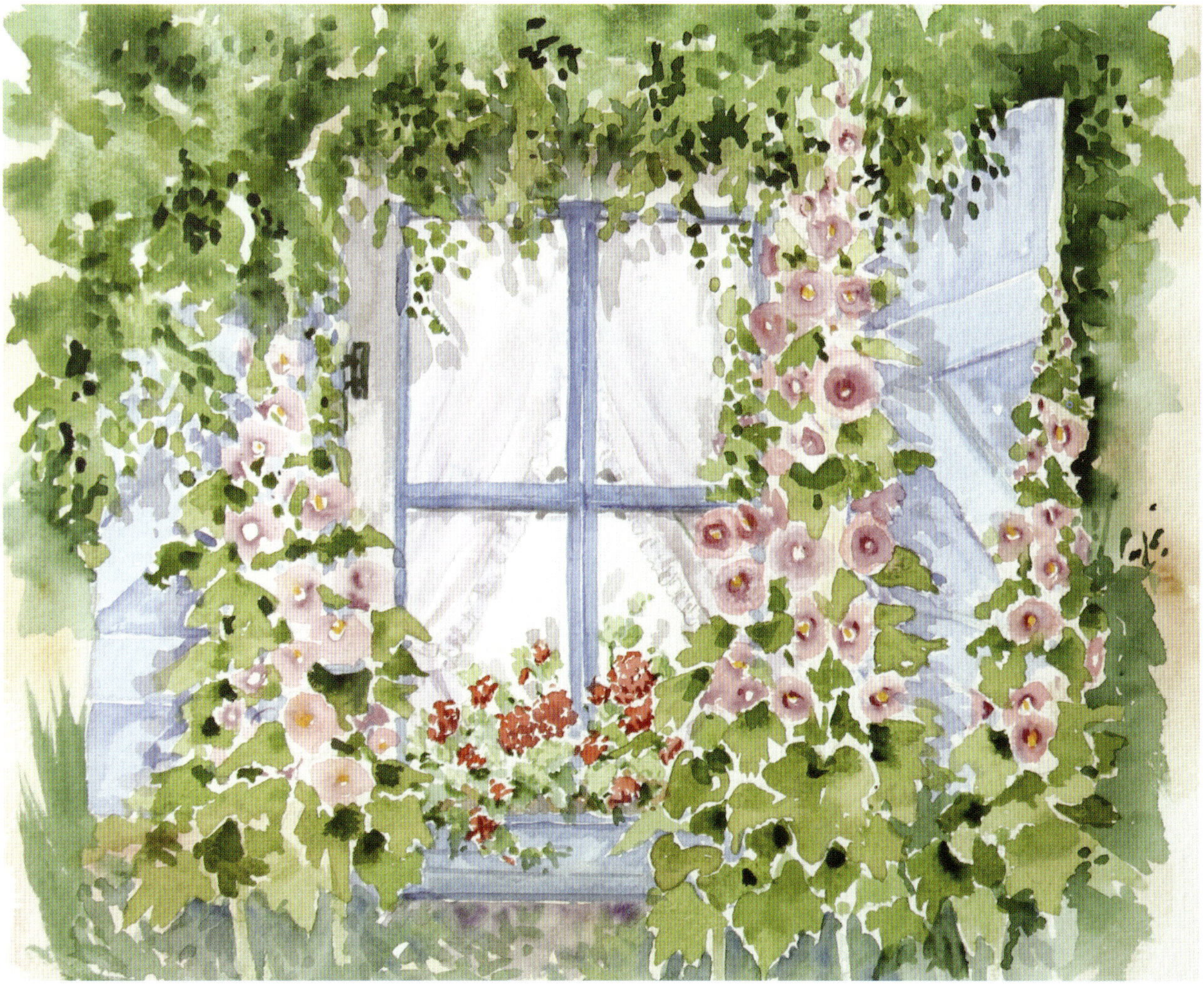

✶ Demonstration: Planning tones

As a help to planning tones, consider the examples below, which are based on the photograph on the right.

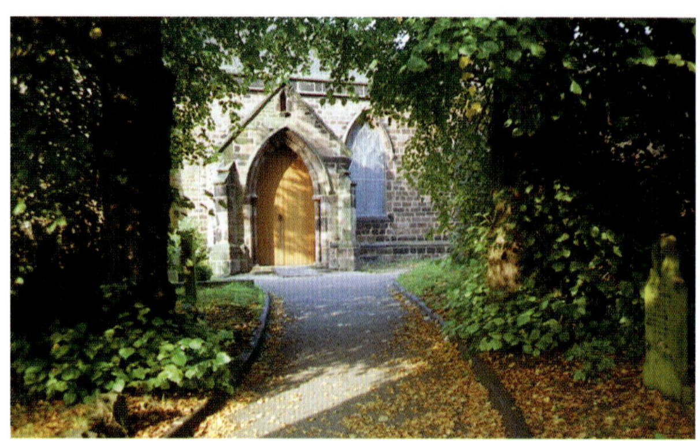

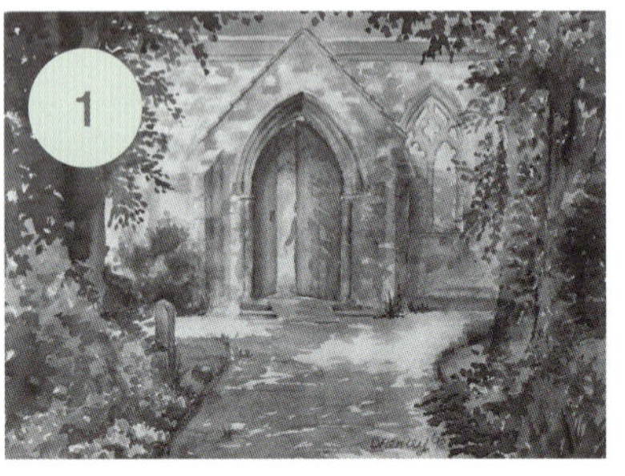

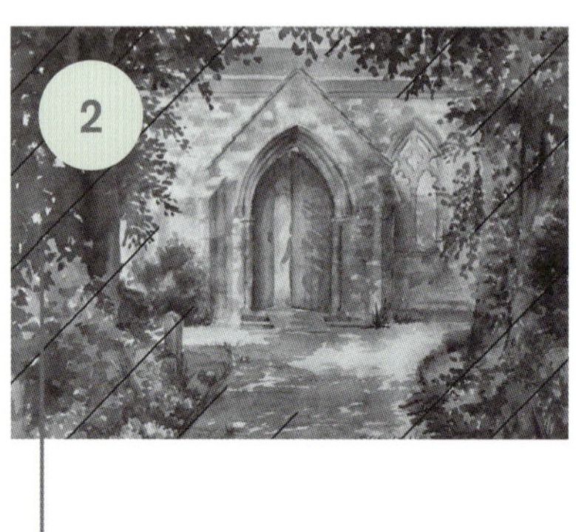

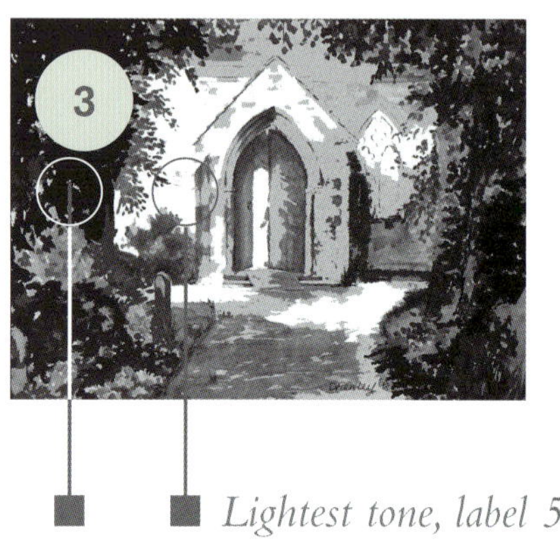

*Mark general areas
of light and shade*

Lightest tone, label 5

Darkest tone, label 1

1 Imagine your picture in black and white and decide whether or not there is a good balance of lights and darks. If you wish, use a viewfinder or piece of card with a hole in – if it is in a neutral/buff colour, then you can judge all the tones against it.

2 Mass together the tones you see with quick scribbles and work out where your general areas of light and dark will be, so that you have a rough idea how the finished pieces will be 'balanced'. Remember that you can alter what you see before you by strengthening tones, linking areas of tones together, as you wish.

3 Divide up the various areas into different tones on a scale of 1–3 or 1–5. Start with three tones – light, medium and dark – then train your eye to differentiate more tones on a scale of 1–5. Sketch in the lightest tones first, then add the darker ones.

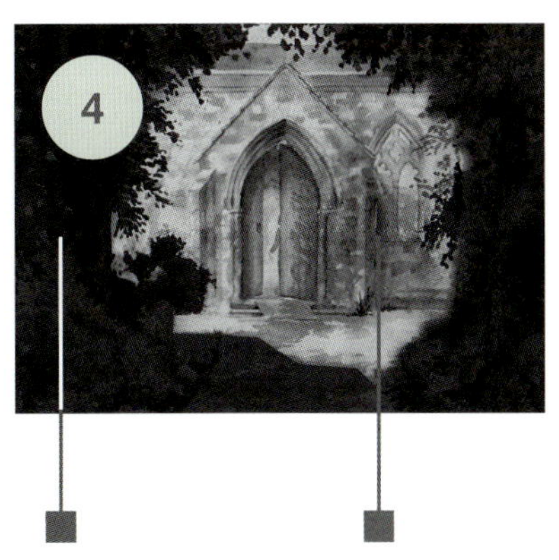

*Two-thirds
of the image
is dark*

*Only one-third
is light*

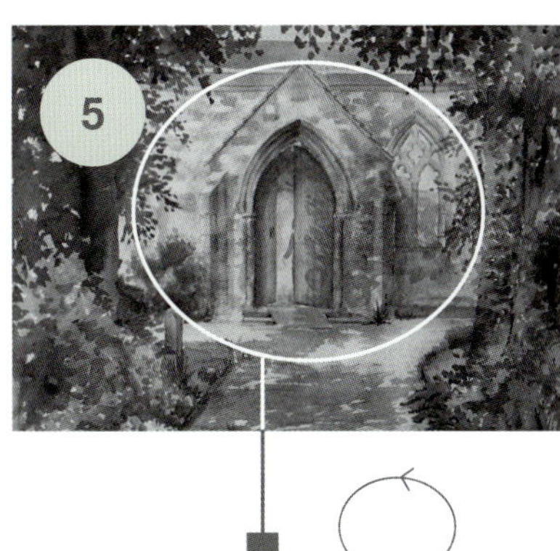

*Where does the
eye lead?*

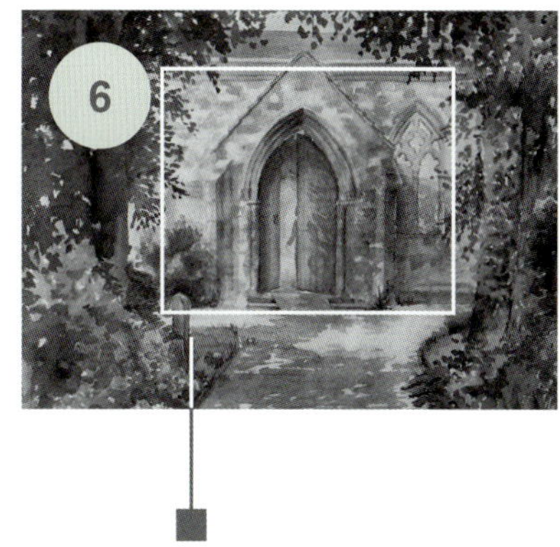

*The area of
strongest contrast*

4 Organize the balance of lights and darks so that it 'feels right' and creates a pleasing composition. Avoid an even amount of darks or lights: make one dominant and the other supportive, aiming for one-third of one (light or dark) and two-thirds of the other.

5 Observe the shapes of things and how they work together – work to a rhythm, with tones leading the eye into and around the picture. Try to avoid too many light bits in dark areas, or vice versa, as these will distract the eye away from the focal point, and disrupt the rhythm.

6 Your strongest contrast will be where lightest lights are next to the darkest darks and this will attract the eye, so make this your focal point. Remember, if you want an area to stand out, it will have more impact if it is a small light area surrounded by darks, or vice versa.

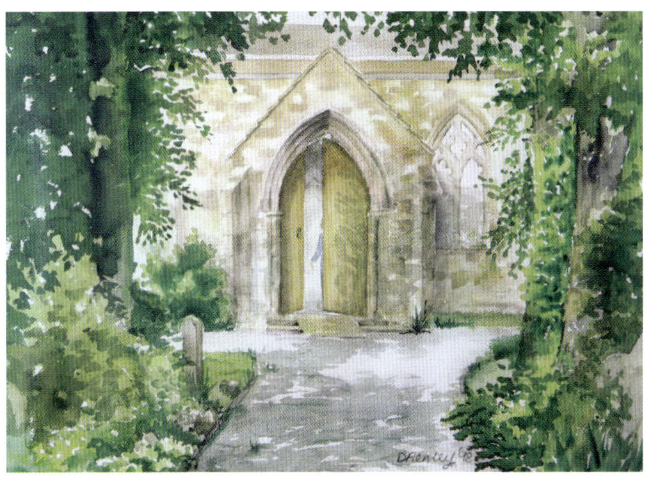

The final painting

Composition

A well-composed painting is pleasing to
look at and has harmony and balance.

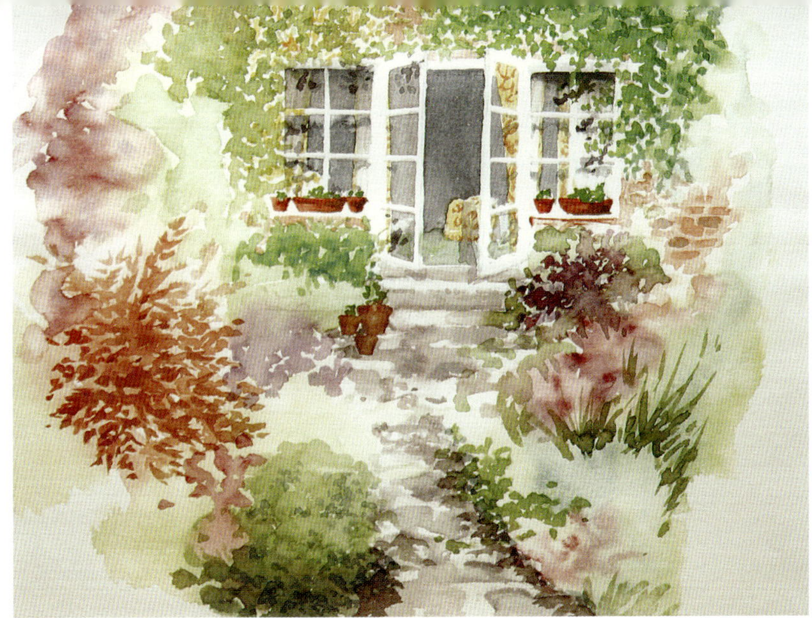

We instinctively know if a painting is 'right' or 'wrong', and we know this often depends on the composition of the work, but beyond that it can be difficult to analyse why it works.

When planning a drawing or painting the rules of composition should be applied subtly, so that the viewer is unaware of how the effect has been achieved, yet finds the results are pleasing. Although there are plenty of rules and theories for good composition, no-one should paint to a set formula. The thought process is what matters, not the rules, and the quality of a work is in its expression not its technique. Remember, for every rule that exists there is a picture which has defied the rule and worked well.

Usually the foreground should be in the tightest focus, with the distance losing detail, but in the painting above the rule has been broken. I didn't want the foreground to be a dominant part of the composition as it is not where the focal point is, so it is less detailed and out of focus.

A good composition can account for 50% of the success of a picture and sometimes it will just present itself – a natural archway of trees, for instance. But 'composition' doesn't just mean the way things are placed, but also the way they are treated in terms of colour, tone and mood. So, it is up to the artist to interpret the situation and create an interesting composition utilizing all these factors – time spent planning this is never wasted.

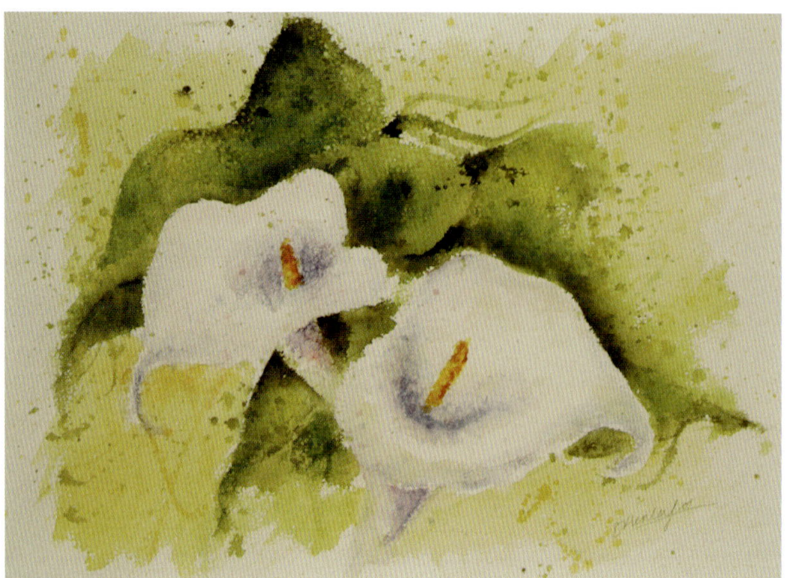 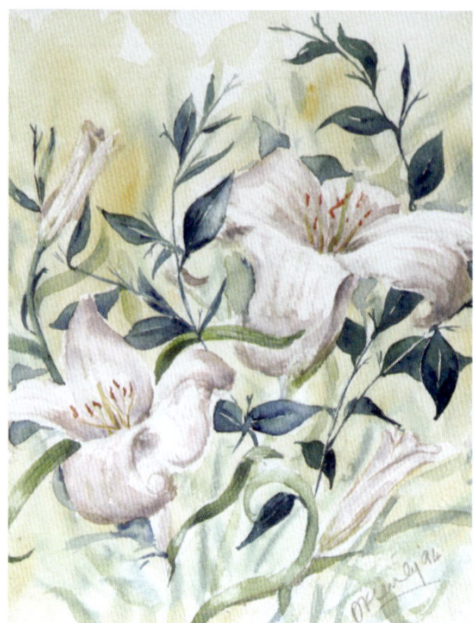

*Of these two lily paintings, I prefer the looser one (above left),
because there is less detail. It may not be as accurate botanically
but, with less to look at, it is easier on the eye*

Atmosphere in composition

As already explained, you don't need to paint exactly
what you see before you. Decide what excites
you about your scene then – just as journalists
predetermine the angle they will give a story by
directing the questions specifically to support their
argument – interpret what you see to fit that mood.

Once you have chosen the way you want to approach
your painting – whether, a 'country-feel' still life, a
pretty flower arrangement, or an exciting and dramatic

abstract – decide what is needed to get that idea across,
then leave out anything that you don't like, exaggerate
what you do like, or even add what you want. Rearrange
everything until you have created the desired image.

You do not need to cover every bit of the paper:
reducing detail gives more impact to what is important.
Suggest just enough detail to allow the viewers to
interpret things for themselves.

Tip: for ease of reference, work out your compositions

in your sketchbook – it's far safer than using scraps

of paper, which you could easily lose.

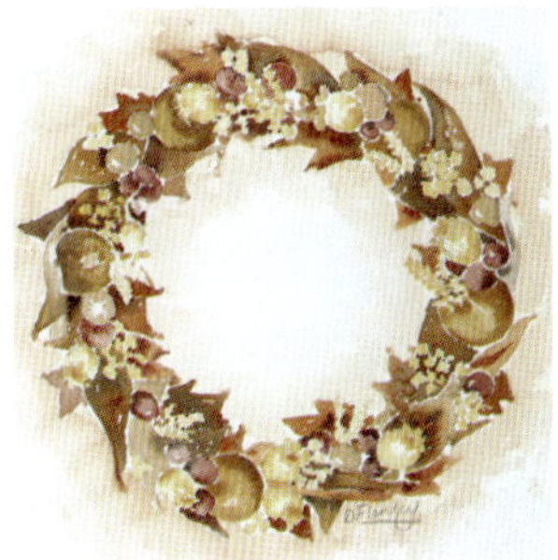 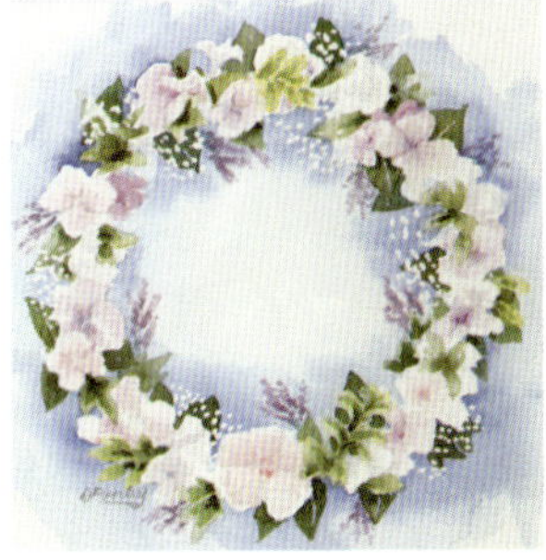 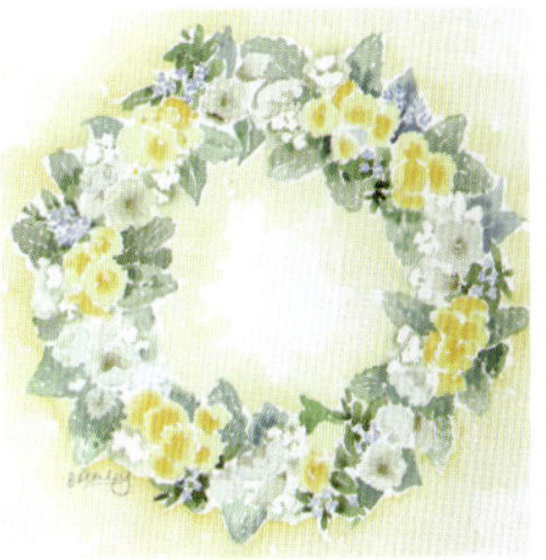 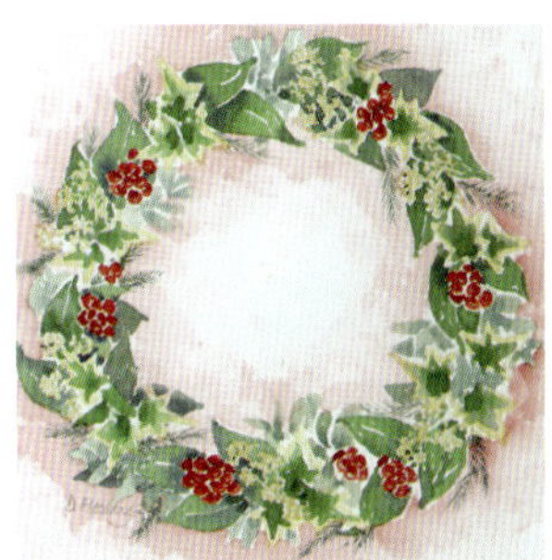

Use colour to your advantage

Note in the images above how each of the rings represents a season of the year by its colour.

You don't need to be told which season each one is for, as the colour does the talking. The same applies to the picture shown below – the season is made obvious by the subject matter and the colour.

Colour plays an important role in establishing the 'feel' of a picture. Fewer colours give a painting harmony, while too many colours can fracture the specific choice of colour. Colour determines the mood and season.

Choose a dominant temperature, warm or cool, have a lot of one and a little of the other, and where you want the most impact have the strongest interplay of colours. Complementary colours (opposite on the wheel) 'sing' when placed together and this creates impact whereas analagous colours (neighbours on the wheel) harmonize and provide a more restful area for the eye. Use these factors to your benefit, bearing in mind that a complex colour scheme requires a simple composition, and vice versa.

Here the warm, limited palette of colours gives the picture an autumnal feel

Your choice of a colour scheme should depend on:

- Subject matter/main interest

- Time (day or night)

- Seasons and weather

- Emotion involved, or story to be told

- Feelings you want to convey

Laying down a wash of pale colours on the paper, before painting commences, introduces a continuity of colour to the work (see page 46). It is best to use transparent colours for this, 'wet-in-wet', and allow them to dry before painting over, as they will then shine through in the unpainted areas, giving a unity and harmony to the work. Alternatively you could use a tinted paper, or glaze over areas of your work (carefully) after they have been painted.

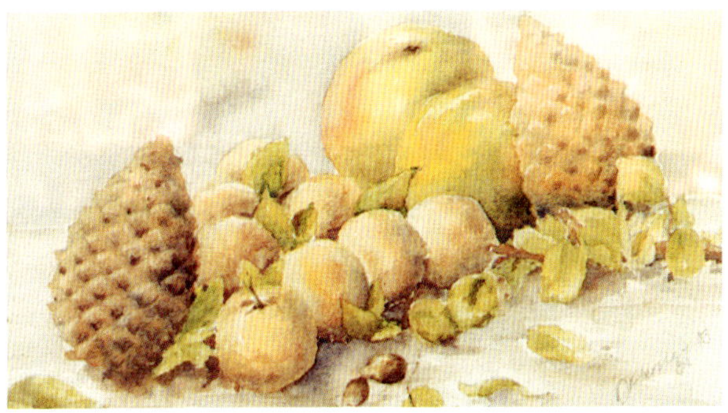

Creating a composition

a   These flowers (top) were placed at the foot of the vase and the leaves on the table were deliberately reaching upwards, towards the foliage that was deliberately falling downwards. In uniting the two, I created a rhythm and unity between them. The composition is unusual, with the bunch of flowers in the corner and partly out of the picture, but the diagonal that it creates is part of the circular pattern of the picture.

b   There is a danger with this picture (below left) that the eye could be led up the steps and have nowhere to go, so I manipulated the tones of the foliage to create a light 'passage' travelling around the picture, to keep the eye moving.

c   Even a small touch like the banana pointing upwards (top right) – towards some foliage that is in turn pointing downwards – creates a unity between the vase and the fruit bowl.

d   This quick study (below right) doesn't work as a painting because the composition is just two parallel lines, so the eye travels across the paper and straight off the page. I should have linked the flowers into a more interesting arrangement.

Rhythm

If you want viewers to be interested in your work, and to retain their interest, you need to keep their eye moving around within the picture. This 'journey of the eyes' can be contrived by the artist: by arranging objects, spaces, tones and colours to suit this purpose you can keep the viewer's eye within the scene, albeit subconsciously.

A way of achieving this is to try to link one part to another, which stops the picture being disjointed and keeps the eye flowing. As each part is linked to the next it stops the eye wandering off out of the picture and leads it towards the focal point. In order to create these links, look for similarities or, if they're not there, create them. For example try to have:

- Lines in a similar direction

- Continuous blends of colour

- Similar tones linked together

- Overlapping shapes

- Repeated shapes echoing each other

- Open doors, gates, arches, and so on, to lead the eye and 'invite the viewer in'.

It can also help to use 'letter-shaped' arrangements, where the rhythm follows a pattern like the shape of a letter. Many artists suggest using certain letter shapes as a basis for composition for instance **C, O, S, T, L, U, V** and **Z.** It's a personal choice, so experiment. I often use a 'C' shape, especially for still-life setups, because this links the vase with the table surface and keeps the eye moving (see p. 142).

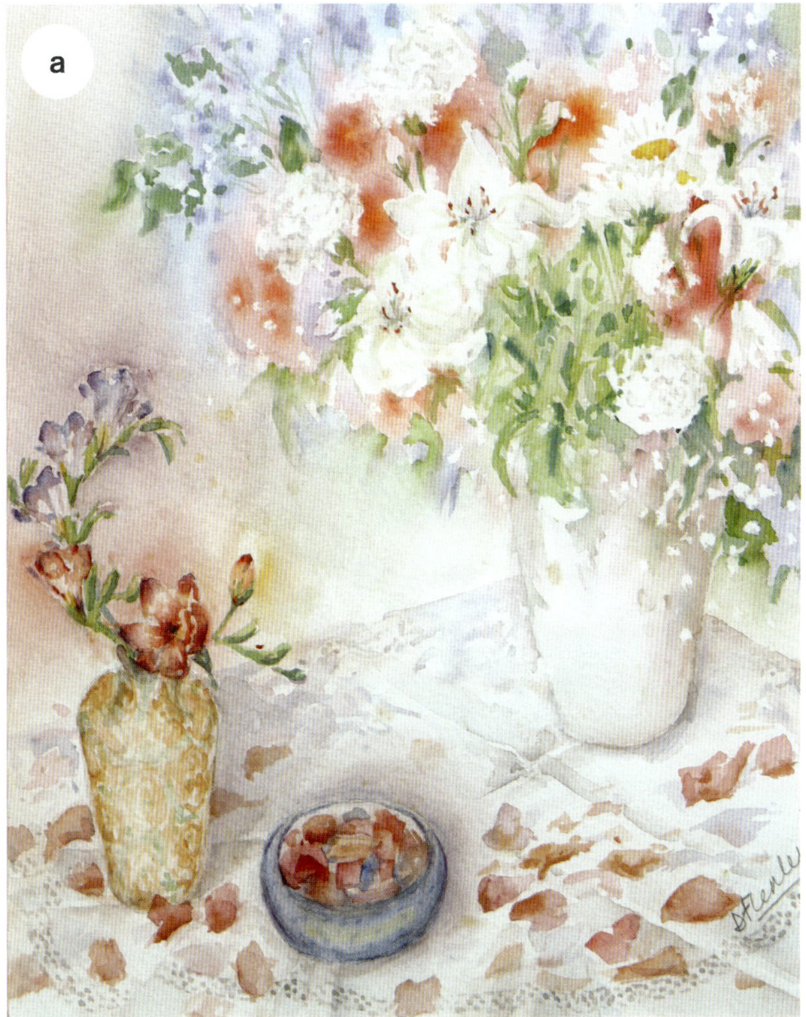

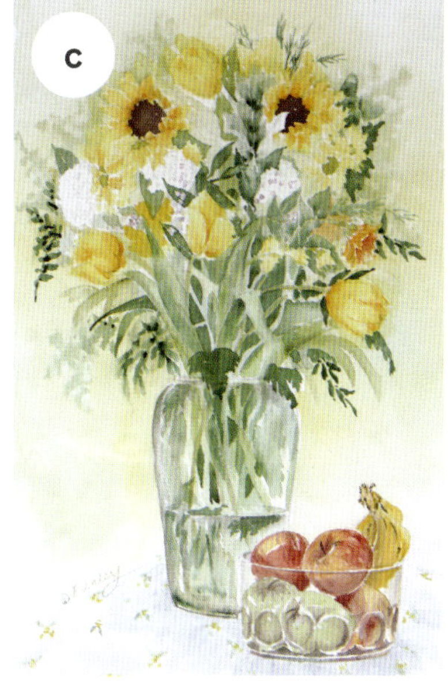

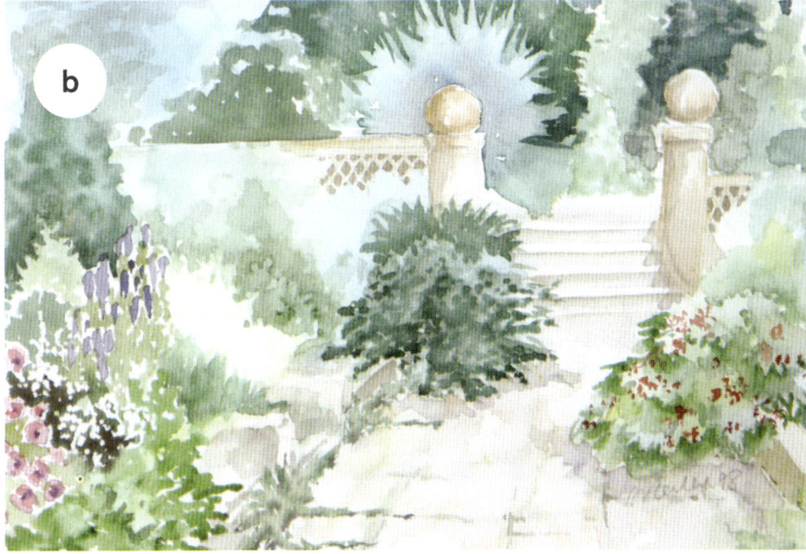

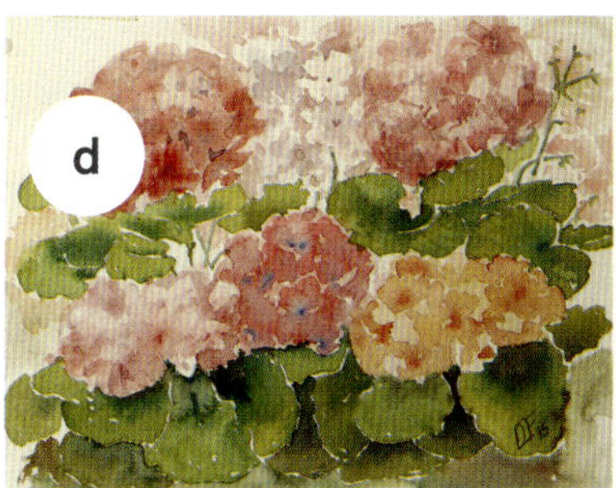

Tip: remember that the viewer's eye usually enters a painting and is led from the bottom left-hand corner.

✳ **Demonstration:** Rhythm

Letter shapes used to link one part of a painting
to another, so manipulating the journey of the eye.

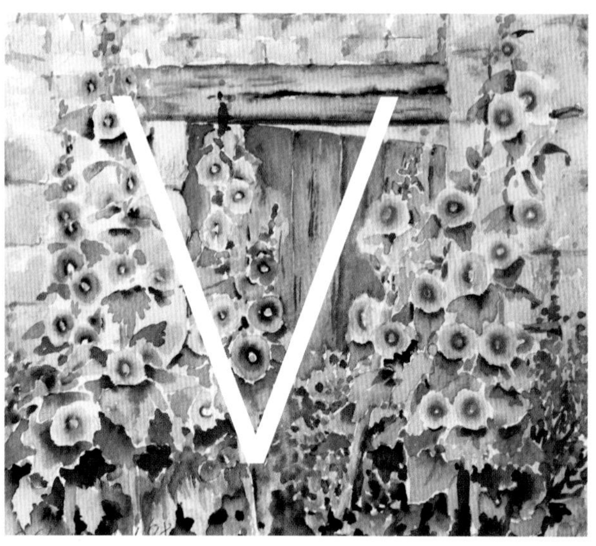

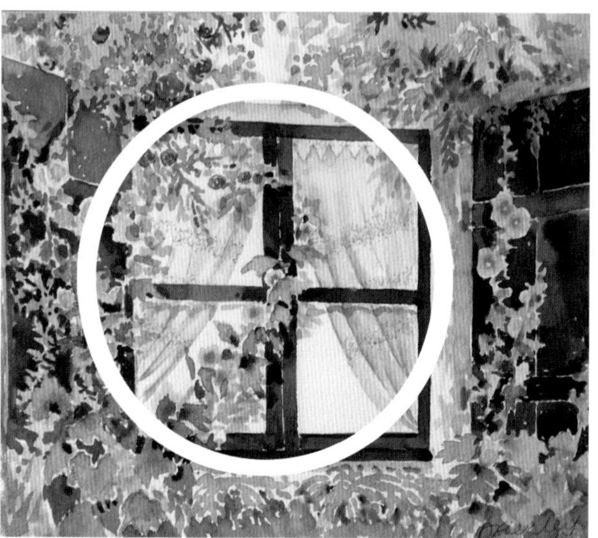

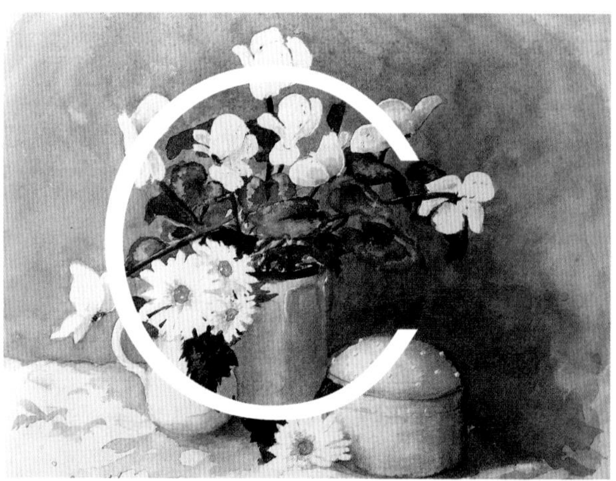

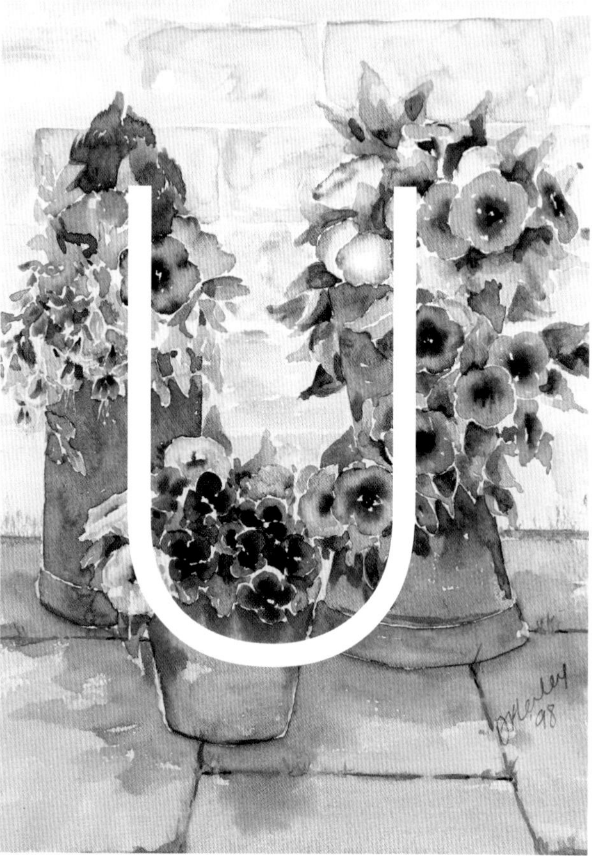

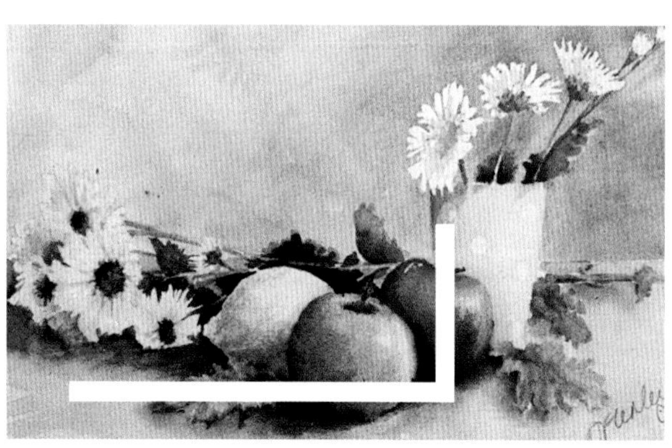

Shapes

It will help your composition if you think about, and plan, your picture in terms of 'shapes' as opposed to 'things'. Shapes can be altered and adapted to suit your composition, you can emphasize pleasing shapes, can overlap or repeat them, and 'lose' or alter awkward ones.

Looking for – and emphasizing – similarities in shapes is a clever way of creating coherency in a picture. For example, I echo certain shapes so that the cloud, the mass of leaves in a tree and patterns of shadow may all be the same shape, and in this way create an almost imperceptible feeling of unity to the picture.

When looking at the tones and shapes and arrangement of objects, make sure the picture is 'balanced'. Whilst you don't want everything to be symmetrical, neither do you want too much emphasis on one side or the other. A lot of this is down to instinct – when you are planning a painting, screw up your eyes and ask yourself if the overall shape of the piece seems right.

Numbers of items

Consider how many things will be in the picture. In theory it is compositionally more interesting and more dynamic if it is an odd number – that way your brain can't even it out and so it retains your interest. It doesn't make any difference what the objects are – the principle is the same and you will probably find this rule follows through in general design, even to the number of items you display on your mantelpiece. If you think about it, three candles – especially at different heights – looks so much more interesting than two standing side by side.

The focal point

Most pictures need a focal point and this is the 'key' part of the picture, where the most interest lies, even though it may only occupy a small part of the scene. All other parts of the picture (if you've taken on board all the notes and planned it correctly) should play a secondary, supporting role, so: be less dominant in terms of strong colours and tones; not distract from the focal point in any way; lead the eye towards the focal point and not intrude or clash with it.

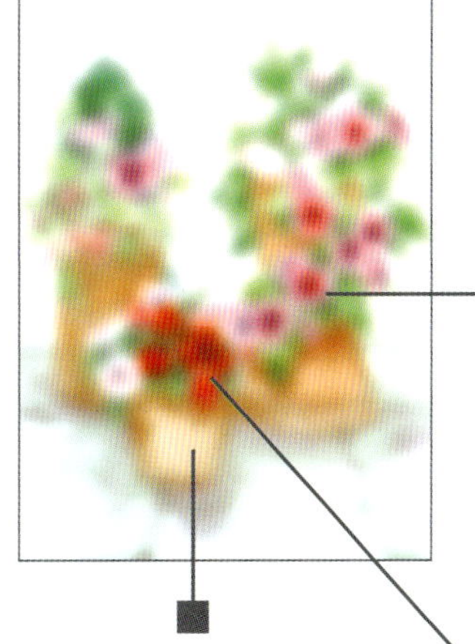

Odd numbers in a painting are more memorable

Squint and the picture becomes blurred, almost abstract, helping you to see shape and tone clearly

The focal point, the key to the picture

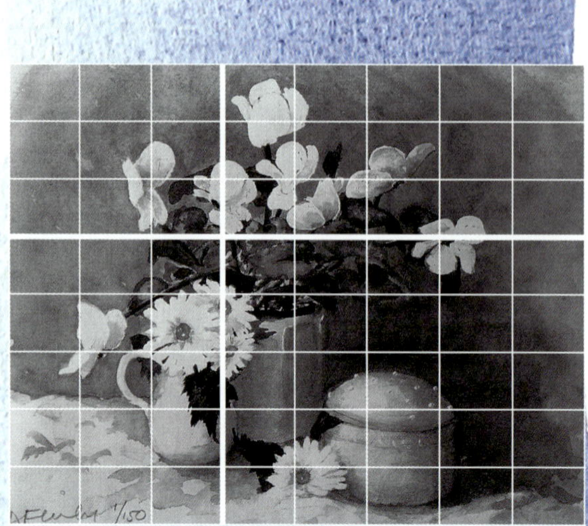

Focus on
The Golden Section

The Golden Section is a classical mathematical formula for distributing the weight in the composition of a picture which, in theory, makes the composition more interesting.

This system creates a series of squares which diminish in size as they follow a pattern curving round towards the centre of the picture. I am not suggesting you learn it or follow it, but it is interesting as it can be translated into many forms including mathematics, music and poetry, and has even been used as a system for predicting the growth of the stock market.

It is also known as the Fibonacci sequence – after Leonardo of Pisa who called himself Fibonacci. He had been educated in North Africa and learned the 'Hindu-Arabic' mathematical system from Moorish teachers. He soon realized the advantages of using this and was one of the people who introduced it to Europe.

Advocates of the Golden Section suggest you should divide your space into eight and look at 3.8 ratio or 5.8, i.e count 3, or 5 along a line vertically then do the same horizontally and the point at which the two meet is the ideal place for your focal point.

Being a lazy soul, rather than divide my painting into 3/8 or 5/8 to get the precise placing on the Golden Section, I tend to divide my painting into thirds, horizontally and vertically, and put my focal point where the two points meet.

Remember though, that although the Golden Section can be very useful as a guide – Michelangelo, Mondrian and Leonardo da Vinci all used it – the rules are that 'there are no rules'. If you feel your focal point needs to be somewhere else, don't let these theories stand in your way.

✱ Demonstration: Composing and planning a painting

These six diagrams illustrate common mistakes made when composing a picture.

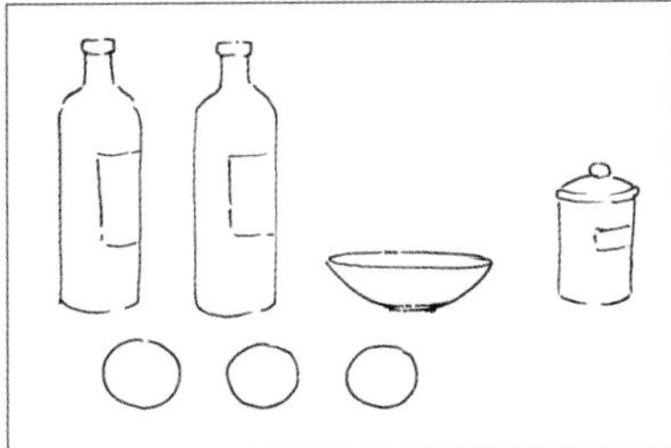

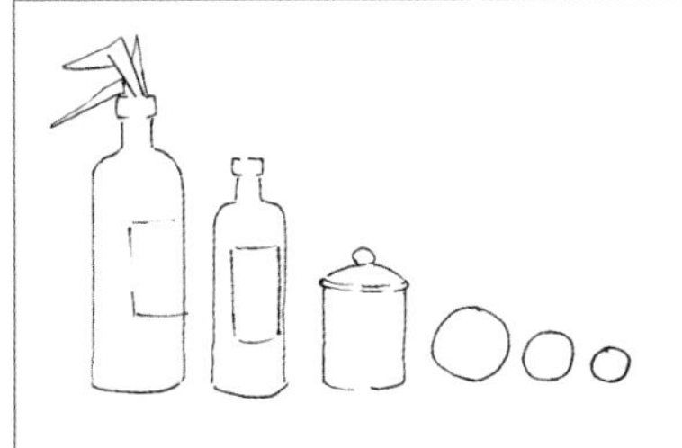

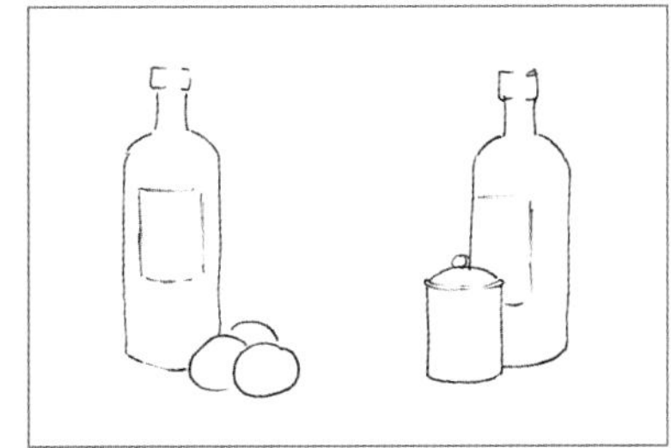

Link objects together so there is a relationship between them. Where they are adjacent, the eye can flow through the picture, following them.

Don't let the eye lead out of the picture – here the eye follows diagonally across the picture and down out of the bottom right-hand corner.

You should only have one main focal point, here both areas are competing for attention and so neither has any impact.

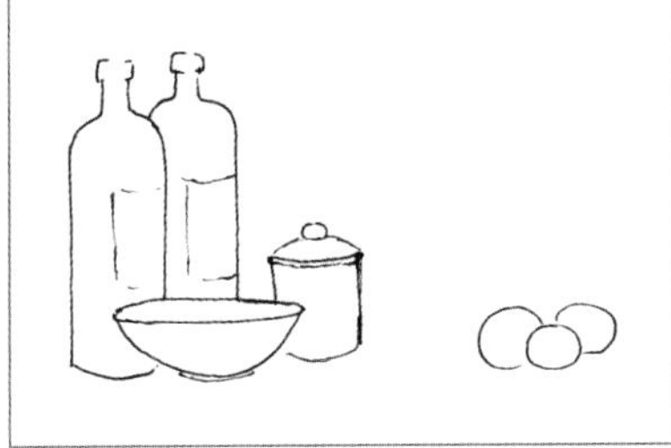

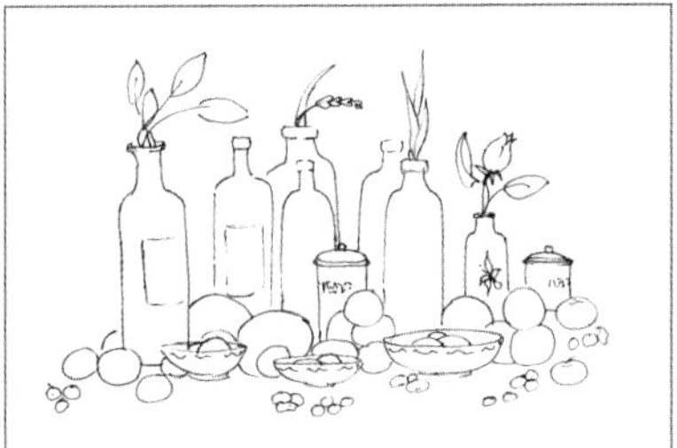

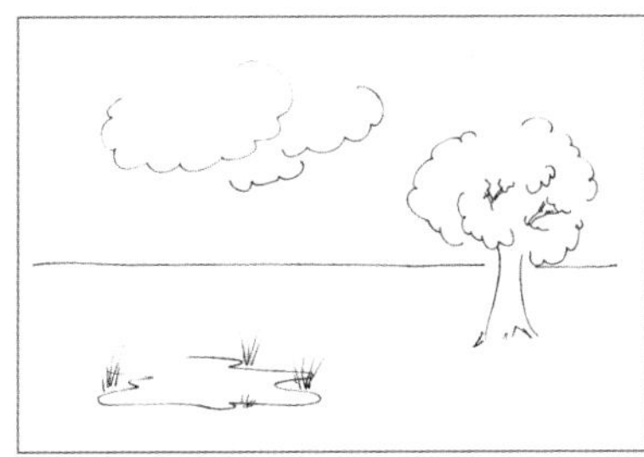

Secondary features should support the focal point, not draw attention away from the main area: these oranges are a distraction.

Less is more: here there is too much information and the composition is cluttered, so nothing has any impact.

Avoid a horizon in the middle of the page: neither area has any dominance so neither area has any impact, and there is no one definitive area for the focal point.

✶ Demonstration: Composing and planning a painting

Three diagrams showing compositions that work.

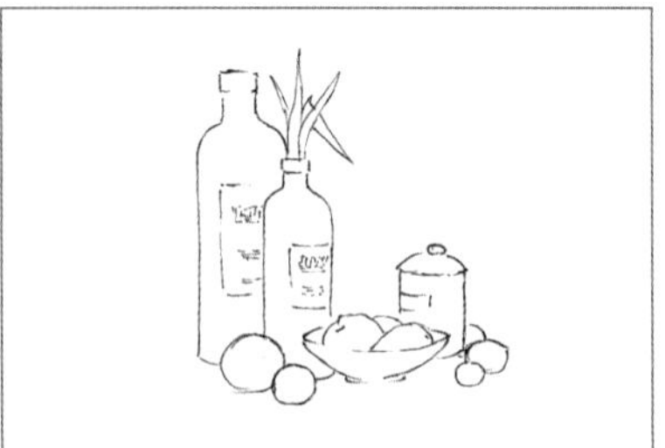

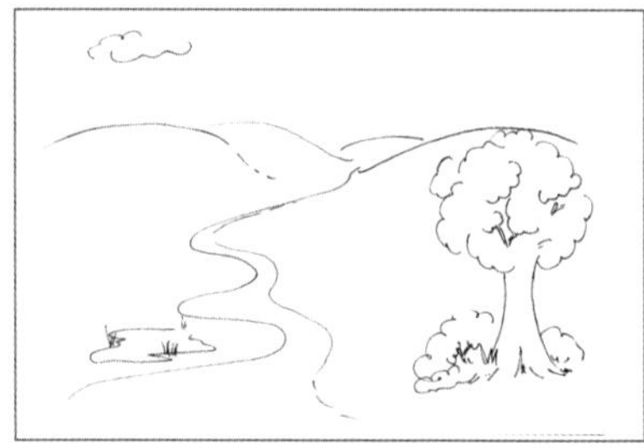

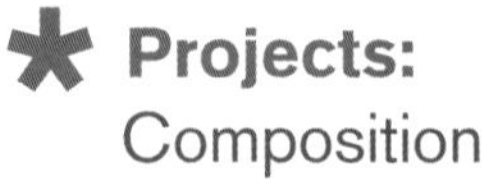

Once the composition is just right, as here, think about the space around it and judge where you will put your edges in framing the image. Too much and the images will be lost in space, too little and they may seem cramped in the scene.

Here the objects are linked together and there is an L-shape to the composition, so the eye flows through the scene. The bent grass in the vase directs the eye back down to the jar on the right, so the eye keeps moving round instead of upwards off the page.

If the background were put in, I would place the 'horizon line' – i.e. the edge of the table – just above the fruit bowl and behind the jar. This would give a one-third/two-thirds horizon line, more pleasing than having it in the middle of the page.

Here we have two-thirds ground and one-third sky, so the focal point is effective in the foreground.

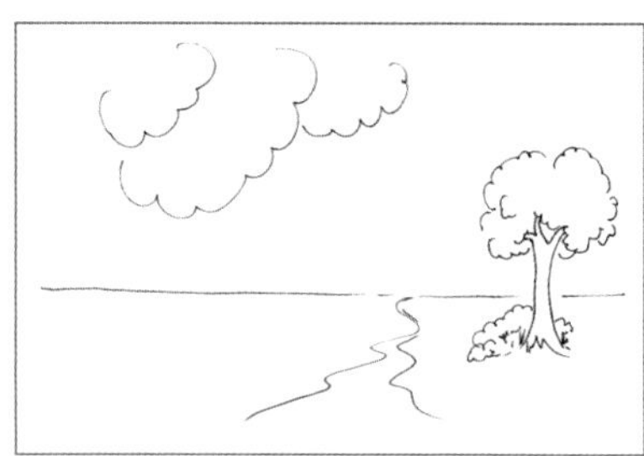

Here the ground occupies one-third and the sky two-thirds of the composition, so the sky has an impact. Note how the shapes are echoed in the tree and the cloud, giving harmony to the composition.

✶ Projects: Composition

1. Choose a scene. Look through a viewfinder and consider different ways that it could be portrayed. Think 'landscape' (with the viewfinder horizontal) or 'portrait' (with the viewfinder vertical). Move the viewfinder around so you can see a number of different options. Practise quick compositional sketches for each possibility and then choose the one you prefer.

2. Arrange some objects and try the same procedure again with a still life. Instead of making the usual assumptions about where things go, try out different angles and views. Aim to surprise yourself.

3. If you like the composition of another artist's picture, or you see, or suddenly think of, a good composition, always record it in your sketchbook.

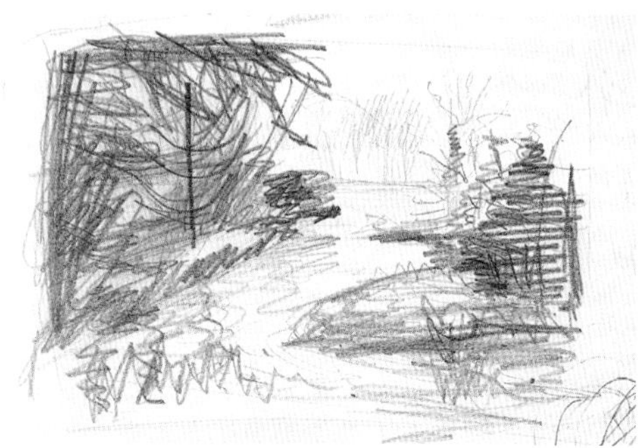

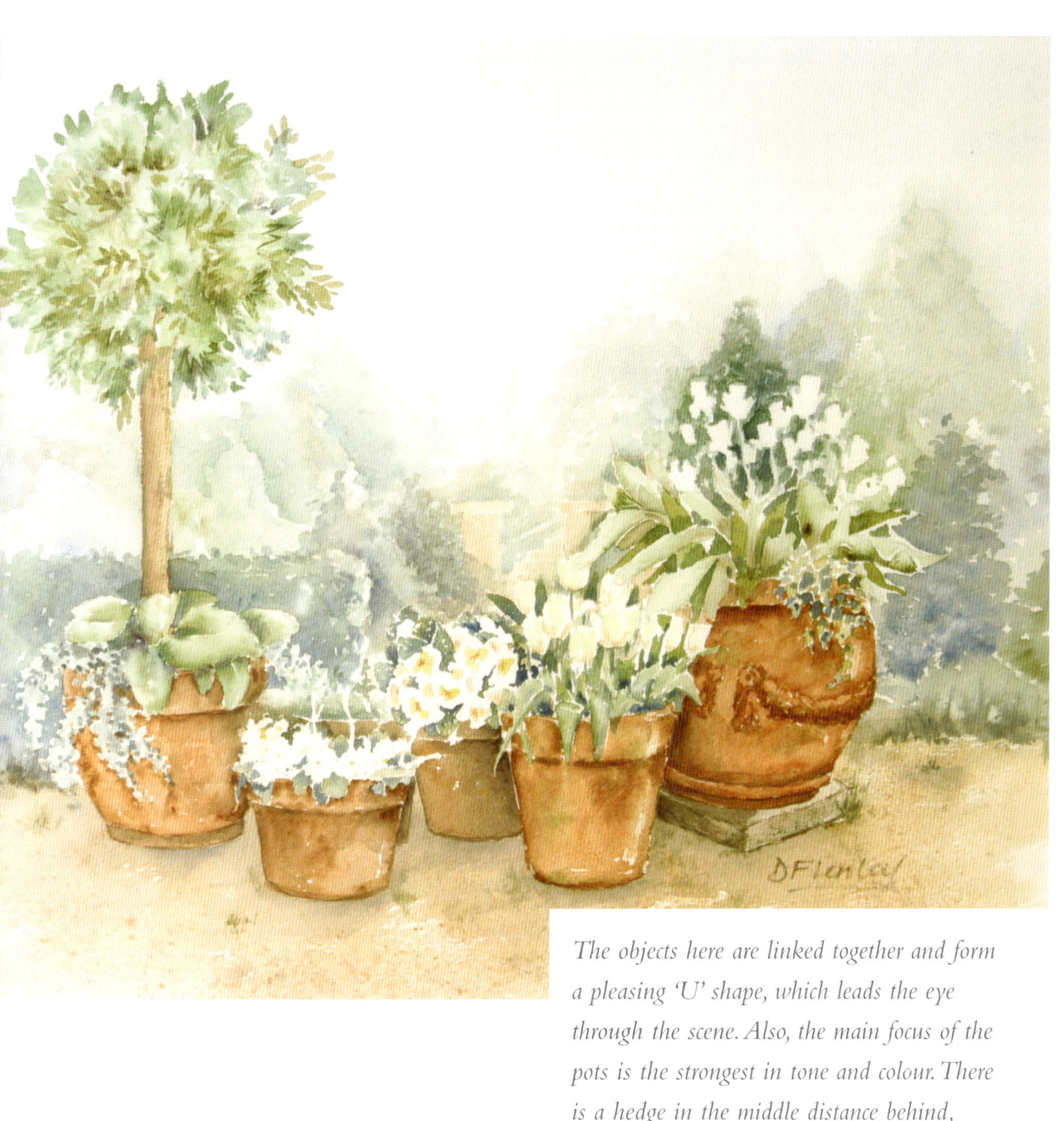

The objects here are linked together and form
a pleasing 'U' shape, which leads the eye
through the scene. Also, the main focus of the
pots is the strongest in tone and colour. There
is a hedge in the middle distance behind,
which is paler and less defined, while the far
distance is very pale, and the least defined

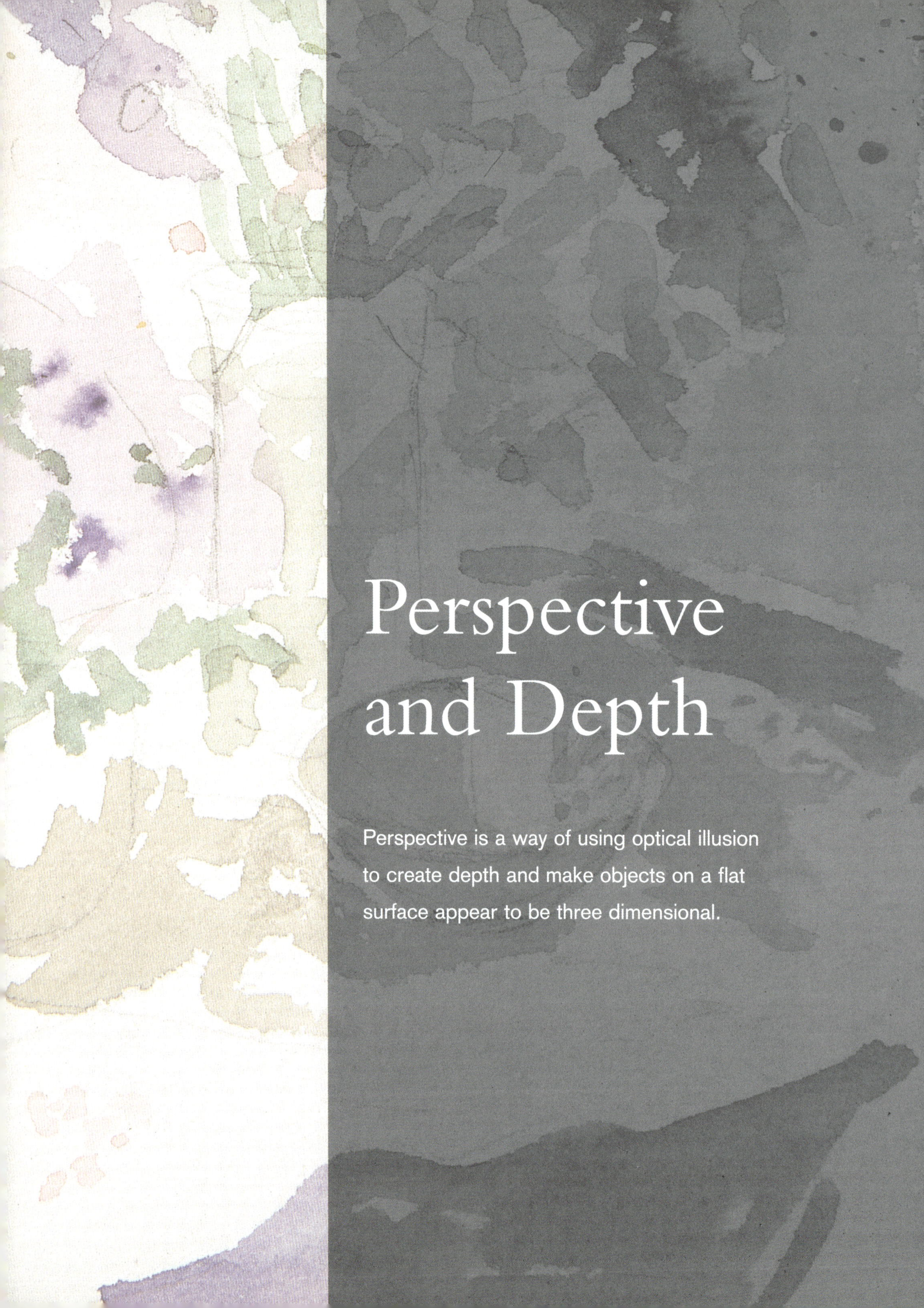

Perspective and Depth

Perspective is a way of using optical illusion to create depth and make objects on a flat surface appear to be three dimensional.

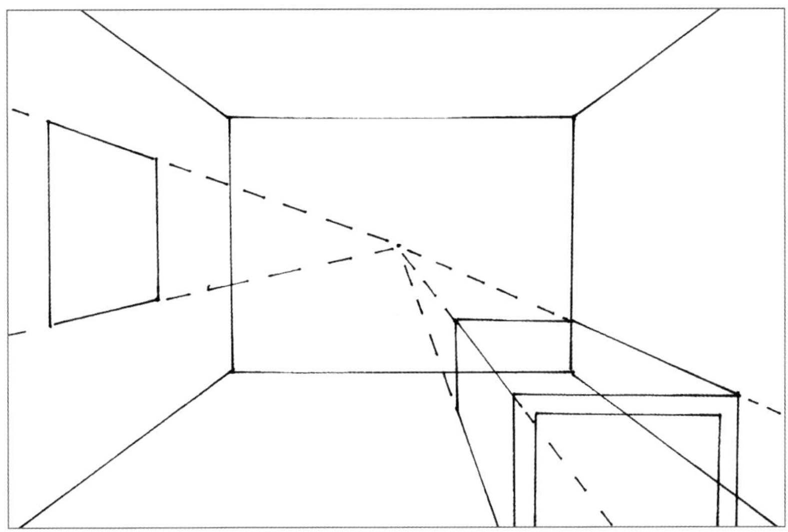

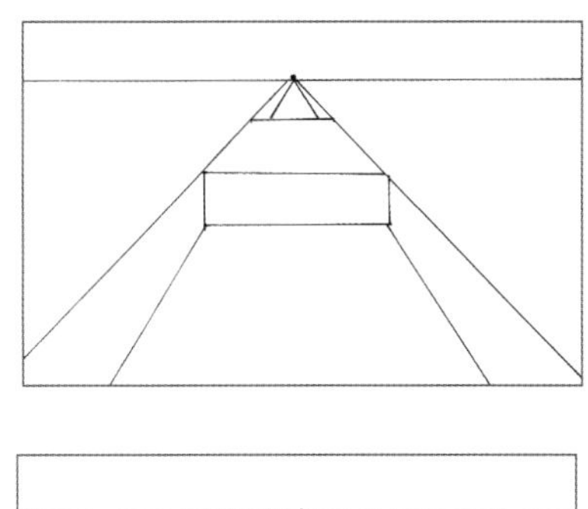

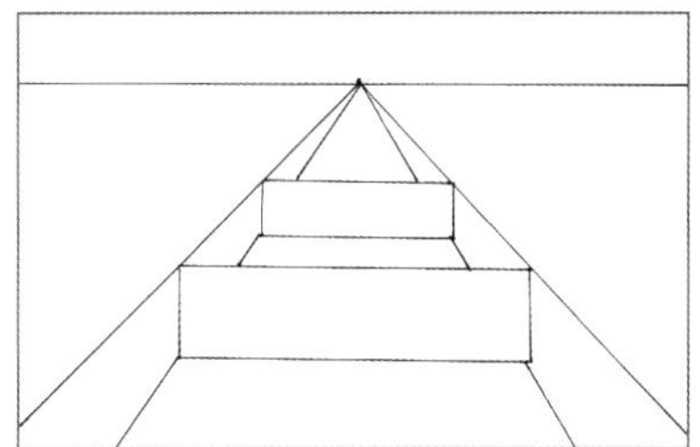

Examples of one-point perspective

The basis of perspective is that objects in the distance appear smaller than those close to the spectator and that parallel lines appear to meet in the far distance (the vanishing point).

Linear perspective

Linear perspective – which evolved from the above premise – is dependent, among other things, upon the correct use of vanishing points. It was first used by the Greeks and Romans but its invention is attributed to the early 1400s with Florentine architect Filippo Brunelleschi's experiments in perspective painting. These ideas continued to be developed and used by Renaissance artists and, in 1436, Leon Battista Alberti's treatise on perspective theory was published. Since then perspective has served a vital role in European art.

One-point perspective

We know that objects that are further away appear smaller, eventually reducing in size to a vanishing point on the horizon. For example, on a flat plane telegraph poles and trees all diminish in size, and we all know from looking at train tracks that parallel lines receding into the distance eventually converge together at the vanishing point. Where lines meet at one point at eye level, it is known as 'one-point perspective'. If the lines are above your eye level they will converge downwards, and if they are below they will converge upwards. For example, the lines of the buildings – or the objects in a picture – are slanted inwards, making them appear to extend back into space.

One-point perspective only works where objects are facing, or are at right angles, to the viewer, for instance a house where only one wall can be seen full on. In this view much of the structure of the building will remain hidden behind the wall.

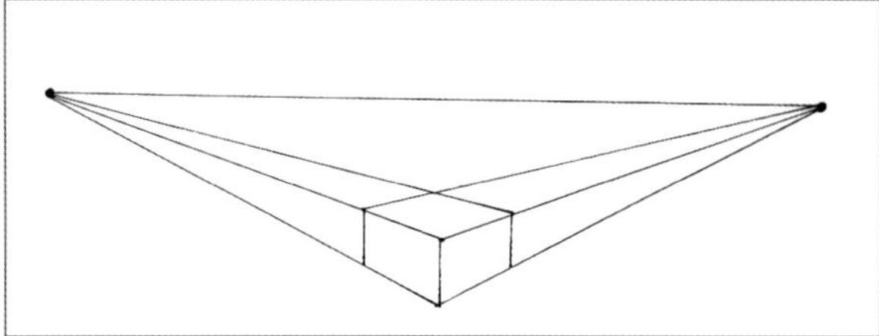

Two-point perspective

Two-point perspective

When you see objects at an angle rather than straight on – for instance the corner of a building, or the corner of a field – you will need two vanishing points instead of one, because the parallel lines still converge as usual. Those on the left of the building converge to a vanishing point on the left, and those on the right converge outwards to a vanishing point on the right. When adding windows and doors to your drawing, be sure to keep the tops and bottoms in line with the walls of the building, as the parallel lines follow for them too. To look realistic, your vanishing points need to be quite far apart. If you can't fit them onto your page, try using long rulers – or even string – and lead them out of the paper onto your table using a dot as your reference point (or drawing pins on the table, if it is not precious).

Three-point perspective

Three-point perspective is probably the most challenging of all and, whilst it is the most accurate way of capturing three-dimensional objects, you will only rarely need to use it. Like two-point perspective, it has two vanishing points somewhere on the horizon, but it also has an additional vanishing point above or below the horizon which the verticals vanish to. It will not work if the vanishing points are too close together as the results will look distorted, but if you take them off the page and spread them far apart it can be dramatically effective.

Overlapping

Another method you can employ to help create distance or depth in a painting is 'overlapping'. This is a useful way of showing that an object is in front of another and, consequently, objects that are behind must be further back.

When you paint the object in front, to emphasize the dominance of its 'forefrontal' position, make sure it is not only comparatively larger, but also slightly stronger in tone and slightly brighter in colour than the object behind. Deliberately soften the edges of what is behind to help reinforce this. Likewise, when superimposing successive planes in landscapes, be sure to stress how much paler and softer the scene is behind.

Sometimes, if objects aren't actually overlapping in real life, it helps to use artistic licence and move things around a little, so that you can employ this strategy to add a sense of depth.

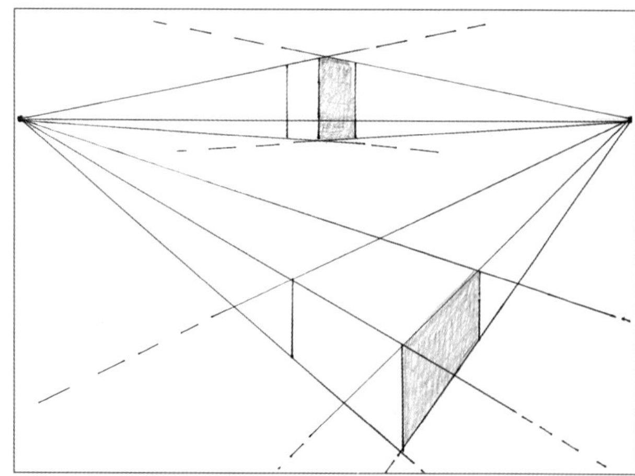

Three-point perspective

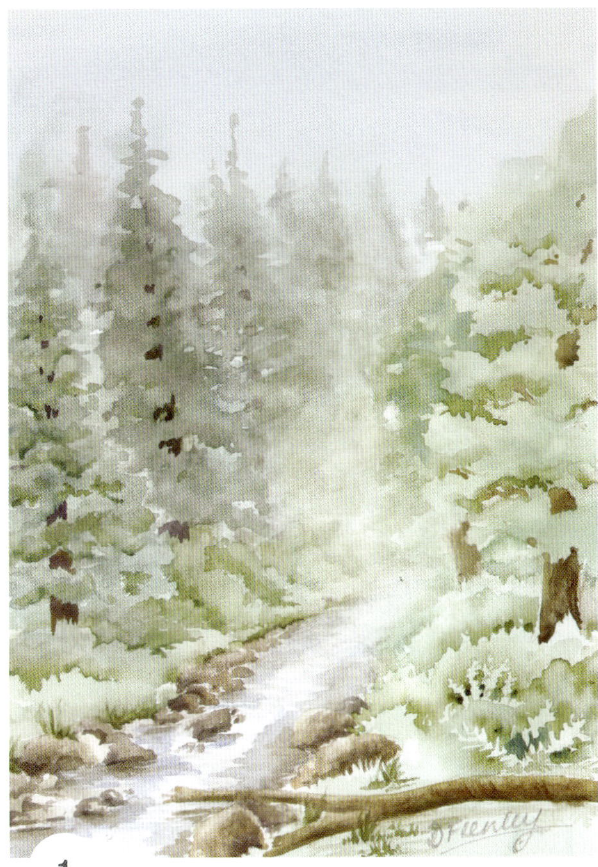

1

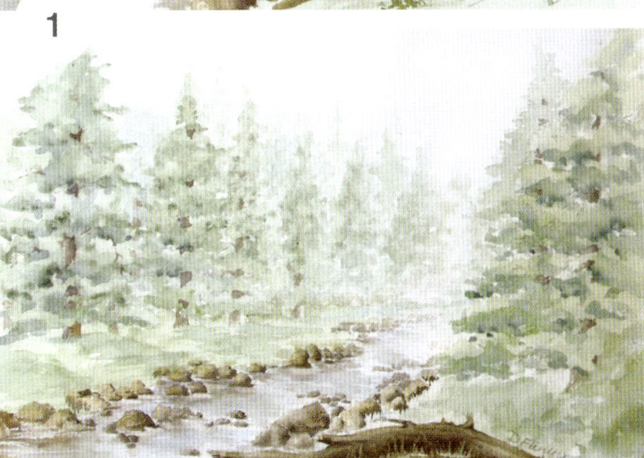

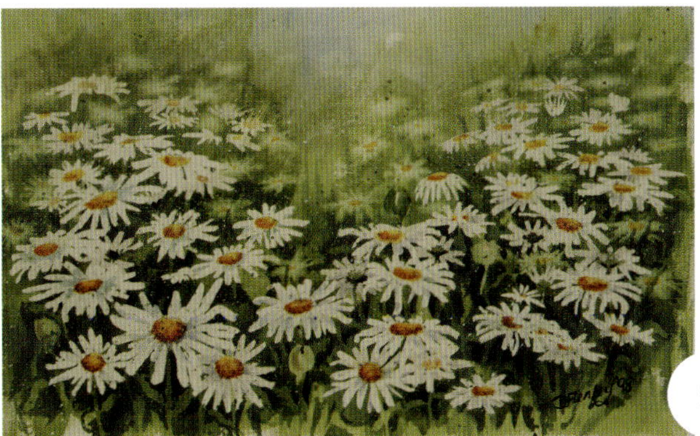

2

Reducing lines

Distance can also be created without vanishing points or overlapping, simply by reducing the spaces between lines. If you combine this technique in a painting along with all the other factors, it will help to play a supporting role in creating depth.

1 Here you can see reducing lines in both the portrait and landscape layouts, and the overlapping trees becoming paler and less defined in the distance.

2 Even though there is little landscape to be seen in the distance, a sense of depth has been achieved in these two pictures by fading out the flowers as they get further away.

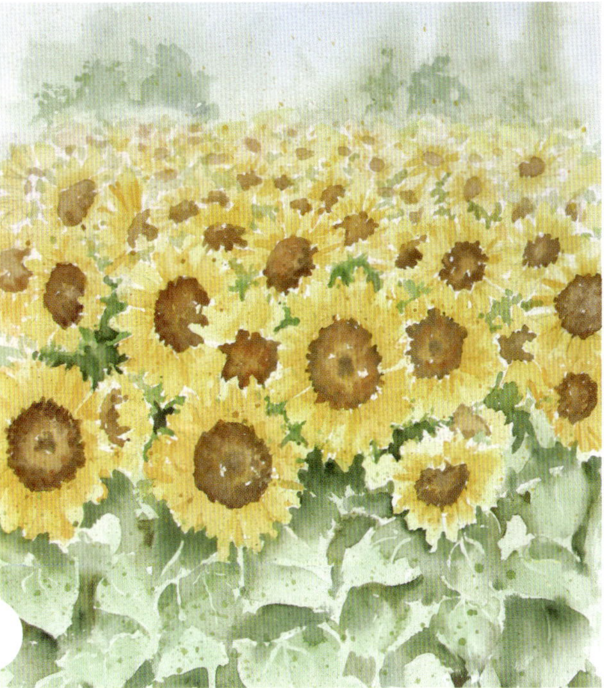

Focus on
Compositional terms

• Eye level

This is your viewpoint. If you have difficulty working out where your eye level is, draw three horizontal parallel lines onto a piece of glass, hold the glass at arm's length, then position the middle line level with your eyes. The parallel lines above and below this middle line will then clarify the angles of the other objects in the picture: those above will slope down (worm's eye view) and those below will slope up (bird's eye view).

• Vanishing point

This is the point on the horizon where parallel lines meet. This will be the horizon if the ground is flat, or you are at the seaside. If you tilt a pencil to the angle of a receding line you will determine where the vanishing point lies. Note, with oblique (two-or-more-point perspective) the vanishing point may be right off the paper.

• Picture plane

The view you would see in a frame, if you held one up – in fact the surface of the painting.

• Light reference

The source of your light, for example the sun, the moon, a lamp or a window.

Aerial perspective or colour perspective

As objects and scenery recede from the observer, the view becomes paler – bluer/greyer – and less defined due to the layers of dust and moisture that are clouding the atmosphere. Aerial perspective – which is used in conjunction with linear perspective – captures this feeling of distance in a painting through change in colour and tonal values.

Aerial perspective is generally used in landscape painting, due to the distances involved, but the principle is still relevant to still-life arrangements, where depth is just as necessary.

To put aerial perspective into practice, imagine you are looking into a three-dimensional box and divide the surface up into three successive planes: foreground, middle distance and far distance. To portray depth in your landscape keep your stronger, warmer, tones and your detail for the foreground, reduce these factors slightly for the middle distance, and reduce them greatly for the far distance. But also consider uniting those planes – by 'linking' each plane to the next – so the picture doesn't become disjointed.

A good way of uniting planes is to repeat shapes elsewhere in the picture. It can be either the same thing travelling back through the planes – telegraph poles, fences and roads, for instance – or a shape repeated in different places, for example the shapes of the foliage on a tree repeated in a cloud or shadow.

This chart details the effect perspective has on a scene.

Foreground

- Objects largest, most detail
- Objects overlap others behind
- Strongest tones and tonal differences
- Lightest lights and darkest darks
- Warmest colours

Middle Distance

- Objects smaller, less detail
- Foreground objects overlap those behind, and those in turn overlap distant objects
- Tones not so strong
- Lights and darks less intense, 'veil' of atmosphere
- Colours cooler – more blueish, less defined

Far Distance

- Objects smallest, detail lost, less definition
- Objects are overlapped by those in front
- Tones merge, least strength of tones and colours
- Least variation in tone and colour
- Colours palest and bluest

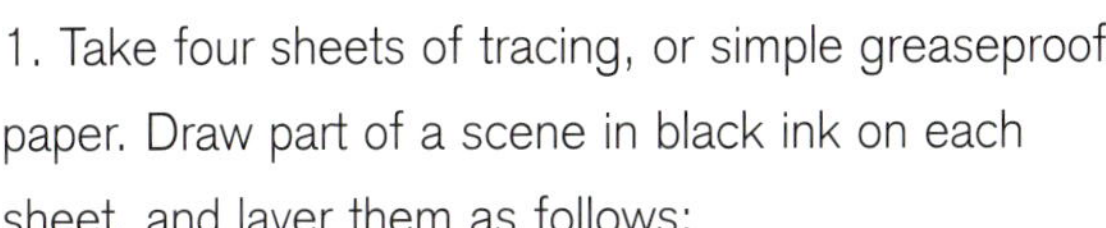 **Projects:** Perspective

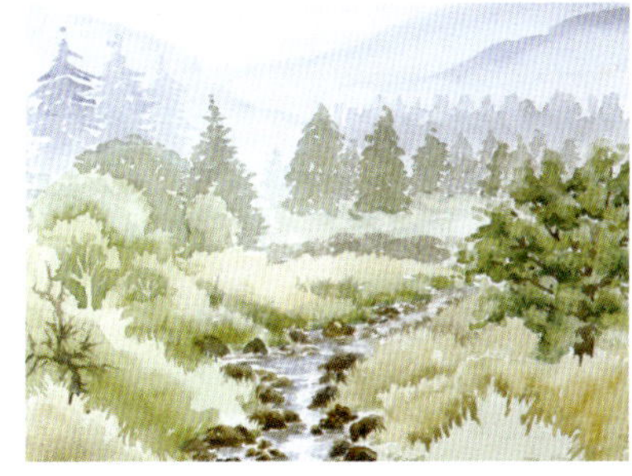

The following projects use layers of paper, to create the effect of aerial perspective. Each layer acts like the atmosphere does, by filtering out the colour, intensity and detail in the distance. They will give you a sense of depth, as each one seems progressively further away, and also an idea of how much paler your distances need to be portrayed.

1. Take four sheets of tracing, or simple greaseproof paper. Draw part of a scene in black ink on each sheet, and layer them as follows:

Far distance on bottom sheet (furthest mountains)

Distance on next sheet to be laid over the top (nearest mountain)

Middle distance (the lake in front of mountain and trees and so on surrounding it)

Foreground (foliage, trees and so on nearest to you)

2. Paint the same landscape, and try to achieve the same sense of depth. Start with the far distance painted palest. Use plenty of water and keep it faint (see chart), then build up successive layers getting warmer, stronger and more detailed as you come forward.

3. Notice, study and copy what gives other work depth, and cut out and stick in your sketchbook any examples you come across. If you are a beginner, also keep the chart above in your sketchbook for reference. When you are sketching out your work, this will help to develop an instinctive approach to planes of depth.

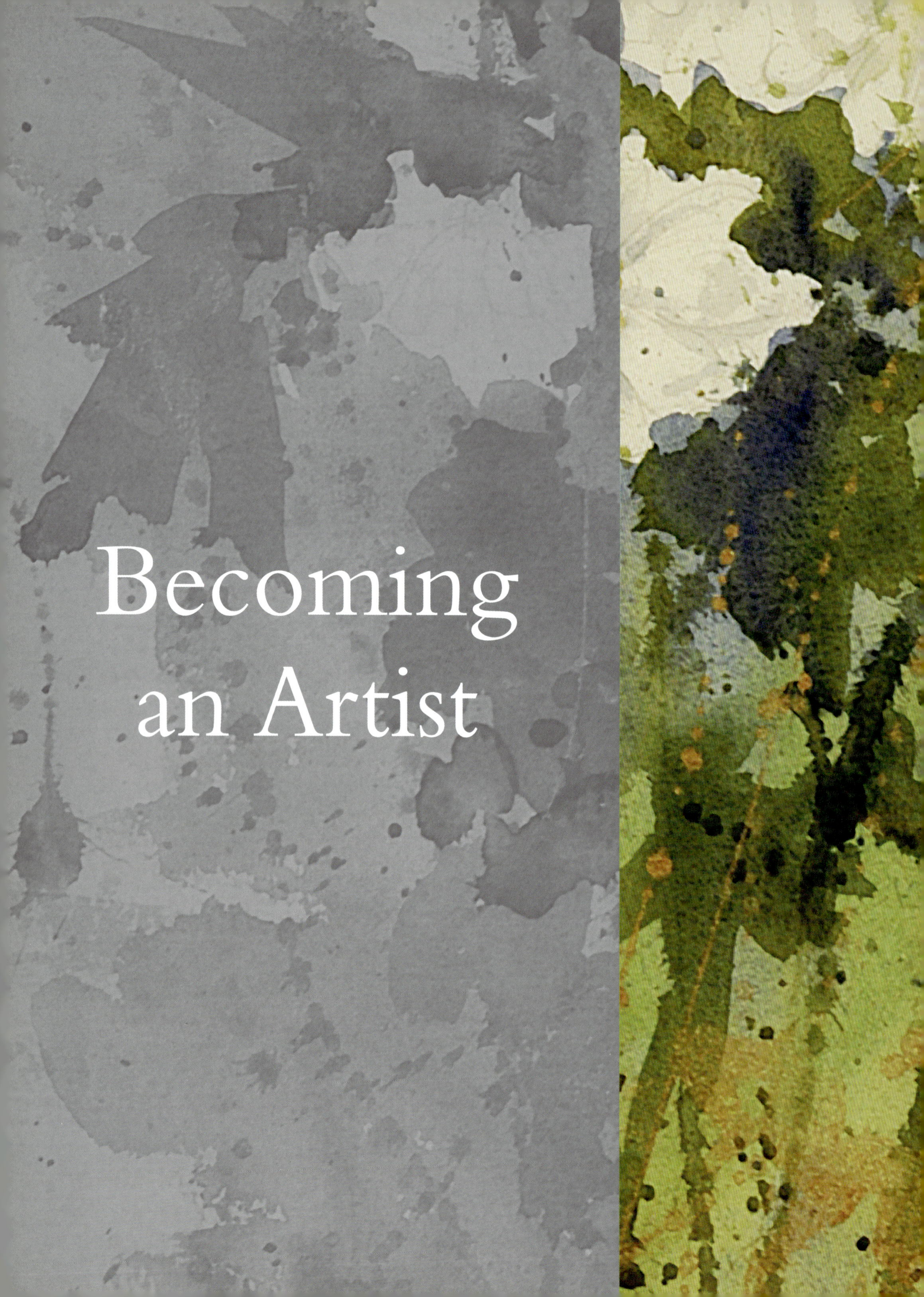

Becoming an Artist

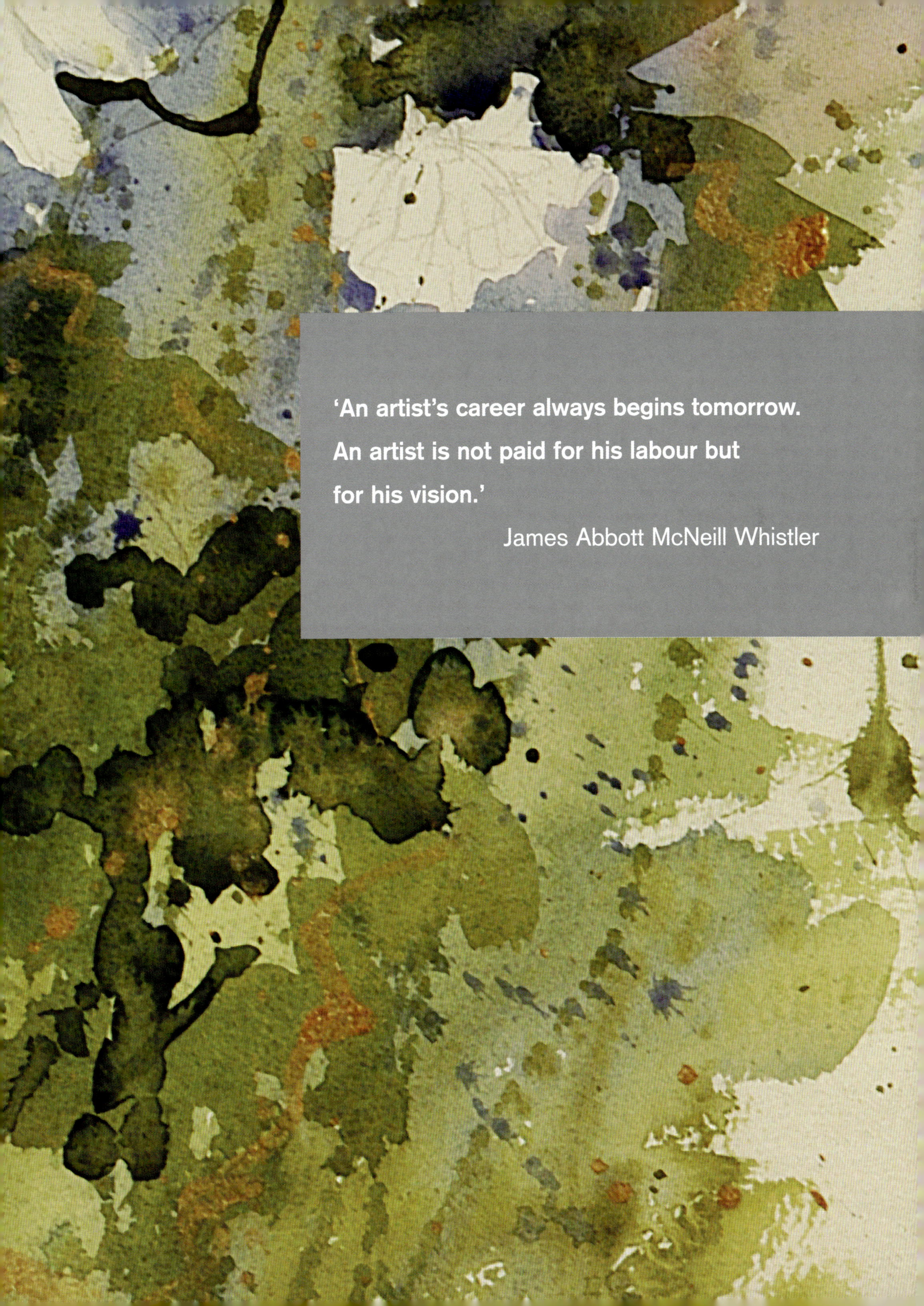
'An artist's career always begins tomorrow.
An artist is not paid for his labour but
for his vision.'
James Abbott McNeill Whistler

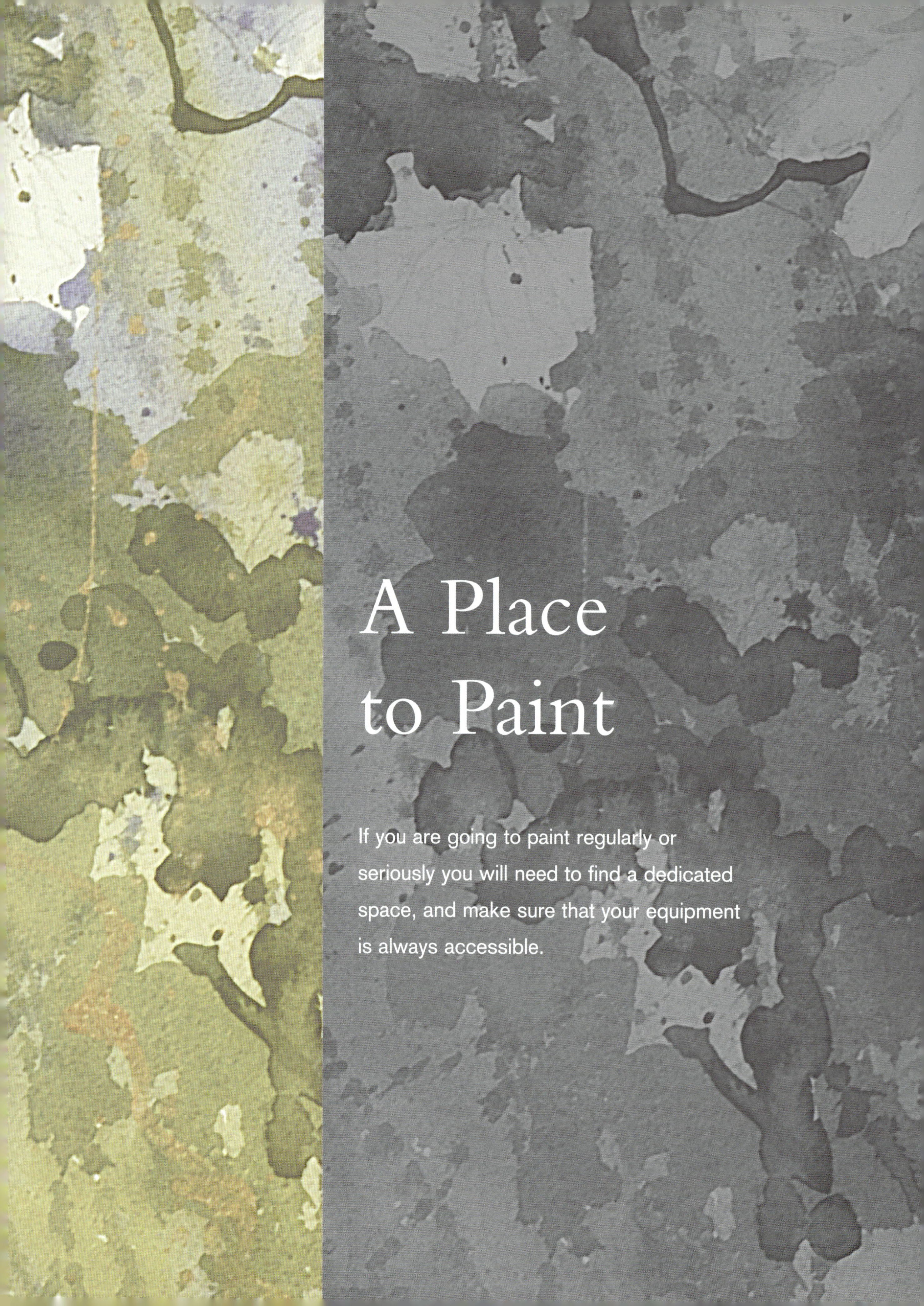

A Place
to Paint

If you are going to paint regularly or
seriously you will need to find a dedicated
space, and make sure that your equipment
is always accessible.

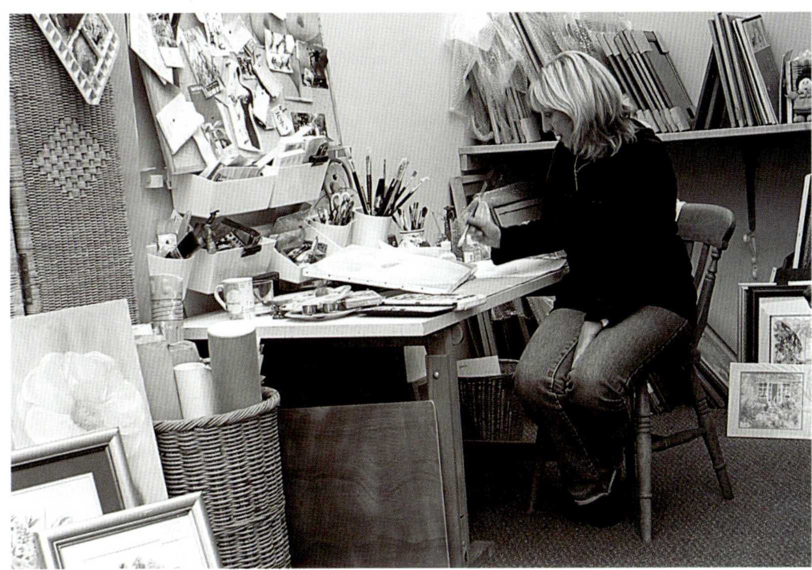

Your space could be a spare bedroom or table in the corner of a room – just somewhere that you can leave out all your stuff and 'dabble' whenever you get a moment, rather than having to set everything up each time and then clear it away again afterwards.

When I started writing this book, my favourite place to paint was on a work station in the corner of a big family kitchen, which allowed me to carry on working while the kids played and the tea cooked (or burnt) around me. I now have a purpose-built studio on the side of the house, which is ideal – great light, lots of shelves, space for everything – but I still like my cosy little corner. So take that as a lesson: don't ever think you have an excuse not to paint if you don't have a studio or designated room – a corner will do.

A friend saw a photograph in a newspaper of me sitting in my little corner. She was horrified that it looked such a mess and said she'd have tidied it up for me if she'd known it was going to be seen by the public. But I would have been more horrified if people had seen it tidy: painting is a messy business, few artists have tidy minds and tidy working spaces and I'm proud of my mess.

So, if you find your space, this is the one place where you don't have to worry. After years of organization, it will be your chance to be as messy as you like!

It's amazingly easy to give up if your equipment is inaccessible. If you really can't find even a corner to make your own, then keep all your art materials and equipment together in a bag, on view and in an easily accessible place. That way it's ready to delve into at any time and take with you whenever you go out, away, or to art classes. Paint every day if time permits – and if it doesn't, try and make time – but this will only be possible if your equipment is ready for you.

A friend of mine followed this advice and had a big canvas art bag that lived in the hall, she brought it to art classes, and her husband knew it had to be the first thing packed into the caravan for holidays – it was always on view and always being accessed. When she moved house though, and no longer needed it every week for classes, it was soon put away into a cupboard and once it was out of sight, it was out of mind and her painting soon forgotten.

If you are not a member already, why not join a local art class, where you can paint without the distractions of home? I can't recommend it highly enough, not only for the value of the instruction but also for the encouragement and support of others like yourself. I reckon my students learn more from each other than they ever do from me. If you cannot find any classes nearby, phone your local Education and Leisure Department and ask if there are any classes in the area. Just having to get up and go every week will keep you painting – much easier than disciplining yourself to paint at home.

Focus on
Things to consider when joining a class

- People join for all sorts of reasons, not of all them are because they want to learn to paint, consequently some are more social gatherings than serious places of study.

- Discover, by asking other pupils, what the class is like. You don't want to commit a large sum of money and then find yourself in a class that doesn't suit you.

- If you are restricted by availability or geography to just one local class, ask the teacher if he/she can help you to meet your agenda, even if it is different from the rest of the class.

- Good communication is vital – make sure you feel you can talk easily to your tutor.

- Find out how the teacher paints. If they are a traditionalist and paint in a tight realistic style, you probably won't have the input you need as a wild impressionist.

- Just as important as the teacher's painting style is how they teach. I found 'handouts', projects and challenges were greatly appreciated by my students who had previously sat through classes where the teacher just walked around saying, 'Um…that's nice, carry on!'

- It's fair to say that the ideal tutor and the ideal class don't exist – so it's a case of how much compromise you are prepared to make.

- Once you have found your class, please don't be narrow-minded – try new things even if you are unsure. I pushed students to do things that they may have considered daft, but it was for a reason – say, to 'loosen them up' or 'stretch' them – and, with hindsight, they were able to see how it helped them.

- Don't expect to go home with a masterpiece every night. Often you learn more from new techniques or exercises and the rush to do a 'nice picture' probably won't pay such dividends in the long term.

- A class is not just a place to paint – gather information, feedback and encouragement from your classmates, see the company as part of the value and, above all, enjoy yourself.

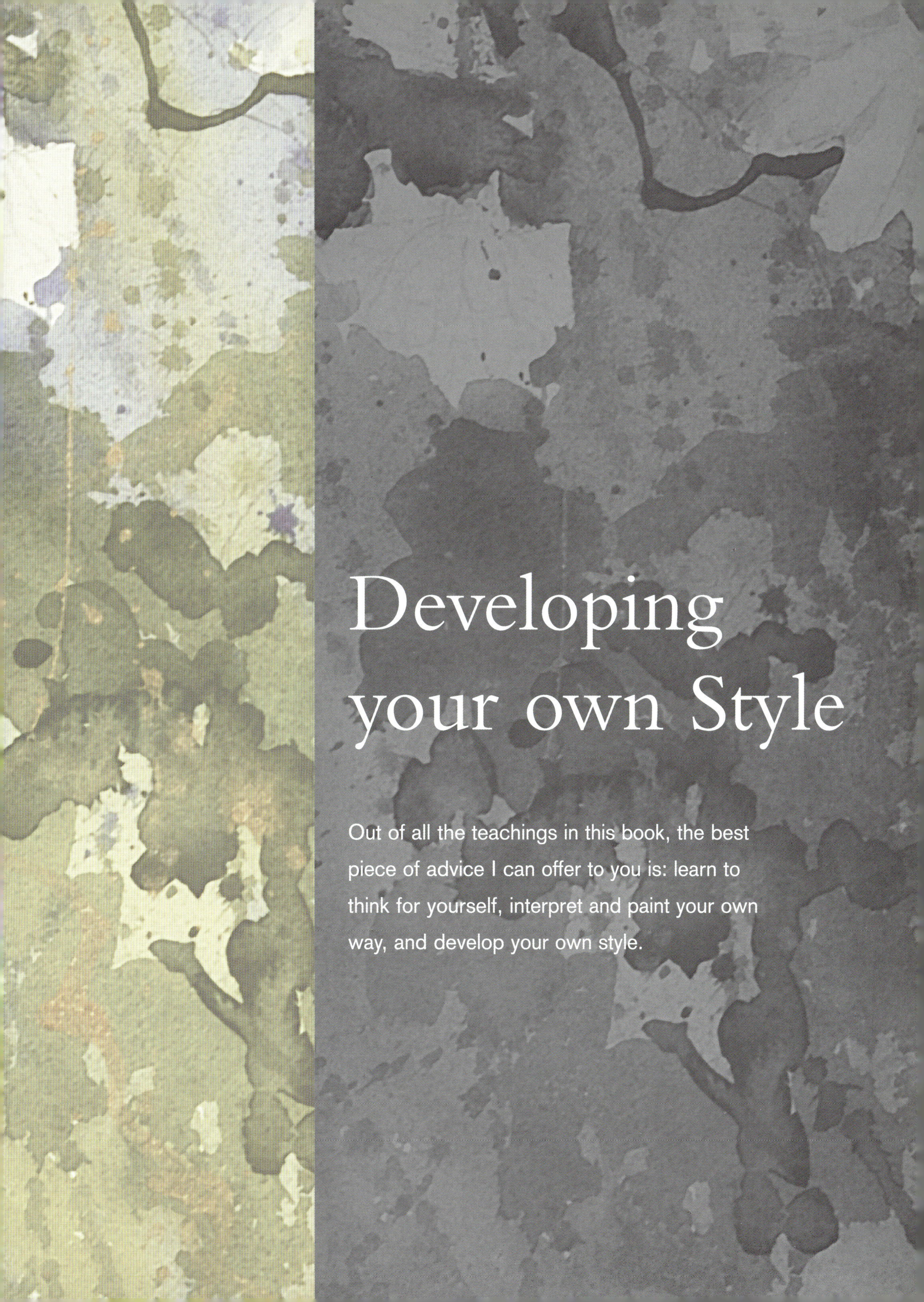

Developing your own Style

Out of all the teachings in this book, the best piece of advice I can offer to you is: learn to think for yourself, interpret and paint your own way, and develop your own style.

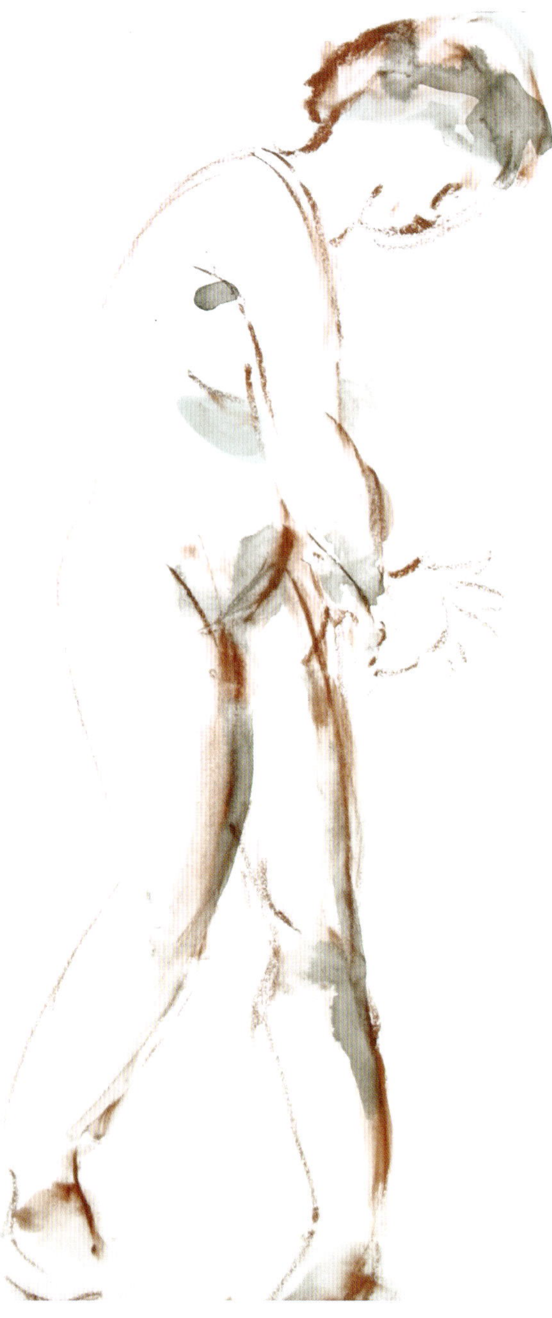

but it's important to keep a varied view and not slavishly follow one person's way. Ultimately you have to decide how YOU want to see things and how YOU want to portray them – that is what will make you an artist.

Students seem to struggle to develop their own style yet, while they're struggling, it is usually developing naturally. When I first started painting my aim (as with most people) was to achieve a realistic portrayal but, after a while I felt these pictures were boring and pushed myself into new areas.

How I loosened up my images

One of the ways I achieve a looser image is to start by rendering a picture realistically, then scrub it and scratch and generally give it a hard time to get a more interesting finish. The lilies on page 162, for example, started life neatly portrayed, but then went into a number of baths of bleach and had a good scrubbing each time, until this more interesting finish emerged.

As my style has 'loosened', I've heard people say, 'Oh she used to be quite good, but she's gone right off'! At a recent demonstration, I painted some flowers in the traditional way, and when I started splattering paint on, there were viewers who were horrified that, in their opinion, I'd messed up the painting. Interestingly, when they saw the finished result, mounted and framed, they liked it, so the message here is be prepared to push yourself into areas that may horrify you at the time.

When you first start it's natural to want to follow a formula and be shown by a teacher or book that 'this is how you paint' but there is no one definitive 'right way' – thankfully, there are as many ways to paint as there are painters. Obviously we all need guidance and there are lots of techniques, rules and tricks to be learnt and I have tried to give you that in this book. It is also helpful to follow the teachings of well-known painters –

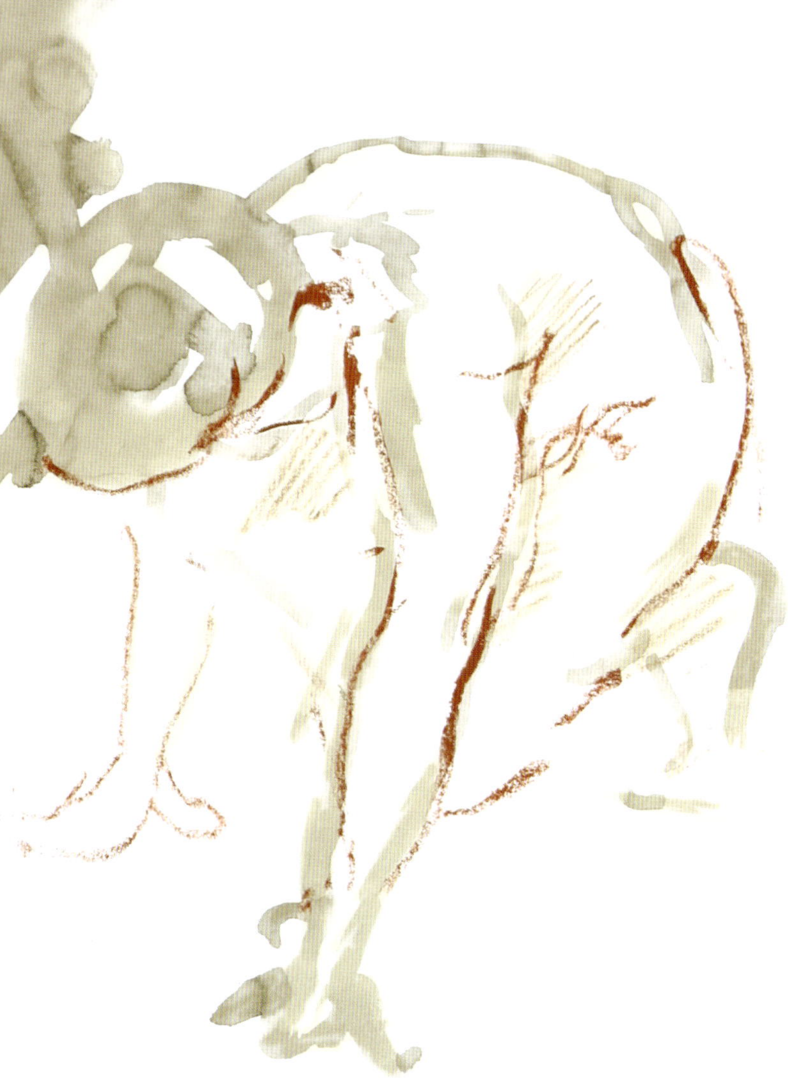

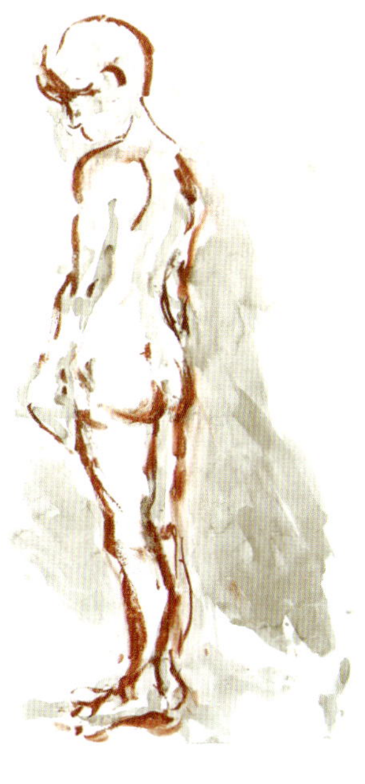

You can see from the sketches on page 39 how my style has loosened and evolved from those early, realistic pieces to the more expressive renditions of the same subjects today. One of the turning points was an evening spent painting with a weird variety of sticks and implements using our bare feet, both hands, a life model and kitchen timer! The model struck a pose for just a minute or two and during that time someone randomly called out, 'Left foot + stick dipped in ink' or 'Right hand + conte stick', 'Right foot + paint brush', every 15 seconds or so.

Trust me, when you have a stick grasped between your toes or you are using your left hand with just a few seconds to convey an image, you haven't got time to worry about neatness. It forced me into a much more expressive way of painting and I loved the results. I am sure that I owe the more free style that I have adapted today to those roots, so push yourself beyond your normal limits – you might surprise yourself.

Focus on
Ideas to help develop your style

● Stop trying to paint like other people. Once you decide to develop your own style, concentrate on your own work instead of that of others.

● Recognize that the most important ingredient in a painting is the 'thinking'. Observation and study are important, but more so is interpreting what you see. A photograph can reproduce a scene, but what makes a painting worthwhile is when your feelings about something shine through and it is reproduced in a way that is unique to you.

● Don't be a slave to your subject but be inspired by it, use it as a launch pad to express your ideas about it. Consider what the character of the scene or subject is. Examine its different aspects: colour, composition, style, light, texture, mood and so on. Decide which particular areas appeal to you, then exaggerate them.

● Get enthusiastic and excited and be confident – timidity is your only barrier.

● Challenge your assumptions, don't be restricted in your thinking.

● Don't always use a brush – try fingers, sticks, sponges, quills – in fact anything you fancy. Try different surfaces: card, newspaper, wood –

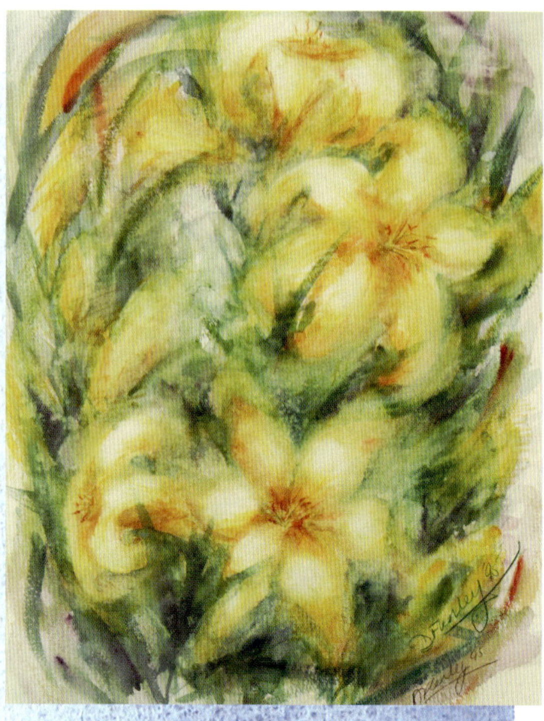

even sandpaper! Don't just use watercolour – add salt, sand, pastel, ink – anything in your larder.

● You don't have to reproduce what is there – move things around, leave them out, exaggerate their shape, size and angles.

● See in terms of shape and colour, try screwing up your eyes to eliminate detail, so you just see the basic forms.

● You don't have to reproduce the 'correct' colours – that tree doesn't have to be green, nor does that sky need to be blue.

● Try using a limited palette so your colours harmonize, or a vibrant mix so they clash. Try mixing your colour on the paper.

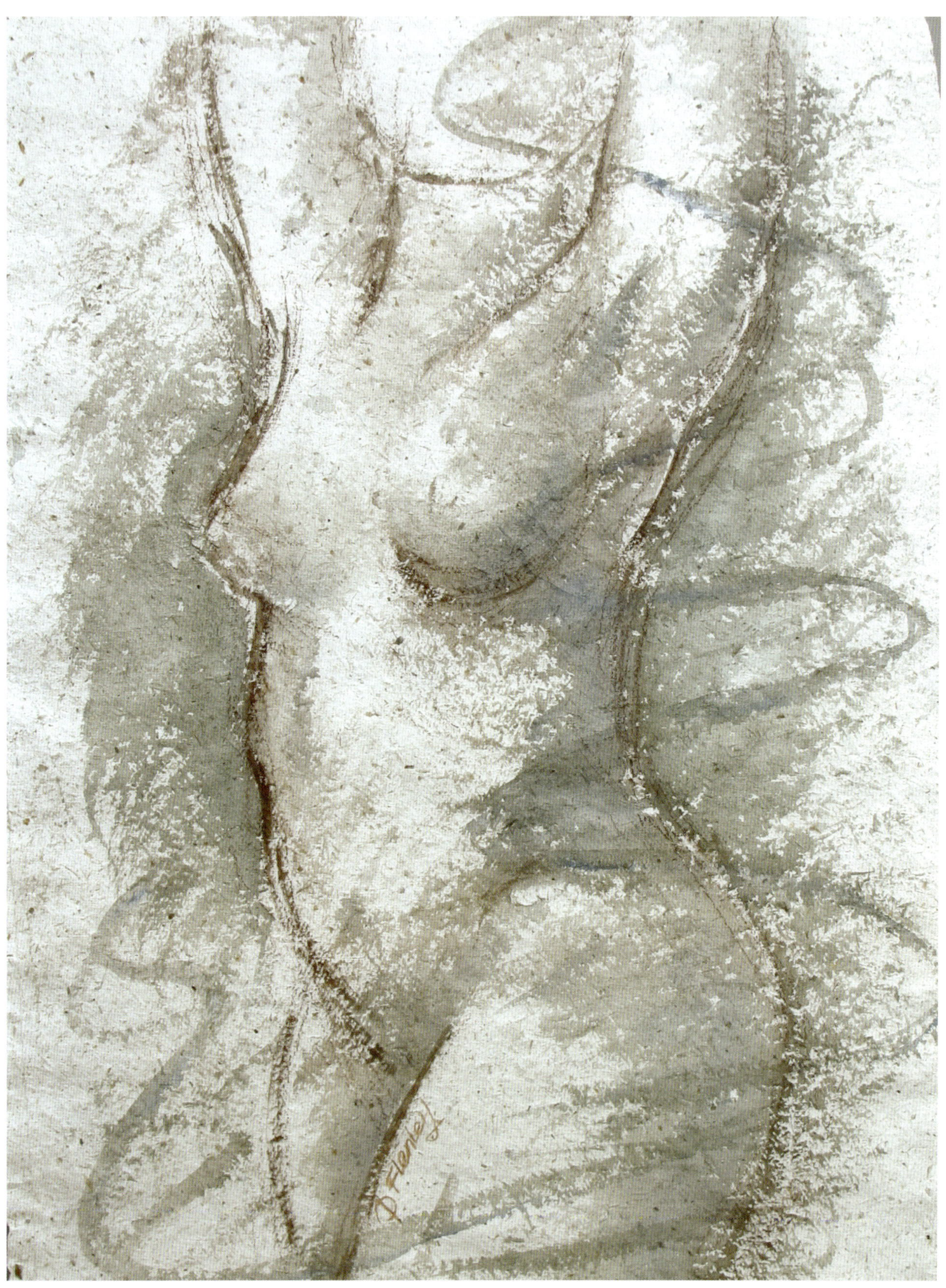

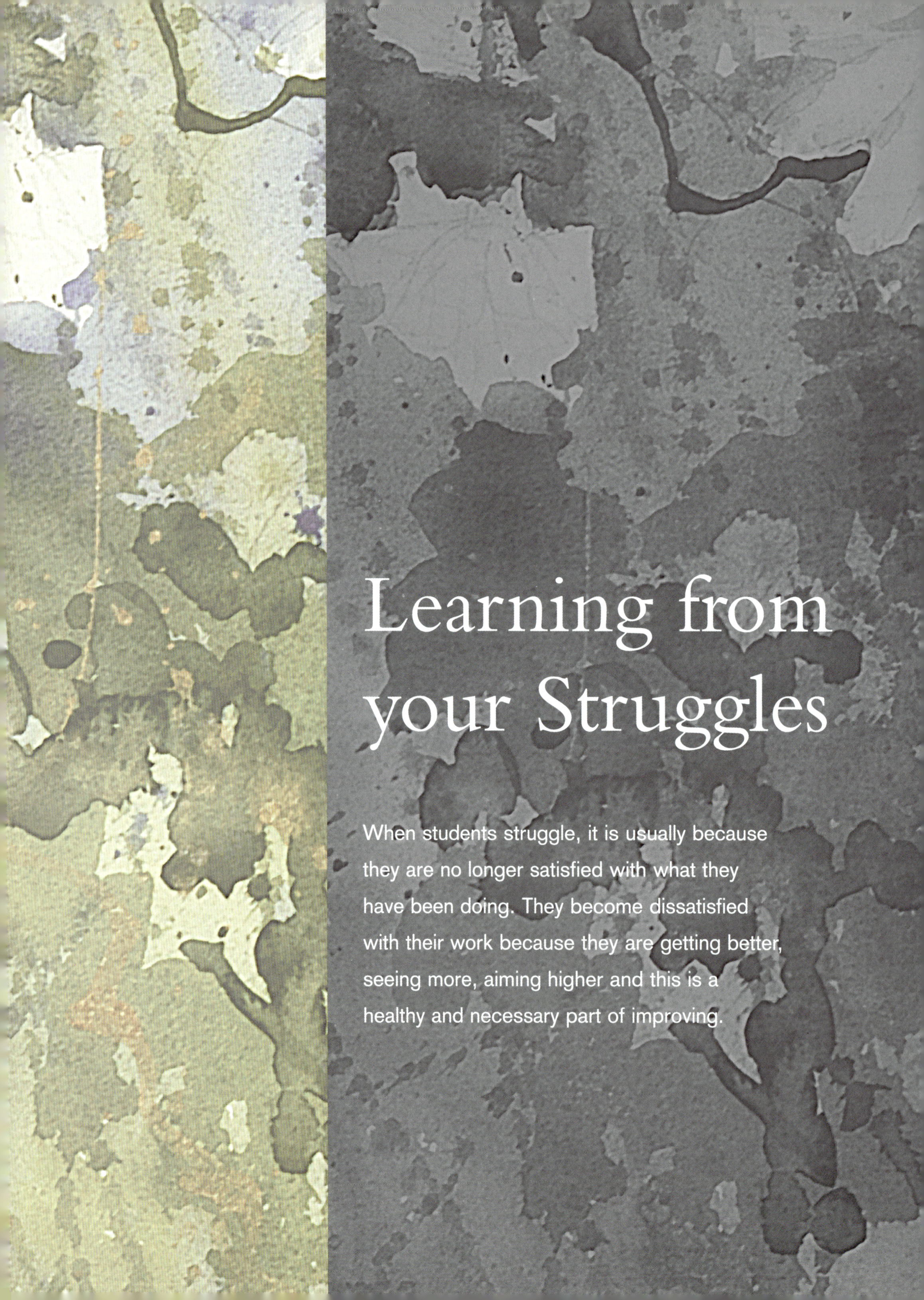

Learning from your Struggles

When students struggle, it is usually because they are no longer satisfied with what they have been doing. They become dissatisfied with their work because they are getting better, seeing more, aiming higher and this is a healthy and necessary part of improving.

If you're reading this, my guess is you probably do some painting but you want to improve.

In my early days I went to every class and gallery I could find. I bought, borrowed, read, and made notes from every picture I saw and every 'how-to-paint' book on the market and was desperate to learn from them all. I'd had to struggle so much when I was learning and I wished someone could have sat me down and simply told it all to me.

So, when I first ran a university foundation course for adults that's exactly what I wanted to do for them, I wanted to teach them so much – I made notes and handouts, and carefully taught them all the basics, perspective and colour theory, tone, and so on. They loved it, collecting their handouts and having it all explained simply to them. But, to my amazement, I was hauled in front of the bosses and 'told off' for making it too easy for them. 'Let them struggle', I was told. 'Let them get really hungry and only then will they learn for themselves!'

Now that I look back, most of what I was teaching was probably going in one ear and out of the other. How many times in life have you been told something, but it's only when you are ready to learn that lesson for yourself – usually the hard way – that you remember it.

I look at some new students now, expectantly waiting for **me** to turn **them** into an artist.

One chap asked for his money back after one session complaining that he hadn't had enough personal tuition and, interestingly, he made the same complaint about his next teacher, too.

There's a lesson he needs to learn, in fact that lots of art students need to learn: teachers can instruct, guide and help you, but the only person who can really make you into a painter is you.

You will never learn as much from my experiences, or from anyone else's, as you will from your own – and that goes for everything in life – not just painting. I still try and explain stuff to my students, but I know now, it only goes in when they've struggled enough to realize that they need to know it and are hungry for it. If you've struggled, and are hungry to find solutions you will (hopefully) then find your answers – and don't give up because of them!

Never was a life story so aptly titled as in Michelangelo's 'The Agony and the Ecstasy'. Most painters will tell you that it's ecstasy when things go well but, likewise, agony when they don't and unfortunately those latter times are inevitable. Yet I regularly find students despondent and thinking of giving up painting when they find they are struggling. They have the notion that their struggle is an indication of their lack of ability and they believe it's easy for us old hands, whereas the truth is quite the reverse.

When students tell me they're going to give up because they're frustrated and feel that they're getting nowhere I usually smile – I know that they're progressing and put all my effort into persuading them to stick at it.

I suggest you photocopy this page and stick it up where you paint or put it in your art box, then re-read it when you get despondent.

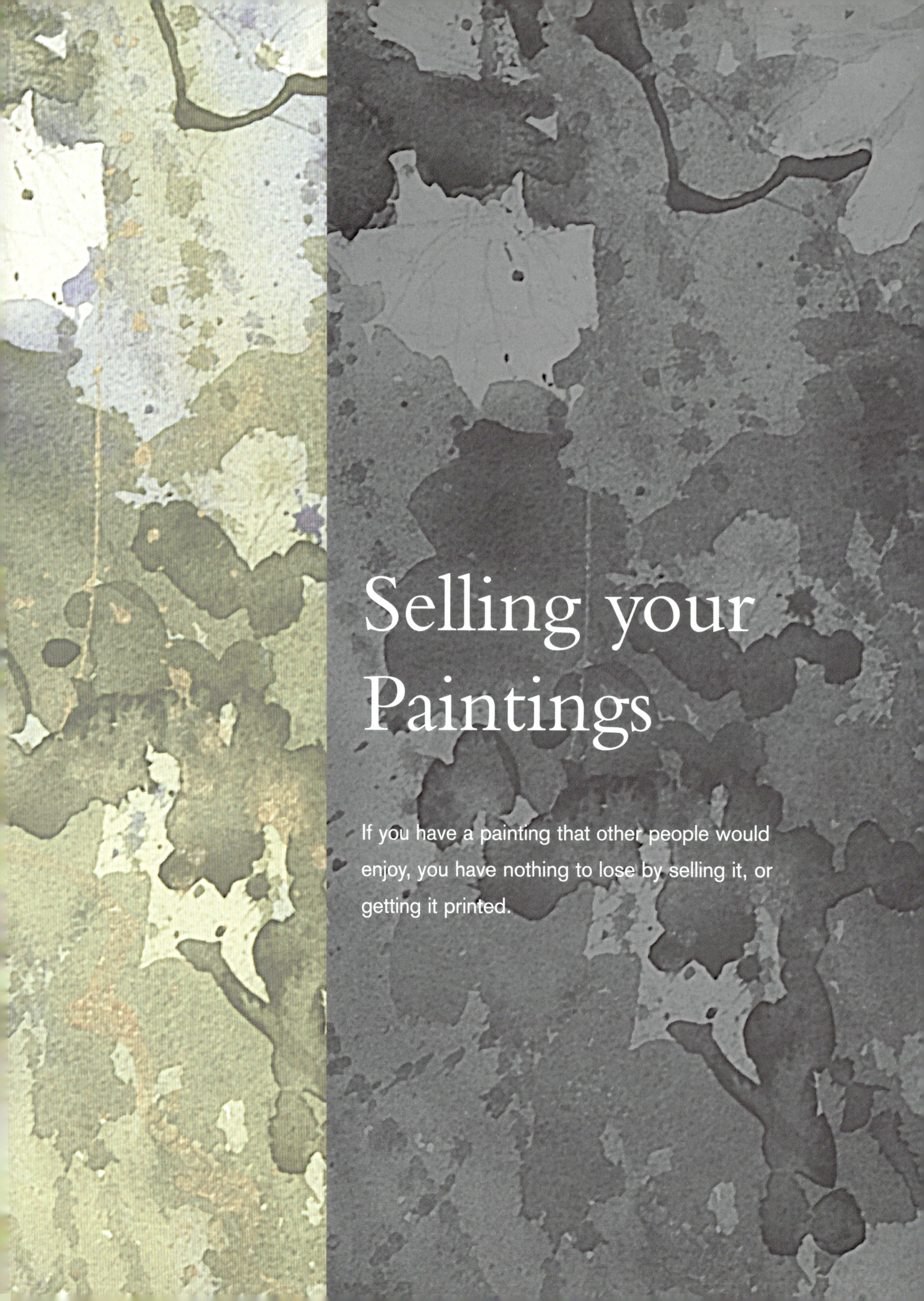

Selling your Paintings

If you have a painting that other people would enjoy, you have nothing to lose by selling it, or getting it printed.

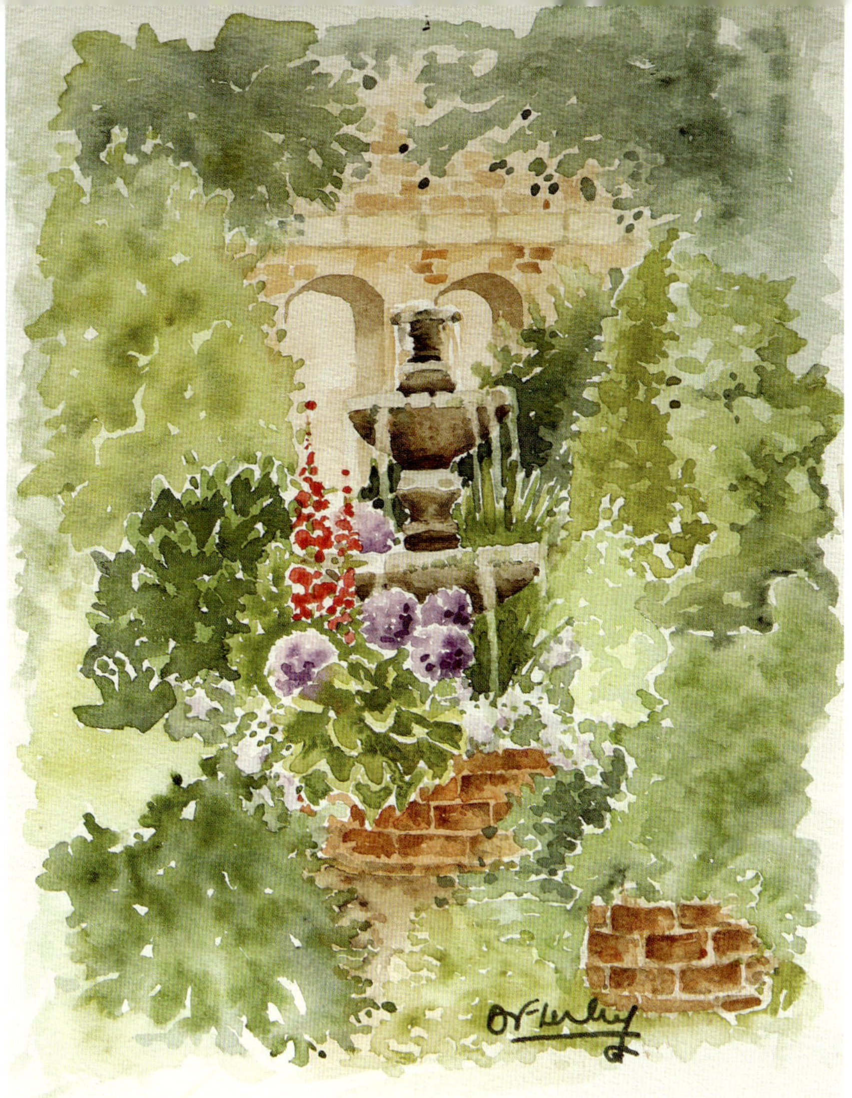

During a church weekend away I did the quick study above of the courtyard. Members of the party suggested that we had copies of it made as a souvenir of their weekend and they all bought them to raise money for a friend who was working in Paraguay. There were a couple spare so my niece had one to raise money for her travels to the Sudan and another went to be auctioned for a missionary.

The moral of this story has to be 'don't hesitate'. Personally, I didn't think this was good enough to be printed and I found the suggestion a bit embarrassing but everyone benefited and, if I had let these minor factors stand in my way, we'd have achieved nothing.

Selling your work is probably your ultimate aim. It is lovely to know that other people like your work enough to part with their hard-earned cash for it and, equally, knowing that they are enjoying having it hanging on their walls is a wonderful feeling for you.

After my last exhibition I received a card from a lady who had advanced cancer. She had bought paintings from previous exhibitions, she had just purchased another and was writing to tell me they had hung the pictures by her bed and how much pleasure they had given her … what can I say? No doubt someone will feel like that about your work and I hope you will enjoy the reward it will bring you.

Don't think this is only relevant to 'real' painters and that you are 'just an amateur' – we all had to start somewhere. It's not that long ago that I looked on in awe as other people demonstrated and exhibited and sold, and now I can't believe it's me doing just that, so there's no good reason why you can't do the same. You will, however, need a lot of confidence. It's no good thinking about your work, 'Oh, this is awful but you can have it if you like.' If you don't believe in the value of your painting no-one else will.

As for pricing – this is difficult. I was told that you should never let a painting go if you are not happy with the price. You don't want to be in a situation where you resent letting someone have a picture. The money has to be an equal compensation for your loss, if you are pleased with the swap then it is the right price.

Never undervalue your work. The price you put on it (within reason) sets the value of it. I heard of a painter whose work didn't sell. She was advised to hike her prices up significantly and, sure enough, it soon sold.

I called together an army of friends to price my work for my exhibition. I chose friends who liked art, bought art and 'did' art, plus other friends who knew nothing about art but gave good advice. Everything sold for the first show, and in the second I had mainly flowers and landscapes with a few large nudes.

The accountant friend suggested pricing the nudes well above what people could afford. I was horrified and thought they wouldn't sell, but she said this price would make them 'aspirational', people would desire and want them and the fact that they couldn't afford them would only add to their appeal. I trusted her and sure enough it worked.

They sold, but only after people went away and thought carefully, so they really meant something to the purchasers.

Don't pass by any opportunities to promote your work – you never know who is going to see it. Watch out for competitions and art fairs, subscribe to all the local magazines and art journals, be ready to enter any competitions – but also be prepared for rejection.

Have a card or leaflet about yourself ready to give to people. If you do commissions, make a list of prices and details and a contact number, you never know when this will come in useful.

You can approach galleries – find one that sells similar style work to your own, but bear in mind that they will take approximately 50% of the price. They may also insist that your work is framed, and you will be liable for this.

You can also set up your own exhibition, but try and do this as professionally as possible, as nothing looks more amateur than someone selling a few pictures from their living room.

Try and create a special event. I paid for full-colour invitations, sold advertising space, bullied my mates into stewarding wearing dinner suits, we had music and professional flowers – in return for free advertising

All this created an ambience and atmosphere that can only impress and improve your chances of selling. To do this takes guts, determination and self-belief but, if you believe in yourself, then others will, too.

Finally, take photographs of any work that you sell, so that you have a record of it, and keep a list of the purchasers.

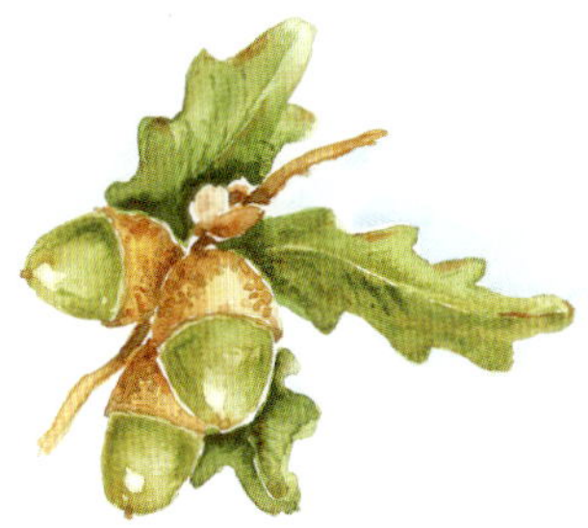

Conclusion – Enjoy your journey

I hope you have found this book to be a valid ticket for your journey into watercolour.

At best it can only be a signpost that can point you on your way and the real journeying has to be done by you, but I want to encourage you to make the trip. Enjoy the journey, savour the sights, experience a lot along the way and especially enjoy the fantastic views and the highs when all goes well.

As with any expedition, most casualties are due to travellers being unprepared before they start off, so prepare yourself, gather together the right materials and start with the right attitude. Take the easy routes and be prepared to be led at first. When you are ready to go it alone, plan your journey so that you are less likely to get lost along the way.

Be determined, aware that at times it will get tough and you will feel like giving up. Be aware that, if you are going to improve, you will need to struggle at times and treat these as learning exercises.

Sometimes you may need to retrace your tracks – it helps to be sure of where you are going. You will need to follow signposts at first but, hopefully, as you become more confident you can challenge and even ignore them when they don't suit you and go off in your own direction.

Soon you will be able to leave the well-trodden path and venture into uncharted territory. You will take new routes, discover hidden treasures that no-one else has ever seen and it will all have been well worth it.

So, bon voyage!

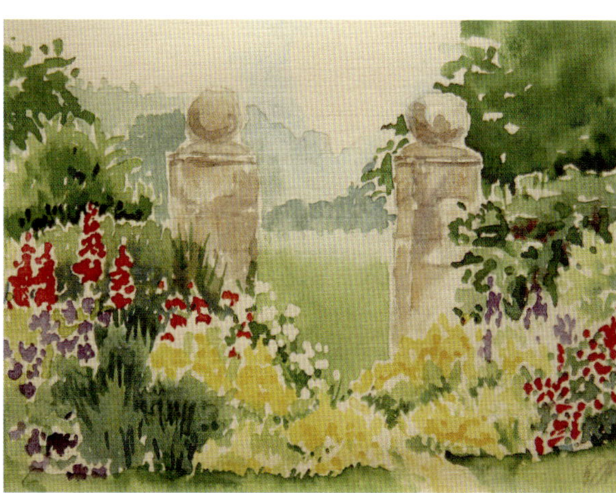

Glossary of Art Terms

• Analogous

Colours that are closely related to each other, i.e. next to each other on the colour wheel. These harmonize when together.

• Atmospheric perspective:

Layers of atmospheres dull out some of the warmer colours and detail, as they come between the viewer and the scene in the distance. Consequently, the further away, the bluer and less detailed a picture becomes.

• Cold colours

Colours with a bias towards blue that are lacking in any red (warm) bias.

• Cold-pressed paper: also known as 'Not'

Watercolour paper that has been pressed between cold presses/rollers so it has just been 'ironed' on the surface, not to a completely smooth finish as in 'hot-pressed'.

• Complementary colours

Those that are opposite on the colour wheel, for example purple and yellow, green and red. These colours have a vibrant effect when put next to each other, but when mixed they neutralize each other.

• Composition

The organization of the subject matter into a pleasing or effective arrangement in a picture.

• Contrast

The difference between two or more factors. The lightest and darkest tones in a painting when put together have the greatest contrast and the most dramatic effect.

• Focal point

The most important point of a painting to which the viewer's eye should be attracted.

• Foreground

The front of a scene that appears to be nearest the viewer.

• Glaze

A transparent wash over another colour.

• Graduated wash

A wash of paint which changes colour as it progresses down or across the page.

• Granulating paint

Paint that has particles which settle on the paper. When disturbed these can make a mix of paint 'muddy'.

• Hot-pressed

Watercolour paper that has been pressed between hot rollers so it has a flat 'ironed out' surface.

• Hue

The name of a colour, such as 'red' or 'green'. It can be used as a term to denote synthetic colour, e.g. lemon-yellow hue.

• Imperial

The original size of a full sheet of watercolour paper before A1, 30 x 20in (85 x 55cm).

• Intensity

The brightness and strength of a colour – also called saturation. In watercolour, colours are more intense when less water is added.

• Linear perspective

Lines in a painting will appear to recede into the distance getting closer together until they converge at the vanishing point.

• Local colour

The colour/hue of the object itself before it is influenced by other factors, such as the shade or reflected colour.

• Medium

The materials used in art to create an image.

• Middle distance

The mid-area between foreground and background/ far distance.

• Mixed media

Where a variety of different materials are used together, for example pastel and watercolour.

• Negative shapes

The space between objects as opposed to the objects themselves. This space, although it is technically 'empty', is important in both composition and drawing.

• Observation

Your most crucial role as an artist – look, look and look again, observe what is really happening as opposed to what you think is happening.

• One-point perspective

Lines converge at a vanishing point on the horizon. This works when you are looking straight on to the image.

• Opaque

A non-transparent quality in paint.

Perspective

A method for depicting three-dimensional objects on a flat surface using linear (one, two or three-point) or atmospheric methods.

• Primary colours

Red, blue and yellow, the three colours that cannot be mixed from other colours, and the main starting points for mixing from the colour wheel.

• Putty rubber

A pliable eraser that can be moulded to suit your specific need.

• Rag content

The percentage of cotton fibre in the paper.

• Rigger

Brush with long, soft hairs suitable for painting thin lines, such as rigging or rope.

• Rough

Surface of watercolour paper that has not been pressed, so it has a rough texture.

• Saturation

The brilliance/vividness of a colour, e.g. the strength, when it is very red.

• Secondary colours

Orange, green and purple, made from mixing two primary colours.

• Size

A glue-like solution added to the paper during manufacture to prevent it from being too absorbent.

• Soft edges (as opposed to 'hard' edges)
Where the edge of an area is gently blended rather than suddenly finishing.

• Stretching
Process of preventing paper buckling when wet by wetting, taping down and allowing it to dry so further wetting will not affect it.

• Tertiary colours
Resulting colours made from mixing two secondary colours or a primary and a secondary.

• Texture
In art terms, the visual or tactile surface of an object.

• Tint
The influential colour in a mix, for example when white has a bluish tint.

• Tone
The lightness or darkness of a shade or colour.

• Tooth
The degree of roughness of watercolour paper.

• Transparent
Watercolours through which you can see the paper or the paint underneath.

• Two-point perspective
If an object is at an oblique angle, two-point perspective needs to be employed, where lines converge on two vanishing points.

• Under painting
A wash laid on the paper first, to condition the colour of the painting.

• Value/tone
How light or dark a colour or shade is.

• Variegated wash
A 'wash' of paint laid onto the paper which changes paint colour during the laying process.

• Warm colours
Those on the side of the colour wheel that are close to red or have a hint of red in their mix, e.g. orange, warm yellow.

• Wash
The laying of paint onto the paper in broad strokes that blend into each other creating a flat surface of paint.

• Wet-in-wet
Adding paint to paint that has been laid and is still wet, so the colours blend and merge.

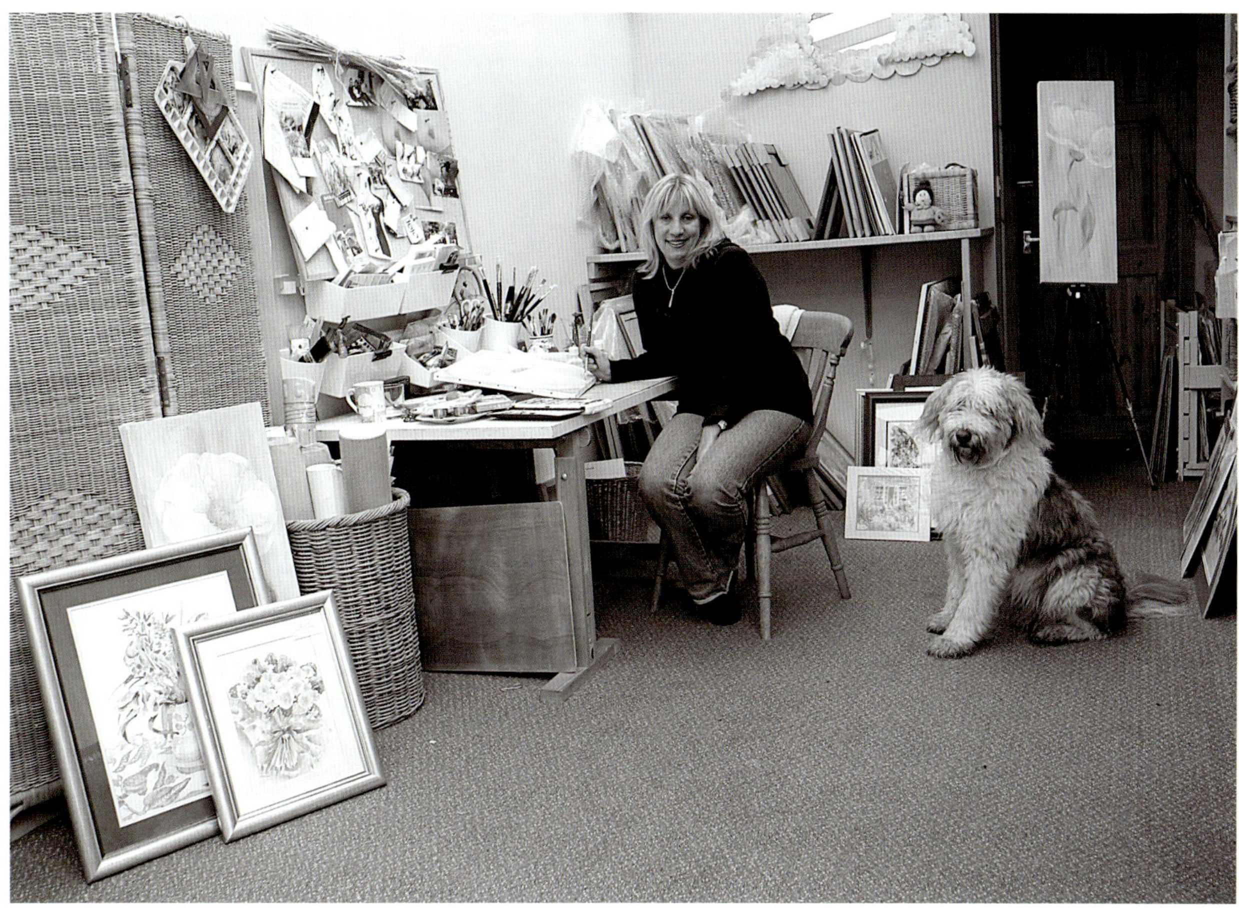

About the Author

After the birth of her first child, Debbie went to art college and juggled motherhood with a passion for painting. Her first solo exhibition in 1996 sold nearly 100 paintings in a couple of hours and she has held further, equally large and successful solo shows since.

Her distinctive paintings range from large, loose and gentle watercolours to oversize semi-abstracts in mixed media. Commissions have been as diverse as 5ft (1.5m) colourful, mixed-media flowers for the walls of a chain of public houses, to even larger monochrome life studies for a health authority, so it is difficult to 'pigeon-hole' her and her work.

Debbie's original degree was in Theology and she has been licensed into the Lay Ministry. Her work is strongly influenced by her faith, especially the beauty of God's creation, hence the paintings contained here are predominantly flowers, landscapes and nudes.

She is married to Colin, they have three children and they live in Aldridge, England, where he is a family doctor. Debbie teaches art, and paints in a studio adjoining their large old house.

Acknowledgements

I couldn't have written this book without the support of Colin, Mum, Dad and Joyce, who always believe in me, so it goes out with special love to you.

Special thanks also go to Ian and Fiona whose friendship and help in starting my career and staging my first exhibition will never be forgotten (miss you!), Chris and Debs for your help. I finally forgive you, as my press officer, for having me photographed for the papers with my slippers on!

Pam and John who encouraged me by buying my first painting, and then subsequently others (which, if the taxman is reading this, never really were for his office you know!), Judy and Roger who not only bought my second, third and probably fourth paintings – but travelled miles to do so, my girlfriends Elaine, Yvonne, Jane and Ella, for teaching me all I know about art (I never knew gouache was a kind of curry!), Aunty Pauline for telling me when to 'put my face straight', Moira, Jenny and Chris for their support, Sally, Hilary, the Evans, Goodhalls and especially McCrieires for commendable longevity in their support, Ken and Jean for having their wine club delivery on the day we heard this book was to be published, the rest of Aldridge Parish Church for being wonderful and my Godchildren and adopted nieces for being special.

Thanks also to all the kind owners of pictures who allowed them to be photographed, and to John who patiently took the pictures.

May God richly bless you all xxxx

Index

GMC Publications Ltd

Castle Place, 166 High Street, Lewes, East Sussex BN7 1XU United Kingdom

Tel: 01273 488005   Fax: 01273 402866   E-mail: pubs@thegmcgroup.com

Website: **www.gmcbooks.com**

Contact us for a complete catalogue, or visit our website. Orders by credit card are accepted.

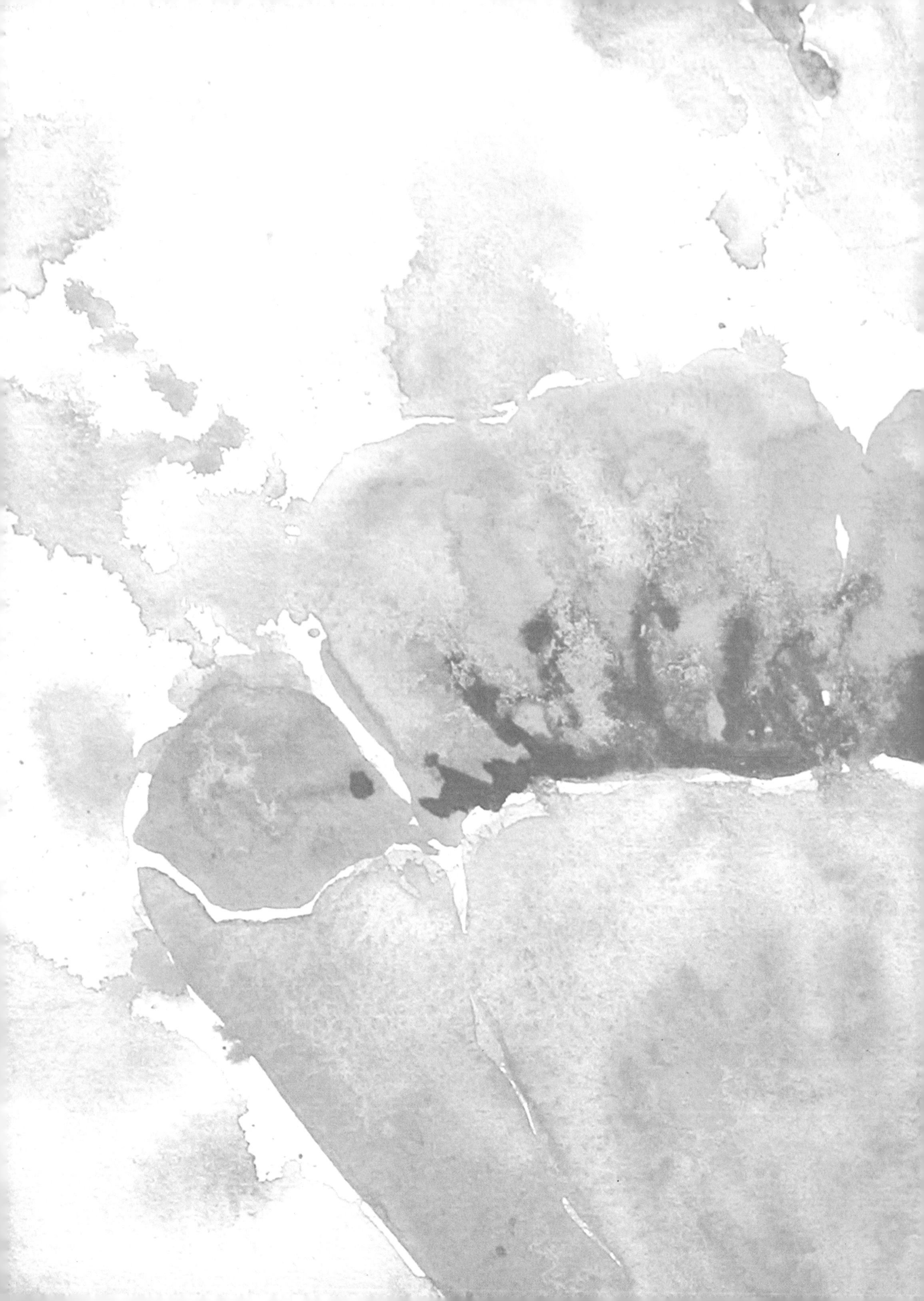